ENGLISH GRAMMAR FOR TODAY: A NEW INTRODUCTION

English Grammar for Today

A new introduction

Geoffrey Leech
Margaret Deuchar
Robert Hoogenraad

MACMILLAN
in conjunction with
THE ENGLISH ASSOCIATION

First published 1982
Reprinted 1983 (with corrections), 1984 (with revisions)
1985
Published by
Higher and Further Education Division
MACMILLAN PUBLISHERS LTD
Houndmills, Basingstoke, Hampshire RG21 2XS
and London
Companies and representatives
throughout the world

Printed in Great Britain by
Redwood Burn Limited, Trowbridge, Wiltshire
and bound by Pegasus Bookbinding, Melksham, Wiltshire

ISBN 0 333 30643 0 (hard cover)
ISBN 0 333 30644 9 (paper cover)

Contents

Foreword

Voices in the English Association have been urging for some time that the moment is ripe for a new English grammar for use in schools, colleges and universities and the Association has been fortunate in bringing together three authors whose distinction and expertise eminently qualify them for the task and a publisher long established in the field.

It is probably true to say that not many years ago such a book could hardly have attracted a publisher, for two very good reasons.

The climate of opinion has for long been unfavourable to giving grammatical teaching to native speakers of English. From causes that we need not go into here, the old tradition of school grammar waned. Grammar for foreign learners was acknowledged to be unavoidable; the rest of us could manage without. And so, of course, many of us did; and perhaps we felt the language survived quite happily when we did not look too closely, whether as teachers or as students or as general users of the language, at the imprecision, the incoherence and – let us confess it – often the incomprehensibility of much of what we read or even wrote in our everyday lives.

A second reason was severely practical. It is, after all, not long since Professor Randolph Quirk complained of the absence of any sound criterion by which to establish what really was acceptable English: 'the writer of a teaching grammar is . . . at the grammatical level . . . almost entirely without a body of descriptive data, and so . . . he has to rely largely on a hesitant and uncertain introspection into his own usage or his intuitive knowledge'.[1]

That the situation has changed is due in great measure to Professor Quirk and his colleagues in the Survey of English Usage, at University College, London, and to its daughter project at the University of Lancaster, where Professor Leech and his colleagues are investigating

---

[1] Randolph Quirk, comment in an article reprinted in his *Essays on the English Language: Medieval and Modern* (London: Longman, 1968) p. 110.

present-day English with the aid of the computer. By far the most important achievement of this new emphasis on the study of English grammar through its usage in the language is surely the monumental *Grammar of Contemporary English*,[1] which is widely regarded as authoritative.

'Authoritative', like the word 'authority', is likely to raise hackles, and so it is proper to point out that it is authoritative statements of the facts of English today that are in question, not rules as to how we should or should not express ourselves. Rules there will be, based on unquestionable fact, but often it is a matter rather of grades of acceptability. We believe there is now a growing body of opinion eager for direction of this kind.

We hope that *English Grammar for Today* will serve as a valuable tool for students, however little their knowledge of grammatical terms, and also for teachers, whether inclined more to a traditional or a modern approach, who believe that a return to a vigilant and well-informed attitude towards the language they use and love is long overdue.

The English Association is grateful to the authors for the care they have given to the preparation of this book, and to those of its members and of its Executive Committee who read earlier drafts and contributed suggestions for improvement. Further suggestions from readers will be welcomed.

GEOFFREY HARLOW
Chairman, Publications Subcommittee,
The English Association,
1 Priory Gardens, Bedford Park,
London, W4 1TT

[1] By Randolph Quirk, Sidney Greenbaum, Geoffrey Leech and Jan Svartvik (London: Longman, 1972).

Preface

This is an introductory course in English grammar for use in English-medium schools, colleges and universities. Lamentably, there is at present no recognised place for English grammar in the British educational curriculum. In fact it is still possible for a student to end up with a degree in English at a British university without having cause to know the first thing about English grammar, or the grammar of any other language. But if we are right in supposing that the time is right for a revival of the subject in schools, there will be a growing need for introductory courses at various levels. Thus this book has a multiple purpose. It is primarily designed as a course book for students at the upper secondary level (sixth forms) and the tertiary level (colleges, polytechnics, universities), but it is also adapted to the needs of teachers interested in exploring a new approach to grammar, or of any person keen to catch up with a subject so wretchedly neglected by our educational system.

If grammar is to become a vital subject in the English curriculum, we have to exorcise finally the spectre of Browning's grammarian who

> Gave us the doctrine of the enclitic *De*
> Dead from the waist down
> (Robert Browning, *The Grammarian's Funeral*)

That spectre still haunts our collective consciousness in the form of a Victorian schoolmaster instilling guilty feelings about split infinitives and dangling participles, and vague fears that grammar may prove to be nothing else than hacking the corpses of sentences to pieces and sticking labels on the resulting fragments. That is why some of this book is devoted to the correcting of preconceptions. Part A, 'Introduction', is meant to provide a reorientation: dispelling myths, and seeking a new appraisal of the value of grammar in present-day education. Part B, 'Analysis', is the main part of the book, presenting a method for describing the grammatical structure of sentences. Part C, 'Applications', shows how this method of analysis can be used in the study of style in its broadest sense, and in the development of written language skills.

The system of grammatical analysis introduced in Part B is influenced by the systemic grammar of M. A. K. Halliday, and more directly by that found in Randolph Quirk *et al.*, *A Grammar of Contemporary English* (1972), and its adaptations in Quirk and Greenbaum, *A University Grammar of English* (1974) and Leech and Svartvik, *A Communicative Grammar of English* (1975). It is a framework which has been widely adopted in the study of English by non-native speakers, making informal use of modern developments in linguistics, but not departing without good reason from traditional terms and categories which are to some extent a common cultural heritage of the Western world. Naturally the framework has had to be considerably simplified. 'Grammar', for our purpose, is defined in a narrow sense for which nowadays the term 'syntax' is sometimes used. It means roughly 'the rules for constructing sentences out of words', and it excludes, strictly speaking, the study of what words and sentences mean, and how they are pronounced.

Exercises are provided at the end of each chapter, but their function in each Part is somewhat different. For Part A the exercises are merely an encouragement towards thinking on new lines about grammar. In Part B the exercises are much more fully integrated into the learning process; it is important for students to test their progress in understanding the system by doing the exercises where indicated. In part C the exercises in Chapters 8-10 invite the student to try out the system of grammatical analysis on different styles and varieties of English. Here grammar will be seen in relation to other levels of language, such as meaning and vocabulary, as part of the total functioning of language as a communication system.

The book can be used as a course book, each chapter providing one or two weeks' work, though the exercises are varied in form and purpose. Some exercises consist of problems with more or less definite answers, and in these cases answers are given at the back of the book (pp.199-214). Other exercises are open-ended tasks to which no answers can be given. The exercises which have answers provided are so indicated by the cross-reference 'answers on p. 00' alongside the heading. Thus those using the book for private study will gain some feedback, while teachers using the book as a course book will find enough material for week-by-week preparation and discussion, in addition to the exercises which students may check for themselves.

Following the Answers to Exercises, we list books and articles for Further Reading (on pp.215-17). The list is alphabetical, and on the few occasions in the text where we need to refer to one of the works listed, references are given by the author's name, the title, and the date of publication: e.g. 'Crystal, *Linguistics*, 1971'. It would be impossible to give due credit to grammarians and other scholars whose work and ideas have influenced this book directly or indirectly; where such ideas have become part of the currency of present-day linguistics, we make no attempt to do so.

Although the book does not include a glossary of technical terms, the function of such a glossary can be matched by careful use of the Index, in which technical terms of grammar are listed alphabetically, together with the pages on which they are introduced and explained.

We thank Martin McDonald for providing us with the material quoted on pp. 151, 153, 155-6.

We owe a general debt to the English Association, which provided the impetus and opportunity for the writing of this book, and a more particular debt to the Chairman of its Publications Subcommittee, Geoffrey Harlow, and to other members of the Association, especially Raymond Chapman, who have given us encouragement and detailed guidance.

Lancaster   GEOFFREY LEECH
August 1981   MARGARET DEUCHAR
                                          ROBERT HOOGENRAAD

Symbols and conventions

The sections where the symbol or convention is first introduced, and where the grammatical category is most fully discussed, are here shown in brackets.

Labels

Function labels

A	Adverbial (2.5.3; 5.1.3)	Mv	Main verb (2.5.3.; 4.5)
Aux	Auxiliary verb (2.5.3; 4.5)	O	Object (2.5.2; 5.1.2)
		Od	Direct object (5.6)
C	Complement (2.5.3; 5.1.2)	Oi	Indirect object (5.6)
Co	Object complement (5.6)	P	Predicator (2.5.2; 5.1.1)
Cs	Subject complement (3.2.3; 5.6)	S	Subject (2.5.2; 5.1.1)
		Voc	Vocative (5.6)
H	Head (2.5.3; 4.1)		
M	(Pre- or post-) modifier (2.5.3; 4.1)		

Form labels

ACl	Adverbial clause (6.1.1; 6.2.2)	NCl	Noun clause (6.1.1; 6.2.1)
		NP	Noun phrase (2.5.1; 4.3.1)
Aj	Adjective (2.5.1; 3.2.3)		
AjP	Adjective phrase (2.5.1; 4.4.1)	p	Preposition (2.5.3; 3.3.4)
		PCl	Prepositional clause (6.2.5)
Av	Adverb (2.5.1; 3.2.4)	Ph	Phrase (2.2)
AvP	Adverb phrase (2.5.1; (4.4.2)	pn	Pronoun (3.1; 3.3.2; 4.3.2)
CCl	Comparative clause (6.2.4)	PP	Prepositional phrase (2.5.1; 4.3.3)

cj	(Subordinating or co-ordinating) con-junction (3.1; 3.3.5)	N	Noun (2.5.1; 3.2.1)
		RCl	Relative clause (6.2.3)
		-'s	Genitive marker (4.1; 4.3.4)
Cl	Clause (2.2) (for Cli, Cling, Clen, see below)	SCl	Subordinate clause (5.2; 6.1)
d	Determiner (3.1; 3.3.1; 4.3.2)	Se	Sentence (2.2)
e	Enumerator (3.1; 3.3.3)	V	Verb (2.5.1; 3.2.2) (used for full-verb or operator-verb)
GP	Genitive phrase (2.5.1; 4.3.4)		
ij	Interjection (3.1; 3.3.7)	v	Operator-verb (3.1; 3.3.6)
MCl	Main clause (5.2)	VP	Verb phrase (2.5.1; 4.5)
		Wo	Word (2.2)

Composite labels

Cl, ACl, CCl, NCl and RCl combine with i, ing, en to form composite labels for non-finite clause types:

Cli	Infinitive clause	⎫
Cling	-ING clause	⎬ (5.8; for AClen, NCli, etc., see 6.4)
Clen	-EN clause	⎭

V and v combine with o, s, ed, i, ing, en to form composite labels for finite and non-finite verb forms:

Vo	Present tense or base form	⎫
Vs	Third person singular present tense form	⎬ (3.2.2, 3.3.6, 4.5.1)
Ved	Past tense form	⎭
Vi	Infinitive (4.5.1)	
Ving	-ING or present participle	⎱ (3.2.2, 3.3.6, 4.5.1)
Ven	-EN or past participle	⎰

Specialised labels

The following symbols are used, mainly in 4.5, for subclasses of *Aux* and v:

Aux: *Mod*	Modality (4.5)		v: be	Primary verb *to be* (3.3.6; 4.5)
Pass	Passive voice (4.5)			
Perf	Perfective aspect (4.5)		do	'Dummy' verb *do* (4.5; 4.5.2)
Prog	Progressive aspect (4.5)		hv	Primary verb *to have* (3.3.6; 4.5)
			m	Modal verb (3.3.6; 4.5)

The following particles (3.3.8) are used as their own labels:

it	'empty' subject *it* (7.7.1)	there	'existential' *there* (7.7.2)
		to	infinitive marker (3.4)
not	clause negation (3.4)		

Bracketing

[ ] around clauses
( ) around phrases   } (2.3.1)
–   separates word constituents
⟨ ⟩ encloses two or more coordinates (6.7)
{ } encloses an optional constituent (2.4.4)
⌐___⌐ links interrupted constituents of a unit (5.1.3): e.g. (*Is (he) kidding*)?

Labelling

The symbol * (asterisk) precedes an ungrammatical construction (2.5.1).

Form labels (2.5.1) have an initial capital for open classes, lower case for closed classes. They are written as subscripts before the opening bracket or before the word: $_{NP}(_{pn}You!)$.

Function labels (2.5.2) are in italics in the text; when writing them, use underlining: e.g. use $\underline{S}$ for *S*. They are written as superscripts before the opening bracket or before the word: $^{Voc}(^{H}You!)$.

Function plus form labels (3.2.1, 3.3.8): the function label is written above the form label; $^{Voc}_{NP}(^{H}_{pn}You!)$.

Skeleton analysis (6.6)

——————— above a directly subordinated constituent (6.5.1, 6.6)
══════ above an indirectly subordinated constituent (6.5.2, 6.6)

The symbol + (plus) stands for the coordinating conjunction in linked coordination (6.7)

The comma is used between coordinates in unlinked coordination (6.7.1)

Tree diagrams (2.3.2)

See 5.9 on how to build up a fully labelled tree diagram.

PART A
INTRODUCTION

1

What grammar is and is not

1.1 Grammar and its role in language

It is important from the outset that we are clear about what we mean by the term GRAMMAR in this book. Many people think of grammar as a rather boring school subject which has little use in real life. They may have come across the concept in Latin 'O' level, in English composition, or in the explanations of teachers as to what is 'good' or 'bad' grammar. So grammar is often associated in people's minds with one of the following ideas: a dead language such as Latin, learning how to write 'good English', or learning how to speak 'properly'. None of these ideas about grammar is completely wrong, but they do not represent the whole picture.

In this book we shall use the term *grammar* in reference to the mechanism according to which language works when it is used to communicate with other people. We cannot see this mechanism concretely, because it is represented rather abstractly in the human mind, but we know it is there because it works. One way of describing this mechanism is as a set of rules which allow us to put words together in certain ways, but which do not allow others. At some level, speakers of a language must know these rules, otherwise they would not be able to put words together in a meaningful way.

Even if they have never heard of the word *grammar* all native speakers of English (i.e. those who have learned English as their first language) know at least unconsciously that adjectives are placed before nouns in English. Thus you would get unanimous agreement among English speakers that *The blue book is on the table* (where *blue* is an adjective, *book* a noun) is a possible sentence, whereas *The book blue is on the table* is not.

If we study the grammar of our native language, then we are trying to make explicit the knowledge of the language that we already have. We might do this out of pure curiosity as to how language works, but we might also find the knowledge useful for other purposes. We might wish

3

to teach English to foreigners, for example, or work out how a foreign language is different from our own. Or we might want to work out how the language of poetry or advertising makes an impact on us, or learn to criticise and improve our own style of writing.

So far we have said crudely that grammar is a mechanism for putting words together, but we have said little about sound or meaning. We can think of grammar as being a central part of language which relates sound and meaning. The meaning of a message conveyed by language has to be converted into words put together according to grammatical rules, and these words are then conveyed by sound. The term PHONOLOGY is often used to mean the system of sounds in a language, and SEMANTICS, the system of meaning. However, in this book we will be concerned mainly with the central component of language, GRAMMAR, which relates phonology and semantics, or sound and meaning. The relationship between the three components in represented in Figure 1.1.

Figure 1.1

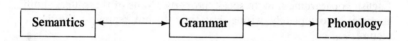

So meanings are conveyed, via grammar, in sound; but what about writing? One of the ideas which many people have about language is that it has to do with the written language. The word *grammar* in fact comes from the Greek *grapho*, meaning 'write', but although statements about the origin of words such as this may be interesting historically, we cannot rely on them to tell us the current meaning of the word, as meanings change in time. Traditionally, grammar did have to do with the written language, especially that of Latin, which continued to be studied and used in its written form long after it had ceased to be generally spoken. But the written form of a language is really only secondary to its spoken form, which developed first. Children learn to speak before they learn to write; and whereas they learn to speak naturally, without tuition, from the language they hear around them, they have to be taught to write: that is, to convert their speech into a written or secondary form. However, writing performs an extremely important function in our culture (see Chapter 8), and in this book we shall view grammar as a mechanism for producing both speech and writing. Therefore we can modify our previous diagram, as shown in Figure 1.2.

Figure 1.2

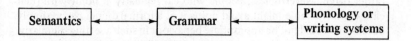

| Semantics | ←——→ | Grammar | ←——→ | Phonology or writing systems |

1.2 'Good' and 'bad' grammar

The terms *good* and *bad* do not apply to *grammar* in the way in which we are using that term in this book. If we view grammar as a set of rules which describe how we use language, the rules themselves are not good or bad, though they may be described adequately or inadequately in a description of how the language works.

Linguists who write grammars are concerned with **describing** how the language is used rather than **prescribing** how it should be used. So if it is common for people to use sentences such as *Who did you give this to?*, then the rules of a descriptive grammar must allow for this type of sentence in its rules. Those concerned with prescription, however, might consider this to be an example of 'bad grammar', and might suggest that *To whom did you give this?* would be a better sentence. What is considered better or worse, however, is of no concern to a descriptive linguist in writing a grammar that accounts for the way people actually use language. If people are communicating effectively with language, then they must be following rules, even if those rules are not universally approved. The role of the linguist is thus analogous to that of the anthropologist who, if asked to describe a particular culture's eating habits, would be expected to do so without expressing a personal opinion as to what they should be like. The latter would be a prescriptive approach. It is probably easier, however, to avoid being prescriptive when dealing with a culture other than our own. As speakers of our native language we are bound to have ideas or prescriptive notions about how it should be used. But we should be able to separate the expression of our own opinions from the activity of describing actual language use.

Although the focus of this book is to be on descriptive grammar, we have to recognise the existence of prescriptive rules, such as that which says that one should avoid ending a sentence with a preposition. This 'rule' was broken in the example quoted above (*Who did you give this to?*) because the preposition *to* is placed at the end of the sentence. Prescriptive rules are clearly not grammatical rules in the same sense as descriptive rules, so it might be appropriate to call them rules of grammatical etiquette. Then we can see that what some people call 'bad grammar' is akin to 'bad manners', i.e. it refers to something you might want to avoid doing, if only to convey a good impression in a particular situation. Some people consider it bad manners to put one's elbows on the table while eating and yet, from a descriptive point of view, it occurs rather often. Nevertheless, people who eat regularly at home with their elbows on the table might avoid doing it at a formal dinner party, simply because it would not be appropriate behaviour in such a setting. Similarly, there are occasions when being on one's best linguistic behaviour means obeying rules which one would not normally obey.

This leads us to the point that, as well as knowing the grammatical rules of a language, its speakers also have to know how to use the language appropriately, and this often involves a choice between different options or different LANGUAGE VARIETIES.

1.3   Variation in language

1.3.1   Introduction

If we were to take a dogmatically prescriptive approach to language, we might suggest that there was just one, 'correct' form of the language which everyone should use. We might recognise that not everyone speaks the 'correct' form of the language, but we would describe any other form as simply wrong.

If, however, we are to take the descriptive approach explored in this book, we cannot dismiss some forms of language as incorrect: we have to be prepared to describe all varieties of language.

A descriptive approach recognises that there are many varieties of a language such as English. We can identify Americans as speaking in a different way from British people, northerners from southerners, young from old, middle-class people from working-class people, and men from women. So language will vary according to certain characteristics of its USER. A user's speech may well reflect several of these characteristics simultaneously: for example, a young woman may well speak differently from both a young man and an older woman.

So language can vary from user to user, depending on the user's personal characteristics. This is not meant to imply that each person speaks a uniform variety of language which never changes. Of course speech may change as personal characteristics change: as a young person becomes older, a northerner moves south, or social-class membership changes as a result of education, for example. In addition, a person's speech will vary according to the USE that speech is put to. For example, the way you talk to a friend will be different from the way you talk to a stranger. The way you talk on the telephone will be different from the way you talk to someone face to face, and you will use yet another variety in writing a letter. Your language will also vary according to what you are talking about, e.g. sport, politics or religion. The variation of language according to its use means that each user has a whole range of language varieties which he or she learns by experience, and knows how to use appropriately. If you talked in the classroom as you would in the pub, you might be considered ill-mannered (this might be using 'bad grammar' from a prescriptive point of view), and if you addressed your friend as you would your teacher, you might be laughed at.

We now consider variation in language according to user and use in more detail.

1.3.2 Variation according to user

Characteristics of the language user which can effect language include the following: regional origin, social-class membership, age and sex. A useful term in connection with these characteristics is DIALECT. This is often used to describe regional origin, as in, for example, Yorkshire dialect, Cockney (London) dialect, but can be used to refer to any language variety related to the personal characteristics listed above.

REGIONAL ORIGIN. We can often tell where a person comes from by the way he or she speaks. Depending on how familiar we are with the variety of a given region, we may be able to identify, for example, Cockney, Yorkshire, Scouse (Liverpool) or Geordie (Tyneside) speech. We can identify speech on the basis of its pronunciation, vocabulary or grammar. For example, in Yorkshire dialect, as in some other northern dialects, the words *put* and *putt* are pronounced alike because the vowel found in the standard or southern pronunciation of words such as *putt*, *bus*, *cup*, etc., is not used. The dialect also has its own vocabulary, for example, the use of the word *happen* to mean 'perhaps'. Finally, on the level of grammar, Yorkshire dialect has *were* as the past tense of the verb *be* in all its forms, so that, for example, *he were* is heard commonly instead of *he was*. So dialect can be identified on the levels of pronunciation, vocabulary and grammar. Vocabulary and grammar are the most basic levels for describing a dialect, since regional pronunciation, or a regional ACCENT, can be used when speaking standard English as well as when speaking a regional dialect.

At this point it should be emphasised that the term *dialect* does not imply an incorrect or deviant use of language: it is simply used to mean a variety of language determined by the characteristics of its user. Sometimes, however, the term may be used to refer to varieties of the language which are not STANDARD. The standard language is in fact just another variety or dialect, but in Britain it happens to be established as that variety which is generally used by southern British, educated speakers of the language, and in writing and in public usage such as on radio and television. It is sometimes known as 'BBC English' or even 'The Queen's

English'. Standard English is not inherently better or more 'grammatical' than non-standard English (all varieties are grammatical in that they follow rules), but it has prestige for social rather than linguistic reasons. Its prestige is due to the fact that it is ultimately based on the speech of educated people living in the south-east of England, where the important institutions of government and education became established. Because standard English is the best-known variety of English in Britain, we shall use it for analysis in Part B of this book.

SOCIAL-CLASS MEMBERSHIP. The extent to which we can identify social-class dialects is controversial, but the social class of the speaker does seem to affect the variety of the language used. In Britain there is an interesting relationship between social class and the use of standard and non-standard speech in that the 'higher' you are up the social scale, the less likely you are to use non-standard or regionally identifiable speech. This means that it is not usually possible to identify the **regional** background of, for example, an upper-middle-class speaker educated at a public school. To make this clearer, imagine that you travel from Land's End to John O'Groats talking only to factory workers, and tape-recording their speech. Then, on the way back, you take the same route, but record only the speech of 'professionals' such as doctors and teachers. On comparing the tape-recordings you would expect to find more variation in the speech of the workers that in that of the professionals. The speech of workers would contain a higher proportion of features which are not found in the standard language. Several of these features would be found in more than one area: for example, *done* as the past tense of *do* is found in both Liverpool and London among working-class speakers (who might say, for example, *I done it* as opposed to *I did it*).

AGE. Less is known about the effect of age on language variation, but there may be grammatical features which distinguish age dialects to some extent. For example, the question *Do you have some money?* would be more likely to be asked by a younger speaker of British English (it is common for speakers of all ages in American English) than an older speaker, as the latter would be more likely to say *Have you (got) some money?* The way young people speak is of particular interest as it may be indicative of the direction in which the language is changing.

SEX. There seem to be some linguistic differences according to the speaker's sex, though little is yet known about them. However, certain grammatical features have been associated more with women than with men, and it has been found that women are more likely to use standard English than men.

It should by now be clear that personal characteristics of the language user can combine to affect the variety of language used. The term *dialect* has been used for convenience to identify the effects of these characteristics, as in, for example, *regional dialect, social-class dialect*, but these are not really separate entities. All the characteristics interact with one another, so that any individual will speak a language variety made up of features from several 'dialects'.

1.3.3 Variation according to use

As was pointed out in 1.3.1, no user of language uses one uniform variety of language. Language also varies according to the use to which it is put. While the term *dialect* is convenient to refer to language variation according to the user, REGISTER can be used to refer to variation according to use (sometimes also known as 'style'). Register can be subdivided into three categories of language use, each of which affects the language variety. These are: TENOR, MODE and DOMAIN.

TENOR. This has to do with the relationship between a speaker and the addressee(s) in a given situation, and is often characterised by greater or lesser formality. For example, a request to close the window might be *Would you be so kind as to close the window*? in a formal situation, compared with *Shut the window, please* in an informal situation. Formality also has the effect of producing speech which is closer to the standard. For example, a witness in court might be careful to say *He didn't do it, Your Honour*, rather than *'E never done it*, which might be said to Cockney-speaking friends outside the courtroom. A speaker has to know which is the right kind of language to use in which circumstances, though sometimes the wrong choice may be made deliberately, for humorous or sarcastic effect.

MODE. This has to do with the effects of the medium in which the language is transmitted. Spoken language used in face-to-face situations makes use of many 'non-verbal' movements such as gestures and facial expressions. On the telephone, however, the visual channel is not available so that, for example, *Yes* has to be substituted for head-nodding. In writing, only the visual channel is available so that the effect of intonation, or 'tone of voice', cannot be conveyed, except, in part, by graphic means such as exclamation- and question-marks. Written language usually involves the additional characteristic that the addressee, who is not present, cannot respond immediately, and this has an effect on the language. For example, in letters, direct questions tend to be less common than in conversation, so that you might be more likely to write, for example, *Let me know whether you are coming* than *Are you coming*? The category of mode is particularly relevant for the distinction between written and spoken language, and this will be given further consideration in Chapter 8.

DOMAIN. This has to do with how language varies according to the activity in which it plays a part. A seminar about chemistry, for example, will involve a wider range of vocabulary, more technical terms and possibly longer sentences than a conversation about the weather (unless by meteorologists!). Similarly, the language of a legal document will be different from that of an advertisement, and the language of a religious service will be different from that of newspaper reporting. We can thus refer to the domains of chemistry, law, religion, and so on.

As with dialect variation, the categories of register variation all affect language simultaneously so that we cannot really identify discrete registers any more than discrete dialects. Also, dialect and register variation interact with each other since both the dimensions of user and use are always present.

To summarise what has been said in this section (1.3), language varies according to both user and use. Certain personal characteristics will be reflected in the speech of a given person, and that person will also have access to a range of varieties appropriate for various uses.

1.4   English and other languages

1.4.1   What is a language?

So far we have shown that a language such as English has many different varieties, which result from a combination of factors. We have also shown that these varieties are not separate entities, and that although they can be described on the basis of linguistic features, they cannot be categorically distinguished from one another.

We have not questioned the assumption, however, that a language made up of such varieties can be clearly distinguished from all other languages. It is true that we have separate labels for different languages, e.g. English, French, Chinese, but the existence of labels should not delude us into believing that these are linguistically well-defined entities. One criterion used to define a language is MUTUAL INTELLIGIBILITY. According to this, people who can understand each other speak the same language, whereas those who cannot do not. But there are degrees of comprehension. For example, southern British English speakers may have difficulty understanding Geordie, and American English speakers may find it virtually incomprehensible. There is even less mutual intelligibility in the group of 'dialects' referred to as Chinese: speakers of Mandarin, for example, cannot understand Cantonese, though both use the same written language. On the other hand, in Scandinavia, speakers of Norwegian, Danish and Swedish can often understand one another, even though they speak what are called different languages. If Scandinavia were one political entity, then these languages might be considered dialects of just one language. So the criteria for defining languages are often political and geographical rather than strictly linguistic.

1.4.2. Grammatical rules in English and other languages

If a language variety is viewed as a standard language rather than as a dialect (usually for non-linguistic reasons), then it has more social prestige. This explains, for example, the insistence of separatists in Catalonia that Catalan is a language rather than a dialect of Spanish. When a language variety does not have social prestige, its grammatical rules are often stigmatised. This is true of the rule of multiple negation in some English dialects, for example. This rule allows sentences such as *I didn't see nothing* ('I didn't see anything'), which would not occur in the standard. The high prestige of the standard leads people to claim that multiple negation is wrong because it is illogical or misleading. However, we have never heard French speakers complain about multiple negation in standard French, which has *Je n'ai vu rien*, containing two negative elements *n'* and *rien*, as a translation of the English sentence. Moreover, Chaucer had no inhibitions about the matter when he wrote (in the *Prologue* to the *Canterbury Tales*):

> He nevere yet no vileynye ne sayde
> In al his lyf unto no maner wight.

> ('He never yet didn't speak no discourtesy
> in all his life to no kind of person'.)

In fact, not content with double negation, he uses four negatives in these two lines! Multiple negation was perfectly acceptable in Chaucer's period.

It is important for English speakers of whatever variety to realise that other languages or varieties may follow different grammatical rules. We cannot assume that other languages or varieties will fit the framework of the one we know well. This kind of mistake was made in the past by classical scholars who tried to describe English in the framework of Latin. For example, the prescriptive rule that *It is I* is right and *It is me* is wrong comes from assuming that the distinction between *I* and *me* must be the same as the distinction made in Latin between *ego* and *me*. This rule is not at all descriptive, since *It is me* occurs often in English.

Many of us first become aware of the existence of grammatical rules different from our own when we learn a foreign language such as French, German or Spanish. We find that, for example, the rules of word order in these languages are different from English. In French a direct object pronoun must precede the verb rather than follow it. So, for example, *I see him* is translated as *Je le vois* (literally 'I him see'). In German the infinitive form of the verb must be placed at the end of the sentence, so that, for example, *I will go tomorrow* is translated as *Ich werde morgen gehen* (literally 'I will tomorrow go'). In Spanish a subject pronoun or noun comes after a past participle in a question rather than before, so that, for example, *Have you forgotten the word?* is translated as *¿Ha olvidado usted la palabra?* (literally, 'Have forgotten you the word?'). However, French, German and Spanish still show considerable similarity to English in their grammatical rules, for all four languages belong to the INDO-EUROPEAN group, and have been in close cultural contact. In all four, for example, you can form questions by changing the order of words in the sentence. This is not true of all languages, however: in Japanese, for example, which is not an Indo-European language, questions are formed by the addition of a particle (*ka*) at the end of the sentence. So *Suzuki-san wa ikimasu* means 'Mr/Ms Suzuki is going', while *Suzuki-san wa ikimasu ka?* means 'Is Mr/Ms Suzuki going?'

These examples have served to illustrate that we must avoid preconceptions about the form which grammatical rules will take in a given language or language variety. Instead, we can find out what these rules are by observing the way people speak or write in different situations. Once we have done this, we can return (as this book does in Chapter 11) to questions of prescriptive usage.

1.5   Grammar and effective communication

The main function of language is to communicate with other people. We said in section 1.2 that there was no such thing as 'good' or 'bad' grammar. It is legitimate, however, to distinguish between good and bad *communication*. In other words, language should not be evaluated according to what type of grammatical rules it follows, but according to whether it conveys its message effectively. It is quite possible, for example, to speak or write according to the grammatical rules of standard English, and yet to produce language which is unclear or difficult to follow. This can be described as 'bad style', and the following examples from written English illustrate the point:

(1)   This is a picture that a girl that a friend of mine knows painted.
(2)   I saw it in a book that a former teacher of mine thought of at one time setting us some exam questions out of.
(3)   If the baby cannot drink cold milk, it should be boiled.
(4)   For sale: a piano belonging to a lady going abroad with an oak case and carved legs.
(5)   The problem of what contribution the public should make to the swimming pool arose.
(6)   She has given the job in London up.

It is interesting to consider why certain sentences are felt to be less successfully constructed than others. In (1) and (2) the sentences are put together in a way which makes them difficult to unravel and understand. For example, in (1) who painted the picture–the girl or the friend? Most people will have to re-read the sentence in order to puzzle out exactly what it is saying. In (3) and (4) the construction of each sentence leads to an ambiguity: what the writer intended to say is not clearly stated. This does not necessarily imply that the reader cannot work out the intended meaning. You are unlikely, for instance, to imagine that the baby rather than the milk is to be boiled in (3). But you arrive at this conclusion **in spite of** grammar rather than **because of** it. The grammar permits a second meaning, which like an after-image lurks distractingly in the background. In (5) and (6) the difficulty is that there seems to be a lack of balance, a 'topheaviness', in the construction of each sentence. To solve this difficulty, one could change the order of the words as follows:

(5a) The problem *arose* of what contribution the public should make to the swimming pool.
(6a) She has given *up* the job in London.

At this stage we shall not attempt to explain exactly what is the matter with (1)-(6); it is enough to note that these are just three types of difficulty in forming and interpreting grammatical sentences.

Since using language is a skill, it is inevitable that some people are more skilled in this respect than others. There is no need to shrink from evaluation of this skill – for example, saying that one writer has a better style of writing than another. It is helpful, for this purpose, to be aware of the grammatical resources of the language, and the various possibilities which may be open to the user who wants to make effective use of the language. In this way we gain conscious control over the skill of using language. This is one of the main reasons for learning about grammar, and we shall return to it in Chapter 12.

1.6   Grammar in prose style

At the other extreme from sentences (1)-(6) are the products of literary masters of prose style. In literature, the resources of the language, including grammar, are used not only for **efficient** communication of ideas, but for **effective** communication in a broader sense: communicating and interpreting people's experience of life, individual and collective. This means using language in special ways, as can be illustrated, on a small scale, by even a short sentence like the following:

(7)　To live is like to love – all reason is against it, and all healthy instinct for it.

(Samuel Butler, *Notebooks*)

The difficulty of making sense of (7) is quite different from that of making sense of (1) and (2). An unusual sentiment is expressed in a striking and unusual way. This is typical of literary expression, and means that much meaning is condensed into a few words. Let us briefly consider how grammar contributes to the effect, particularly through *parallelism*: the matching of one construction with another, similar one. Figure 1.3 is a visual representation of this parallelism.

Figure 1.3

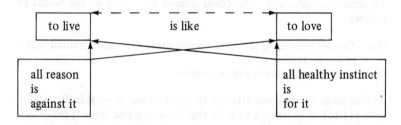

As the diagram shows, sentence (7) is cleverly constructed so as to bring out two parallelisms. The first is one of similarity (*to live. . .to love*) and the second is one of contrast (*all reason. . . all healthy instinct*). The parallelisms are expressed by symmetry in the actual choice and combination of words, so that almost every word in the sentence is balanced significantly against another word. Even the sound of words helps to underline these relationships: the analogy between *live* and *love* is emphasised by similar pronunciation, and the word *like*, which 'mediates' between the two, resembles the former in appearance and the latter in meaning.

Sentences exist primarily in time rather than in space, and so the order in which words occur is important for literary effect. Suppose (7) had read like this:

(7a)　To live is like to love – all healthy instinct is for it, and all reason against it.

The result would have been to stress 'reason' at the expense of 'instinct' – almost as if the writer were inviting us all to commit suicide. This is because there is a general principle (see 12.2.3) that the most newsworthy and important information in a sentence tends to be saved to the end. Sentence (7), as Butler writes it, is optimistic rather than pessimistic – for he places 'instinct' in a triumphant position at the end, adding the word *healthy* for further optimistic emphasis. The first part of (7) provides a further example of the significance of ordering. Let us imagine that Butler had written *To love is like to live*. . . In that case he would be comparing 'loving' with 'living' rather than vice versa. As it stands, (7) in effect says: 'You know about love being the triumph of healthy instinct over reason, don't you? Now I'm telling you that life itself is like that.' That is, the sentence begins with what we may call shared general knowledge (the traditional conception of love defying reason), and extends this well-known idea to a new sphere – or rather, generalises it to the whole of life. So if Butler had written 'To love is like to live', the whole effect would have been altered, to the bafflement of the reader.

This extremely simple example shows how much the way we construct a sentence – the way we put the parts together – can contribute to the effect it makes on a reader or listener. If we want to understand the virtues of good writing, whether as students of literature, or as writers ourselves, we need to understand something of the grammatical resources of the language, and the ways in which they may be exploited.

1.7 Grammar in poetry

The same applies to poetry. Poetry and grammar seem to be poles apart – the one suggestive of 'the spark o' Nature's fire', the other of the cold eye of analysis. But a poet would be foolish to proclaim 'I am above grammar', for it is by grammatical choice that many of the special meanings of poetry are achieved. Often these effects show 'poetic licence' – the poet's acknowledged privilege of deviation from the rules or conventions of everyday language. Without the rules, of course, the poet's deviation from the rules would lose its communicative force. The following short poem, on a nun's taking the veil, shows some of the characteristics (in addition to those of metre and rhyme) which we may expect to find in the language of poetry:

(8)   *Heaven–Haven*

I have desired to go
Where springs not fail,
To fields where flies no sharp and sided hail
And a few lilies blow.

> And I have asked to be
> Where no storms come,
> Where the green swell is in the havens dumb,
> And out of the swing of the sea.

(Gerard Manley Hopkins)

As in (7), but more obviously, words strike up special relationships with one another because of similarities of sound and meaning, and also because of similarities of grammatical structure. The first tendency is best illustrated by the pun in the title, linking the words *heaven* and *haven*. The second tendency is evident in the marked parallelism of the two stanzas, as shown in this 'skeleton' version:

(8a)   I have ____ ed to –   And I have ____ ed to –
              Where _____   Where _____
          To fields where _____   Where _____
              And _____   And _____

We could study, further, the unEnglish grammar of the second line (*Where springs not fail*, rather than *Where springs do not fail*); the inversion of the normal order of words in the third line (*To fields where flies no sharp and sided hail*); and the postponement of the adjective *dumb* to the end of the seventh line. Such unusual features of grammar contribute to a strange dissociation of words from their expected context, so that simple and ordinary words like *springs, flies, blow, swell* and *swing* seem to attain abnormal force. It is enough here to point out that the poet's artistry in language involves both extra freedom (including freedom to depart from the rules of grammar), and extra discipline (the discipline which comes with the superimposition of special structures on language). We shall later (Chapter 10) explore the application of grammar to the study of literature, through specimen analysis.

1.8 Conclusion

In this chapter we have aimed to provide a backcloth for the study of English grammar. We began with an attempt to 'demythologise' the subject: that is, to dispel some misconceptions about grammar which have been prevalent in the past, and still have influence today.

We showed how the notion of grammar must allow for variation in language, and that we cannot prescribe the form which grammatical rules will take. We thus rejected the possibility of evaluating grammar itself, but went on to show how language can be used for more or less effective communication. In Part C of this book we will return to some of the points which we have managed to raise only briefly and simply so far, and we will also illustrate the practical benefits of studying grammar for understanding our language and using it more effectively.

Part B, which follows, aims to make you aware of your knowledge of how standard English is structured. We shall be introducing grammatical terminology and techniques of analysis that will enable you to describe this structure. Part of understanding grammar is learning how to do it, so we would urge you to work through the exercises in each chapter in order to apply your new knowledge.

Exercises

Exercise 1a   (answers on p. 199)

True/false questionnaire (to test your understanding of the chapter)
The following statements should be labelled 'true' or 'false':

1. The study of grammar must include the study of Latin.
2. Grammar can be seen as a set of rules which we follow when we use language.
3. We can follow the grammatical rules of our native language without knowing them consciously.
4. The study of grammar will improve your spelling.
5. Grammar only deals with the study of writing, because it originally meant 'to write' in Greek.
6. Children have to be properly tutored in their language if they are to learn to speak grammatically.
7. Studying grammar involves learning how people should speak.
8. It is incorrect to end a sentence with a preposition.
9. American English is less grammatical than British English.
10. The way we speak depends, among other things, on our personal characteristics.
11. The way we speak to friends is identical to the way we speak to strangers.
12. Dialect is inferior to the standard language.
13. Factory workers in the north and south of Britain differ more in their speech than do doctors.
14. The term TENOR refers to the pitch of your voice in a given situation.
15. Whatever you can convey in speech, you can also convey in writing.
16. Medicine could be considered a language domain.
17. All languages follow the same grammatical rules.
18. A sentence which is difficult to understand must be ungrammatical.
19. The use of language in literature is the same as in conversation.
20. Poetic licence is official permission to write poetry.

Exercise 1b (answers on p. 199)

Classification of sentences
All of the following sentences have something 'wrong' with them. Try to work out whether each is:

A   ungrammatical in the sense that it does not follow a rule observable in the language behaviour of native speakers of English;

B   'bad etiquette' from the point of view of prescriptive grammar (see 1.2); or

C   'bad style' in the sense that it does not communicate effectively.

1. I can recommend this candidate for the post for which he applies with complete confidence.
2. I ain't going nowhere tonight.
3. We need more comprehensive schools.
4. To was or not to was, that be the ask.
5. There lives the dearest freshness deep down things.
6. How are you, it has a long time that we don't have heared from you again.
7. I gave him the present that I had bought in the shop in which I had met the man to whose house I went yesterday.
8. Him and me are going to the beach today.
9. Eggs should be stamped with the date when they are laid by the farmer.
10. This is the sort of English up with which I will not put.

Exercise 1c (answers and sources on p. 200)

Identifying categories of language use (see 1.3.3)
Identify the categories of language use in these samples of language, as follows:

Tenor   formal or informal
Mode   spoken or written
Domain   advertising, journalism, or religion

Example   After reading this, other central heating systems won't look so hot.

Tenor: informal;   *Mode*: written;   *Domain*: advertising.

1. The Senate yesterday announced the creation of a nine-man committee to investigate the relationship between Billy Carter and Colonel Qaddafi's government in Libya.
2. Praise and glory and wisdom, thanksgiving and honour, power and might, be to our God for ever and ever! Amen.

3. Anywhere return, still only 50p.
4. Contour tiling, it looks superb, it feels marvellous.
5. So what's likely to happen now? Well the report has been sent to the Director of Public Prosecutions, in view of er certain evidence.

PART B
ANALYSIS

2

Sentences and their parts

Grammar can be briefly described as a set of rules for constructing and for analysing sentences. The process of analysing sentences into their parts, or CONSTITUENTS, is known as PARSING. In this and the next five chapters we shall gradually build up a simplified technique for parsing English sentences. If parsing seems at first a negative process of taking things to pieces, remember that by taking a machine to pieces one learns how it works. Analysis and synthesis are two aspects of the same process of understanding. This chapter introduces the main concepts of grammar, with examples. If you find parts of it difficult, it will be a comfort to know that all the classifications of Chapter 2 will be dealt with in more detail later on.

2.1 Prologue: parts of speech

2.1.1 A test

First, here is a short test, which may be seen as a very easy general-knowledge test about English grammar. Its purpose is simply to start you thinking on the right lines; in some cases, no doubt, this will mean remembering what you learned many years ago, and have rarely thought about since.

(a) In sentences (1)-(4) make a list, in four columns, of the italicised words which are (i) **nouns**, (ii) **verbs**, (iii) **adjectives**, and (iv) **adverbs**:

(1) *New cars are very expensive nowadays.*
(2) I *understand* that even *Dracula hates werewolves.*
(3) I have *won* more *rounds* of *golf* than you have *had hot dinners.*
(4) Mother Hubbard *went* to the cupboard, *looking vainly* for *food* to *give* her *dog.*

(b) Now that you have made the list, say **why** you classified the words as you did. This will require some kind of definition of what a noun, a verb, an adjective, or an adverb is.

If you remember about traditional word classes, or PARTS OF SPEECH as they are called, your lists will be something like the following: *cars, Dracula, werewolves, rounds, golf, dinners, food* and *dog* are nouns; *are, understand, hates, won, had, went, looking* and *give* are verbs; *new, expensive* and *hot* are adjectives; *very, nowadays* and *vainly* are adverbs. In order to explain your lists, you may have used familiar definitions like these:

(i)   'A **noun** is a naming word: it refers to a thing, person, substance, etc.'

(ii)   'A **verb** is a doing word: it refers to an action.'

(iii) 'An **adjective** is a word which describes or qualifies a noun.'

(iv)   'An **adverb** is a word which describes or qualifies other types of words, such as verbs, adjectives and adverbs.'

These are largely **semantic** definitions, i.e. definitions in terms of **meaning**. Such definitions are a useful starting-point, especially in the early days of learning about grammar, but they have two drawbacks: (a) they are often vague, and (b) they are sometimes wrong.

For example, *golf* and *dinners* in sentence (3) are nouns, but do not fit the definition given: *golf* names a type of game, and *dinners* a type of meal. This defect could be mended if we included games and meals under the 'etc.' of (i); but having extended the definition of nouns in this way, we would have to extend it in other ways, to include other words such as *rounds*. The truth is that it is difficult to see anything in common between all the 'things' to which nouns can refer, except the fact that nouns can refer to them. On the other hand, it *is* true that the most typical or central members of the class of nouns refer to people, things and substances. These are often called CONCRETE NOUNS.

Similarly with verbs, the definition of a 'doing word' applies naturally to *went, looked, won* and *give*, but does not so easily apply to *are, hates* and *understand*. We could improve the definition by saying that a verb can denote 'states' as well as 'actions', but the difficulty is partly that words like *state* and *action* are themselves vague in meaning. When we say *The girls seem hungry*, for example, does *seem* refer to a state? The adjective *hungry* fits the definition of 'state word' more easily than *seem*. And what about *Two twos are four*? Saying that *are* refers to a 'state' here seems to be pressing the meaning of 'state' a bit too far.

An additional problem is that such definitions fail to keep the parts of speech apart. Compare *hates* in *Dracula hates werewolves* with *hatred* in *Dracula's hatred of werewolves*. It is generally accepted that *hates* here is a verb, whereas *hatred* is a noun; but this cannot be due to the meaning of these words, for they both refer to the same 'thing' - that is, to an emotion which is the opposite of love. We could make the same point about many ABSTRACT NOUNS which, like *hatred*, are related in form to a verb or an adjective: *reduce/reduction; love/love; increase/ increase; kind/kindness; different/difference; cold/cold.*

2.1.2 An example: 'Jabberwocky'
So we cannot always rely on meaning in defining word classes. The point is made irrefutably when we notice (as many have noticed before) that in nonsense poems such as Lewis Carroll's *Jabberwocky* we can tell the word class of the nonsense words even though we do not know their meaning:

> 'Twas brillig, and the slithy toves
> Did gyre and gimble in the wabe:
> All mimsy were the borogoves,
> And the mome raths outgrabe.

We know, for instance, that *toves* and *borogoves* are nouns, that *gyre, gimble,* and *outgrabe* are verbs, and that *slithy* and *mimsy* are adjectives. But **how** do we know? Certainly not on account of meaning! Rather, we classify each word on the basis of its form and its position. *Borogoves* is a noun because it ends in -*s* (the regular plural ending of nouns), and because it follows *the*. *Slithy* is an adjective because it comes between *the* and the plural noun *toves*. *Outgrabe* is a verb because it has a common verb prefix *out-* (cf. *outwit, outdo*), and also because if it were not a verb, the sentence would not be complete. These are only partial explanations, but they show the kind of intuitive skill in grammatical analysis which all of us possess, and which a book on grammar has to explain. They also show that this intuitive skill is not primarily dependent on meaning.

2.1.3 The fuzzy boundaries of grammatical classes
We learn, then, that semantic definitions are fallible and are also dispensable. But this does not mean that they are useless. Defining grammatical terms like *noun* and *verb* is like defining many other words of the language, such as *cup, chair, bird, dog, mountain.* We can easily identify the features of the most typical members of the class: for example, a 'prototype' chair has four legs, is made with wood, has a back, and is used for sitting on. But there are other objects which we would be less inclined to call chairs, though they are marginally so; for example, a sofa, a settle, a pew, a chaise longue, a bench. In such cases, we cannot easily give a yes-or-no answer to the question 'Is this a chair?' Similarly with birds: the typical bird has two legs, two wings, feathers, a tail; it flies, lays eggs in a nest, and sings. In this, sparrows and robins

are typical, whereas eagles, ducks and penguins are in increasing degrees less 'birdy'. The same concept of categories with fuzzy edges applies to grammar. Just as some chairs are less 'chairy' than others, and just as some birds are less 'birdy' than others, so some nouns are less 'nouny' than others, and some verbs less 'verby' than others. The typical, or prototype, nouns are those which refer to people, animals and things – and these happen, incidentally, to number amongst them the nouns which children learn first, and the nouns which are most common in adult language as well. Similarly, the typical verb is a 'doing word' – even though the most common verb of all, *to be*, is not typical in this respect.

In what follows, then, we shall often, when defining grammatical notions, use words such as 'typical' or 'generally', rather than 'every' and 'always'. This is not a weakness; it is a reflection of the fuzzy boundaries of grammatical classes, especially in the area of meaning.

This concept of a 'fuzzy' category applies not just to meaning, but also to formal aspects of definition. For example, a **typical** noun has a plural in *-s* and a **typical** verb has a past tense in *-ed*; but there are nouns which have a plural in *-en* (e.g. *oxen*), and others which have no plural at all (e.g. *sunshine*); there are also verbs which have an irregular past tense, such as *win/won*.

Grammar is not a precise logical or mathematical system, but has much in common with biological systems, in that it involves overlapping criteria, and has fuzzy edges. There are plenty of linguistic parallels to the duck-billed platypus. This means that there is not always a single, uniquely correct parsing of a sentence; there is scope for legitimate disagreement about what is the best analysis of a sentence. [Now try Exercise 2a.]

2.2   The hierarchy of units

The SENTENCE is the largest unit of language that we shall be concerned with here. A sentence is composed of smaller units, CLAUSES, PHRASES and WORDS:

GRAMMATICAL UNITS OF ENGLISH	SYMBOL
Sentence	Se
Clause	Cl
Phrase	Ph
Word	Wo

For convenience in parsing, we give each grammatical category we introduce a shorthand symbol. The symbols and abbreviations used in this book are listed on pages xiv–xvi.

The units SENTENCE and WORD need little introduction, as they are fairly clearly represented in our writing system. In general we shall identify them according to the usual conventions: that is, a sentence will be delimited by an initial capital letter and a final full-stop (or question-mark or exclamation-mark), and a word will be delimited, for most purposes, by a space (or punctuation mark other than a hyphen or apostrophe) on each side.[1]

CLAUSES are the principal units of which sentences are composed. A sentence may consist of one or more clauses. For example:

(5)   Jack Sprat could eat no fat.

This, standing on its own, is a sentence. But (5) can also occur as part of a larger unit:

(6)   [*Jack Sprat could eat no fat*], and his wife could eat no lean.
(7)   Every child knows [*that Jack Sprat could eat no fat*].

Here (6) and (7) are sentences, but the parts of them in square brackets are clauses.

PHRASES are units intermediate between **clause** and **word**. Thus (8) consists of nine words, but these words are grouped into four phrases:

(8)   (My Uncle Olaf) (was munching) (his peach) (with relish).

Like words, phrases belong to a number of different classes. *My uncle Olaf* is a NOUN PHRASE, *was munching* is a VERB PHRASE, *his peach* is another NOUN PHRASE, and *with relish* is a PREPOSITIONAL PHRASE.

Although it is possible to break words down into smaller units (known as MORPHEMES), this is not generally necessary for parsing, and we shall deal with such cases as they arise.

The units of grammar can be ordered in terms of RANK:

Higher A **sentence** consists of one or more clauses
        A **clause**   consists of one or more phrases
        A **phrase**   consists of one or more words
Lower   A **word**

It is **very important** to notice that we are using 'high' and 'low' in a special way here: what we mean is that a unit of the higher rank consists

---

[1] But note that these conventions are not always followed; e.g. *I want to stay here. With you.* and *Did we despair? Not at all.* Here *With you* and *Not at all* are not complete sentences. Also, the boundaries of words, particularly of noun compounds (see section 6.5.1), are not always clear; e.g. we can write the sequence *piggy + bank* in three different ways: *piggy bank, piggy-bank*, or *piggybank*. There is no easy way of deciding whether this is one word, or two.

of **one or more** of the units of the next lower rank. So a sentence can consist of **only one clause** (such sentences are called SIMPLE SENTENCES) and a phrase can consist of **only one word**. Compare sentence (8) with the following:

(8a)   [(Olaf) (munched) (peaches) (contentedly)].

The whole of this sentence is a single clause (as signalled by the square brackets), and each word also constitutes a phrase (in round brackets). For that matter, a whole sentence can consist of a single word: *Shoot!* is a **sentence** consisting of **one clause** consisting of **one phrase** consisting of **one word**.

At first glance this concept of rank may seem strange; but the following analogy may help to clarify it. For another human activity – not talking, but eating – we could set up a rank scale of four units: meal, course, helping, mouthful. A meal may consist of one or more than one course; a course may consist of one or more than one helping; and a helping may consist of one or more than one mouthful. Such a rank scale is adaptable enough to account for a wide variety of human eating behaviour – ranging from a seven-course banquet at which every one has second helpings, to a brief snack when, literally, someone has a 'bite to eat'. Similarly, the rank scale of grammar accounts for a wide range of language behaviour. Obviously, the rank of a unit is not necessarily related to its size, in terms of number of words; for instance, the sentence in (8a) consists of only four words, whereas the clause in square brackets in (7), which is of lower rank, consists of as many as seven words.

2.3   Grammatical notations

For both clarity and brevity, it is essential to have a way of representing grammatical structure on paper. In fact, it is useful to have two different graphic notations: bracketing, and tree diagrams.

2.3.1   Bracketing

We have already used a simple set of BRACKETING conventions:

(a)   Sentences are marked with an initial capital letter and a final full-stop.
(b)   Clauses are enclosed in square brackets: [ ].
(c)   Phrases are enclosed in round brackets: ( ).
(d)   Words are separated by spaces.
(e)   If we need to separate the grammatical components of words, we can use a dash: – .

So in (9)-(11) we have as complete a parsing as can be managed at present:

(9) [(Our land—lady) (keep—s) (a stuff—ed moose) (in her attic)].
(10) [(Uncle Olaf) (savage—ly) (devour—ed) (his six—th peach)].
(11) [(They) ('re play—ing) (Arsenal) (at home) (next week)].

Notice that *'re* in *They're playing* (11) belongs with *playing* rather than with *They*. To see this, we expand *'re* to *are*, which clearly belongs to the verb phrase *are playing*.

2.3.2 Tree diagrams
The bracketings of (9)-(11) are easy to use, but they do not give a very clear visual picture of the relation between constituents. For this, when we want to, we can replace the brackets by a TREE DIAGRAM (see Figure 2.1).

Figure 2.1

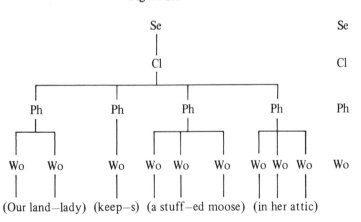

The symbols Cl, etc., which we introduced earlier are here used as LABELS for nodes on the tree, so that all units of the same rank (as shown on the right-hand side) appear at the same level of the tree. Each 'branch' of the tree represents a relation of 'containing'; for example, the left-hand part of the diagram means 'The phrase *Our landlady* **contains** two words, i.e. *Our* and *landlady*.'

The conventions of bracketing and diagramming should be our slaves and not our masters: we should use them only to show what is pertinent for our purpose. For example, if a sentence contains a single clause, it is often unnecessary to show the clause level, and it is often unnecessary

to label the words. The tree shown in Figure 2.2, which may be called
an ABBREVIATED tree diagram, shows some simplifications.

Figure 2.2

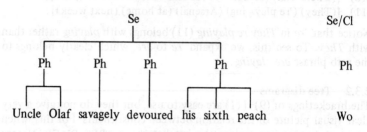

We may even want to simplify things even further, and produce an
UNLABELLED tree diagram (see Figure 2.3).

Figure 2.3

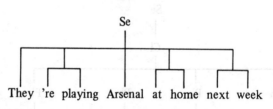

Thus we can use the notations flexibly, to show whatever information
we consider important. But it is also important to be able to do a complete parsing when necessary, and for this, we need to be able to draw a
FULLY LABELLED tree diagram, such as Figure 2.1, where every constituent is labelled. [Now try Exercise 2b.]

2.4   Using tests

In bracketing and drawing tree diagrams we have tools for parsing a
sentence. But it will become more and more clear that we often cannot
tell the structure of a sentence merely by passively observing it; we need
to investigate actively the relations between its parts by using various
GRAMMATICAL TESTS.

2.4.1   Expansion tests

In *They're playing* (11) we expanded *'re* into *are*, and so made it clear
that *'re* is a separate verb, belonging to the phrase *'re playing*, rather than

with *They*. We can also expand a word by adding other words to it, to show that the word is acting as a phrase. For example, each of the words of (8a) can be expanded into a word group:

(8a) [(Olaf)   (munched)   (peaches)   (contentedly)].
(8b) [(*Uncle* Olaf) (*has* munched) (*his* peaches) (*very* contentedly)].

Such additions, although they add something to the meaning, do not change the relations between the parts of the sentence. Hence the round brackets in (8a) correctly show (*Olaf*), (*munched*), etc., as phrases, like the phrases of (8b).

2.4.2 Substitution tests

Sometimes, even though we cannot use an expansion test, by substituting a word sequence for a word we can see that the word is actually behaving as a phrase. For instance, in (11) we marked *They* and *Arsenal* as phrases:

(11a) [(They) (are playing) (Arsenal) (at home) (next week)].

And to help show that this analysis is correct, we can replace each of these constituents by a word group having the same function, and a similar meaning:

(11b) (Their team) (are playing) (our team) (at home) (next week).[1]

2.4.3 Subtraction tests

The opposite of an expansion test is a subtraction test, i.e. omitting some part of a construction. In *Jabberwocky* in 2.1.2, *toves* in *the slithy toves* was recognised as a noun, and this in part was because intuition tells us that *tove* (without the -*s*) would also be grammatical. Equally, in (10), we marked the -*ed* as a separate grammatical suffix of *devour–ed*, and this is partly justified by the fact that the remaining part of the word, *devour*, is itself capable of standing alone as a separate word.

2.4.4 Movement tests

In (10), *Uncle Olaf savagely devoured his sixth peach*, we treated *savagely* as a separate phrase rather than as part of a phrase *savagely devoured*, and this was because *savagely* can be moved elsewhere in the clause,

---

[1] On the use of the plural *are* following *team*, see 3.2.1, p.46, and 11.5, p.177.

without noticeably changing its meaning or function in the clause, and without dragging *devoured* with it:

(10a)   [(Savagely) (Uncle Olaf) (devoured) (his sixth peach)].

These tests will be refined as we go, and at the moment must be used with caution. Also bear in mind that, because grammatical categories have fuzzy edges, one test is rarely enough; we often have to rely on a number of different tests in deciding which analysis is the correct or best one. Nevertheless, the tests are already useful, and this is particularly evident in recognising types of phrase. Each phrase class has a 'keyword' which is essential to it, and which provides it with a name. For example, in (12) the 'keywords' of the phrases are as follows:

(12)

	noun	verb	adjective	adverb
	↓	↓	↓	↓
	[(Aunt *Gladys*)	(has *seemed*)	(rather *grumpy*)	(just *recently*)]
	noun phrase	verb phrase	adjective phrase	adverb phrase

And we can see that these words are essential to the structure, in that if we reduce the sentence to a minimum by subtraction or substitution, we end up with them alone:

(12a)   [(Gladys) (seemed) (grumpy) (recently)].

If we want to indicate which constituents are optional, we can place them in curly brackets, as in (12b):

(12b)   [({Aunt} Gladys) ({has} seemed) ({rather} grumpy)
           ({just} recently)].

[Now try Exercise 2c.]

2.5   Form and function

This brings us to the general question of how to classify grammatical units. To explain how sentences are constructed, it is not enough to identify constituents such as clauses, phrases and words; we also need to identify these as belonging to various classes.

2.5.1   Form classes

As we have seen, words are divided into word classes such as **noun** (N), **verb** (V), **adjective** (Aj), **adverb** (Av). Similarly, phrases are sub-divided into **noun phrase** (NP), **verb phrase** (VP), **adjective phrase** (AjP), **adverb phrase** (AvP), **genitive phrase** (GP) and **prepositional phrase** (PP). We

shall look at these phrase classes and word classes later (see 3.2, 4.3–4.5).
For the moment, notice that one reason why we need to identify such
classes is to explain the order in which elements of the sentence occur.
It would not do to put the phrases of (9) into any order:

(9a) [(Our landlandy) (keeps) (a stuffed moose) (in her attic)].
(9b) *[(Keeps) (a stuffed moose) (our landlady) (in her attic)].[1]
(9c) *[(A stuffed moose) (keeps) (in her attic) (our landlady)].

Nor would it do to put the words in any other order within the phrases:

(9d) *[(Landlady our) (keeps) (stuffed a moose) (in attic her)].

The tree diagram shown in Figure 2.4, adapted from sentence (12),
shows how the extra information about phrase and word classes can be
included, by using CLASS LABELS.

Figure 2.4

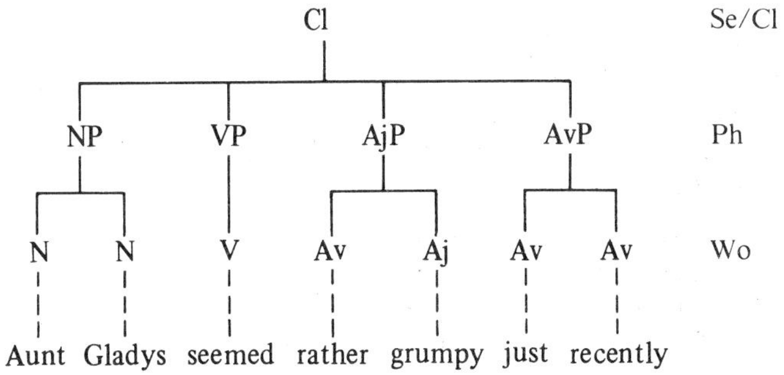

Alternatively, we can show the same detail by LABELLED BRACKET-
ING, placing the class label as a subscript before each word and opening
bracket:

(12c) Cl[NP (NAunt NGladys) VP(Vseemed) AjP(Avrather Ajgrumpy)
AvP(Avjust Avrecently)].

Grammar has to state which orders are permitted. For example, the
order VP NP NP AvP in (9b) is normally ungrammatical in English.

2.5.2 Function classes: elements of the clause
Classes such as NP, VP, and AjP are called FORM CLASSES because the
classification of phrases in this way depends on how the unit is com-

---

[1] An asterisk (*) before a sentence marks it as being *ungrammatical*.

posed of smaller units, or on how its form can vary. But it is also necessary to classify units into FUNCTION CLASSES: that is, to classify them according to how they are used to form larger units. A unit's function class determines such things as what positions it can fill, and whether it is optional.

The need for function classes is illustrated by another version of (9):

(9a) [(Our landlady) (keeps) (a stuffed moose) (in her attic)].
(9e) [(A stuffed moose) (keeps) (our landlady) (in her attic)].

The sequence of phrases is the same in both (9a) and (9e): NP VP NP PP. But the relationship between phrases in the clause is quite different, and this is reflected in the very different meaning of (9e). In traditional terms, *our landlady* in (9a) is the SUBJECT (*S*) of the clause, and *a stuffed moose* is the OBJECT (*O*). In (9e) these functions are reversed, so that *a stuffed moose* is the subject, and *our landlady* is the object. We shall use these traditional terms, but we shall also combine them with a less traditional, but useful, term for the verbal element: we shall call *keeps* in both sentences the PREDICATOR (*P*). To exemplify the concept of function, we shall limit our attention at this point to these three elements, *S*, *O* and *P*, leaving till 5.1 the fuller treatment of clause functions, including those of units such as *in the attic*. We use the term ELEMENT for function classes such as *S*, *O* and *P*. These three elements can be distinguished as follows:

1. *P* is the only element of a clause which is a verb phrase, and so there is little difficulty in identifying it.
2. *S* typically comes before *P*, whereas *O* typically comes after *P*.
3. *S* typically denotes the 'actor' of the action represented by *P*, whereas *O* typically denotes the 'sufferer' of the action.
4. *S* must normally be present (in a main declarative clause), whereas *O* is often omitted.

Using this starting-point, we can identify the functions of the phrases in (13)-(17). Notice, by the way, another piece of notation – we mark the function class of a unit by a raised italic letter immediately in front of it:[1]

(13) [^{S}(He) ^{P}(works)].
(14) [^{S}(A big red apple) ^{P}(might have fallen)].
(15) [^{S}(Many gentlemen) ^{P}(prefer) ^{O}(blondes)].
(16) [^{S}(My aunt) ^{P}(rides) ^{O}(a yellow tricycle)].
(17) [^{S}(Everyone) ^{P}(will enjoy) ^{O}(Uncle Olaf's funeral)].

---

[1] When writing function labels, use underlining: e.g. for *P* write P̲.

2.5.3 Function classes: elements of the phrase

To finish this brief survey of grammatical classes, let us take a look at the functions of words in phrases. We shall identify two function classes: HEAD (*H*) and MODIFIER (*M*). In the examples shown in Table 2.1 (though this is not always the case) modifiers come before the head.

Table 2.1

	MODIFIERS (*M*)	HEAD (*H*)
Noun phrase (NP)	my that strange both his rich elderly spinster the steam-driven explo- dable hairless	Boris bicycle feeling great-aunts toupée
Adjective phrase (AjP)	more much much extremely	pleasant careful happier narrow
Adverb phrase (AvP)	too very very	now slowly often

In general, the head is the word which cannot be omitted from the phrase, whereas modifiers are optional. This applies to NP, AjP and AvP. In verb phrases, however, the relation between the constituents is different from this, and instead of the terms modifier and head, we use the terms AUXILIARY verb and MAIN verb (see Table 2.2).

Table 2.2

	AUXILIARIES (*Aux*)	MAIN VERB (*Mv*)
Verb phrase (VP)	had must be may have been	is received working broken

Prepositional phrases, on the other hand, are essentially noun phrases (NPs) with an initial preposition (p) such as *of, in, on, under* (see Table 2.3).

Table 2.3

	p	MODIFIERS (*M*)	HEAD (*H*)
Prepositional phrase (PP)	in		luck
	of	strong	convictions
	under	the squeaky old oak	floor-boards

We can now represent sentence (12) as a tree diagram, this time using FUNCTION LABELS instead of FORM LABELS for each node (see Figure 2.5). (Here two further function classes, *C* = complement and *A* = adverbial, have to be used – see 3.2.3 and 3.2.4.)

Figure 2.5

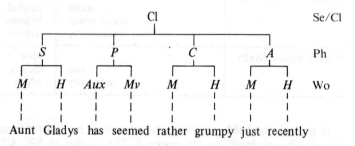

Alternatively, we can represent the same sentence as a bracketing with function labels:

(12d) [^{S}(^{M}Aunt ^{H}Gladys) ^{P}(^{Aux}has ^{Mv}seemed) ^{C}(^{M}rather ^{H}grumpy) ^{A}(^{M}just ^{H}recently)].

[Now try Exercises 2d and 2e.]

2.6 Summary

In this chapter we have introduced in a preliminary way:

(a) **A rank scale** consisting of four units: sentence (Se), clause (Cl), phrase (Ph), and word (Wo).

(b) **Form** classes of word: noun (N), verb (V), adjective (Aj), adverb (Av), and preposition (p)

(c) **Form** classes of phrase: noun phrase (NP), verb phrase (VP), adjective phrase (AjP), adverb phrase (AvP), genitive phrase (GP) and prepositional phrase (PP).

(d) **Function** classes within the phrase: modifier (M) and head (H); auxiliary verb (Aux) and main verb (Mv).

(e) **Function** classes within the clause: subject (S), object (O), predicator (P) (two further elements, complement (C) and adverbial (A), will be considered later).

(f) The following conventions for brackets:

( ): round brackets enclose a phrase
[ ] : square brackets enclose a clause
{ }: curly brackets enclose an optional constituent.

Exercises

Exercise 2a

It is a significant point about nonsense words, such as those in *Jabberwocky*, that we can put these words to work in new sentences which we know to be grammatical. For example:

1. A tove is mimsier than a rath, but a borogove is mimsiest of all.
2. Did you see that slithy tove gimbling and outgribing?

But the following, for example, is not grammatical:

3. * I momed a rath mimsy.

Think up five new examples of (a) sentences which are grammatical, and of (b) sentences which are ungrammatical, using Carroll's nonsense words. Discuss the reasons for the differences between (a) and (b). Also, see how many grammatical forms of the same word (e.g. *mimsy/mimsier/ mimsiest*) you can find.

Exercise 2b   (answers on p. 200)

Draw tree diagrams like Figure 2.1 (p. 29) for the following sentences:

1. [(Those students) (have made) (an interesting discovery)].
2. [(Without doubt) (the play) (has been) (tremendously successful)].

Now reduce these diagrams to (a) abbreviated tree diagrams, and (b) unlabelled tree diagrams. Lastly, translate the tree diagrams shown in Figures 2.6a and 2.6b overleaf into bracketed sentences like 1 and 2:

Figure 2.6a

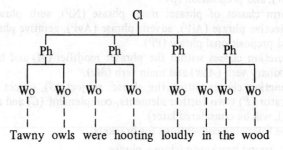

Tawny owls were hooting loudly in the wood

Figure 2.6b

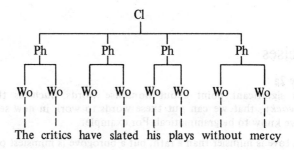

The critics have slated his plays without mercy

Exercise 2c

Using expansion and substitution (2.4.1–2.4.2), convert the one-word phrases in the following sentences into units of two or more words (choose your own vocabulary, and make minimal changes to the sentence as it stands):

1. [(Tonight) (we) (leave) (London)].
2. [(Sometimes) (she) (looks) (young)].

Now, using subtraction and substitution (2.4.2–2.4.3), reduce the phrases of the following sentences to one-word phrases, so that each sentence consists of just four words (you may use pronouns such as *he, she, it* and *they* as substitutes):

3. [(The paintings in the Ducal Palace) (are considered) (without doubt) (his greatest masterpieces)].
4. [(Her first novel) (had made) (Emily Brontë) (almost as famous as her sister)].

Exercise 2d   (answers on p. 200)
1. Translate the tree diagram shown in Figure 2.7 into a sentence
    with bracketing labelled with form labels, like (12c), p. 33.

Figure 2.7

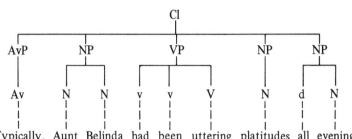

2. Translate the following sentence into a labelled tree diagram, like
    Figure 2.4, p. 33:

    Cl[NP(N Jane) VP(v is v finding) NP(Aj modern Aj French N literature)
    AjP(Aj fascinating)].

3. Translate the tree diagram shown in Figure 2.8 into a sentence
    with bracketing labelled with function labels like (12d), p. 36.

Figure 2.8

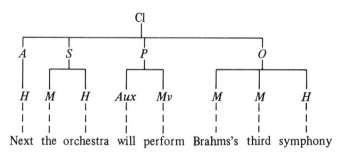

4. Translate the following sentence into a labelled tree diagram like
    Figure 2.8:

    [S(H Gertrude) P(Aux can Mv type) O(M business H letters) A(M very
    H rapidly))].

Exercise 2e (answers on p.202)
Insert the function labels *S* (subject), *P* (predicator), and *O* (object) as appropriate in front of the phrase brackets in the following sentences. *Tip*: first identify the predicator, then the subject, and then the object (if any):

1. [(^{M}Little ^{H}Joanna) (^{Aux}was ^{Mv}sleeping)].
2. [(^{M}This ^{H}job) (^{Aux}must ^{Aux}be ^{Mv}finished)].
3. [(^{M}The ^{M}poor ^{H}girl) (^{Aux}has ^{Mv}seen) (^{M}seven ^{H}ghosts)].
4. [(^{H}You) (^{Aux}must ^{Mv}meet) (^{M}my ^{H}wife)].
5. [(^{M}My ^{H}train) (^{Aux}is ^{Mv}leaving)].

3
Words

In the next three chapters we extend and explain in greater detail the concepts of grammar introduced in Chapter 2. It is simplest for us to start at the bottom of the rank scale, focusing on **words** in this chapter, then ascending the scale to **phrases** in Chapter 4, and to **clauses** in Chapter 5. It will become clearer, however, that we cannot fully understand one unit without taking proper account of the others.

3.1 Open and closed word classes

Our first task is to elaborate on the form classes, or parts of speech, introduced in 2.1. There are two major kinds of word classes in English: open classes and closed classes. The OPEN CLASSES we shall recognise are shown in Table 3.1.

Table 3.1

OPEN CLASS	Symbol	Examples
Noun	N	*girl, chair, water, thing, beauty, thought*
Verb (= full-verb)	V	*sing, walk, go, become, seem, water*
Adjective	Aj	*good, watery, calm, unlimited, friendly, able*
Adverb	Av	*now, there, calmly, actually, past, away, today*

These classes are known as open classes because we can readily coin new words to add to them (either real words, or nonsense words such as *slithy* and *tove* - see 2.1.2). Their membership is fairly open-ended; for instance, the word *blackbox* is a noun which was coined fairly recently (referring to an electronic device). But in our library, there is a notice on a book-rack: *Books to be blackboxed*. Here *blackbox* has become a verb, and refers to the action of putting books through a black box! This is a small illustration of how English vocabulary is continually being

41

extended to meet new demands. Note that a member of one class may be identical in spelling and/or pronunciation with a member of another class - for example, *water* can be a noun or a verb: *We* ᵥ*water our plants with rain* ₙ*water.*

The CLOSED CLASSES, on the other hand, have a fairly fixed membership. We rarely invent new words like *the, she, which, must* and *in*, so it is possible to give a reasonably full listing of each closed class; in the lists shown in Table 3.2 we give some common members of each.

Table 3.2

CLOSED CLASS	Symbol	Examples
Determiner	d	*the, a, this, that, some, any, all, many*
Pronoun	pn	*I, me, you, he, she, it, her, them, one, some, someone*
Preposition	p	*of, in, on, at, before, under, past, from, to, by, for*
Conjunction	cj	*and, or, but, if, when, because, that, so*
Operator-verb	v	*can, may, will, shall, have, be, do*
Interjection[†]	ij	*oh, ah, ooh, gee, ugh, hell, shoo, hey*
Enumerator[†]	e	*one, two, three, first, second, eighteenth*

[†] In some ways interjections and enumerators are like open classes, but for our present purpose they are more happily placed among the closed classes.

You will see that we use small letters for the closed class symbols, whereas we used (initial) capitals for the open class symbols. The closed classes are straightforward enough, but they are not quite so simple as they seem. First, like open classes, and grammatical classes in general, they have 'fuzzy edges'; for example, on the edge of the preposition class are idioms like *instead of, away from, with reference to,* which behave in some ways like a single preposition, and in other respects like a sequence of words. Second, again like the open classes, they have members which are identical in form to members of other classes; for example, *this* may be either a determiner or a pronoun (see 3.3.2), and *since* may be either a preposition or a conjunction. We can distinguish these words, when we like, by using separate labels: ₐ*this* and ₚₙ*this.* There are even cases where the same form is shared by an open class word and a closed class word: for example, *past* may be either an adverb or a preposition; *round* can be either an adjective or a preposition.

This raises another complication about open and closed classes. Although this distinction is generally very useful and important, it cuts right across a traditional word class, that of verbs. In functional terms, there is a distinction between a main verb, and a 'helping', or auxiliary verb (see 2.5.3). This usually corresponds to a distinction of form between an open class of 'full-verbs', and a closed class of 'operator-verbs' – the latter being verbs which can act as **operator** (see 4.5.2, 5.4.1) in the formation of questions, negation, etc. We distinguish these, in our labelling system, simply by the capital and lower case 'V'. When we wish to refer to 'verbs' in general, we shall use the capital 'V'.

3.2 The open classes

In defining the open classes of N, V, Aj and Av, we shall use three types of test, or criterion:

(a)   FORM: We can tell the class of a word partly from its form:

(i)   Certain suffixes are characteristic of certain word classes; e.g. *electric–ITY* (noun); *electri–FY* (verb); *electr–IC, electric–AL* (adjectives).

(ii)   Certain suffixes can be added to change the form of a word: *box, box–ES* (noun); *work, work–ED* (verb); *tall, tall–ER* (adjective). These purely grammatical endings are called INFLECTIONS; compared to some other well-known languages (e.g. Latin, German, Russian, French) English has only a few of them. The main ones are: *-s/es, -ed, -ing, -er, -est, -'s.*

(iii) In some less regular cases, English words have inflections which involve some other change in the form of a word, e.g. a change of vowel (*man/men, sing/sang*), or in the extreme case a complete change in the word (*go/went, good/better/best*).

(b)   FUNCTION: We can tell the class of a word by the way it behaves, i.e. from the function or functions it has in phrases, and therefore indirectly in clauses. For example, in *The cook does not actually cook the meal* we can recognise the first *cook* as a noun and the second as a verb because of their function; obviously there is no overt difference of form to help us.

(c)   MEANING: This is a supportive criterion, in that if you learn to recognise certain semantic types of word (i.e. word types classified according to meaning), such as action verbs, state verbs, abstract nouns, etc., this will help you to check the purely grammatical criteria, those of form and function.

These three tests (a)-(c) may be placed in the following order of importance:

   Function is most important
   Form is next most important
   Meaning is least important

Why this order? First, we have already seen (2.1) that **meaning** is not a reliable guide to word class; for example,

(1)   I $_V$*love* money, but my $_N$*love* of humanity is greater.

In (1), $_N$*love* and $_V$*love* have the same meaning; but differ in word class. Second, we cannot always rely on a word's **form**, because many words contain no suffix (*help, water, male, much, rather*), and many words are invariable (i.e. they do not change their form by inflection). Just as with word-forms, we must also allow for multiple classification of suffixes; e.g. -*ing* marks three different word classes in:

(2)   It is very $_A$j*amusing* to watch Mungo $_V$*trying* to paint the $_N$*guttering.*

Similar cases are:

> -*ed* can end an adjective as well as a verb (e.g. *conceited*)
> -*ic* can end a noun as well as an adjective (e.g. *a comic*)
> -*ly* can end an adjective as well as an adverb (e.g. *friendly*).

Even suffixes which seem to be thoroughly safe indicators of a word class can sometimes be deceptive, e.g. -*tion* usually indicates a noun, but forms like *position* and *sanction* can also be used as verbs.

Where it can be used, the criterion of **inflection** is often conclusive (e.g. the verb *position* can take an -*ed* ending, while the noun *position* can only take an -*s* ending). But English has few inflections, and this criterion applies in the main only to nouns and verbs.

Because of the limitation of form and meaning as criteria, we mainly rely on a word's **function** as a criterion of its class. With this preparation, let us look at the four major word classes in turn.

3.2.1   Nouns (N)
The class of of NOUNS (N) is by far the most numerous word class.

(a)   FUNCTION: Nouns can function as the **head** (*H*) of a noun phrase (NP) - see 2.5.3: $_{NP}$(*^{H}donkeys*) $_{NP}$(*^{M}our ^{H}town*) $_{NP}$(*^{M}the ^{M}worst ^{H}journey ^{M}ever*) $_{NP}$(*^{M}Stanley's ^{M}historic ^{H}meeting $_{PP}^M$*(with Livingstone)).[1]

A good way to recognise an NP is to see whether it will fit into a frame such as *Have you heard about. . .?* or *Did you know about. . .?* It is generally possible for an NP to begin with *the*, and so a good test for a

---

[1]   Notice that now, for the first time, we are combining function labels (*M, H*) with form labels (NP, PP). As these examples show, the head may be preceded or followed by modifiers.

noun (which does not apply, however, to **proper** nouns - see (ii) below) is whether it can fit the frame '*the* −'. *The*, the most common word in English, has a special name: the DEFINITE ARTICLE.

(b) FORM: (i) Many nouns have characteristic suffixes: e.g. *-er* (*singer*), *-ist* (*hypnotist*), *-ism* (*fascism*), *-*{*a*}{*t*}*ion* (*station, caution*) *-ity* (*divinity*), *-hood* (*falsehood*), *-ence* (*preference*), *-ness* (*goodness*). There are many exceptions, however, e.g. *longer* is an Aj, *linger* is a V. (ii) Most nouns can change their form from SINGULAR to PLURAL by adding *-s* or *-es* (*goal, goals; dress, dresses*) or by some other change of form (*woman, women; foot, feet; bacillus, bacilli*). Such nouns are **count** nouns, as opposed to **mass** nouns (see (i) below).

(c) MEANING: Nouns typically refer to physical phenomena: people, objects, places, substances, etc. Such nouns are called CONCRETE nouns; but there are also ABSTRACT nouns referring to events, states, activities, processes, times, occasions, etc.: *birth, happiness, refinement, revival, birthday, meeting*.

Members of such a large class of words as nouns will obviously not all behave in the same way. We can distinguish these subclasses in terms of form, function and meaning:

(i) COUNT/MASS: Count nouns (e.g. *table, dog, idea, mile*) refer to things that can be counted, and can therefore have a plural form (*tables*, etc.). Mass nouns, on the other hand, refer to substances, qualities, etc., that we do not think of as coming in countable 'lumps'; such nouns normally have no plural (**golds, *happinesses*). Notice, however, that the same noun may belong to both categories: in *Her hair is brown, hair* is a mass noun, but in *I found a hair in my soup*, it is a count noun. *A/an* is termed the INDEFINITE ARTICLE, and, like the numbers *one, two*, etc., is a marker of count nouns: *a hair* makes good sense, but not **a sunshine*.

(ii) PROPER/COMMON: Proper nouns denote an individual person, place, etc., whereas common nouns classify things into types. A proper noun normally begins with a capital letter: *John, Goldilocks, London, Africa*, etc.; it generally has no plural form (**Johns, *Africas*), and cannot generally occur after *the* or *a/an*: (**a John, *an Africa*).[1] Common nouns, on the other hand, can occur after *the*. So all the count and mass nouns discussed in (i) are common nouns.

(iii) COLLECTIVE NOUNS: These are generally count nouns, but even in the singular they refer to groups of people, animals or things:

[1] Sometimes, however, proper nouns are treated like common nouns: *There's a London in Ontario; I know several Johns*, etc.

family, government, committee. Grammatically, the thing to notice about collective nouns is their ability, sometimes, to go with a plural verb even when they themselves are singular: *Her family live/lives in Manchester* (see 2.4.2, 11.5).

In languages like German and Latin, nouns vary their form for CASE (e.g. subject versus object function) and have differences of GENDER (e.g. masculine, feminine). These notions usefully apply to English pronouns (see Exercise 4e, p.73), but not to English nouns. [Now try Exercise 3a.]

3.2.2 Verbs (V)

(a)   FUNCTION: Verbs as we discuss them now are FULL-VERBS, that is, they always function as the main element of a VERB-PHRASE. They can stand on their own as a predicator, or they can follow other (operator) verbs: $[^S$(Most wombats)^P($_V$*bite*$)]$, $[^S$(One peach) ^{P}(had been $_V$*eaten*$)]$, $[^S$(The cat) ^{P}(was $_V$*purring*$)]$, $[^S$(I) ^{P}(must have been $_V$*dreaming*$)]$.

Because the predicator is the central or pivotal element of a clause, and because every predicator contains a main verb, it is always a good idea to begin an analysis by **looking for the verbs** first.

(b)   FORM: (i) Some verbs have characteristic suffixes like *-ise* (*realise*) and *-ify* (*clarify*), but these are not very important. (ii) Much more important, each verb has up to five different forms, which we symbolise as shown in Table 3.3. Notice that most verbs are REGULAR, and have forms like those of *ask*. For these verbs, the Ved and Ven forms are identical. For IRREGULAR verbs, of which there are about 200 in English, the Ved and Ven forms can vary in a number of different ways; for example, we call the latter 'Ven' because they sometimes have the distinctive suffix *-en* (as in *beaten*), instead of *-ed*.

Table 3.3

	Vo	Vs	Ved	Ving	Ven
Regular	ask	asks	asked	asking	asked
Irregular	show write put give	shows writes puts gives	showed wrote put gave	showing writing putting giving	shown written put given

(c)   MEANING: Verbs can express actions, events, processes, activities, states, etc. Such actions, etc., can be physical (*eat*), mental (*think*), perceptual (*see*), social (*buy*), etc.

An easy test for a verb is: Can the word vary its form for PRESENT TENSE and PAST TENSE? The forms Vo and Vs are used for the present, and the form Ved for the past tense. [Now try Exercise 3b.]

3.2.3 Adjectives (Aj)

(a) FUNCTION: Adjectives in general have two functions:

(i) as head of an adjective phrase (AjP):

(3) [Dukes can be $_{AjP}(^M_{Av}very \, ^H_{Aj}rich)$].

(ii) as modifier in a noun phrase (NP): $_{NP}(^Ma \, ^M_{Aj}rich \, ^Hduke)$.

If a word can fill both these positions we can feel confident that it is an adjective.

(b) FORM: Most common adjectives are GRADABLE (see below), and can vary for comparative and superlative: *rich, richer, richest*. Thus we can often tell an adjective by its ability to take *-er* and *-est* as suffixes.

(c) MEANING: Adjectives typically denote some quality or property attributed to nouns; most commonly they are used to narrow down, or specify, the reference of nouns, as *red* specifies what kind of *hen* in:

(4a) $_{NP}$(the $_{Aj}red \, _N$hen).
(4b) [(The $_N$hen) $(_V$is$)$ $(_{Aj}red)$].

There are various types of adjective meanings, for instance:

(i) physical qualities of colour, shape, etc.: *green, large, heavy, tall*
(ii) psychological qualities of emotion, etc.: *funny, brave, sad, amazing*
(iii) evaluative qualities: *good, wrong, foolish, beautiful, clever*.

In the clause of (4b), *(red)* is called the COMPLEMENT (*C*) (more precisely, the SUBJECT COMPLEMENT - see 5.6), because it follows the predicator, and attributes some quality to the subject. It is a good test of adjectives that they can follow the so-called COPULA verb *to be*, acting as the head of an AjP in the frame 'NP *be* ——':

(5a) $[^S$(The building) ^{P}(is) $^C(green/large/old/tall)]$.

It is also a good test of adjectives that they can occur between *the* and the head of an NP, in the frame '*the*—— N'. This is because as modifiers they come after articles and other determiners:

(5b) $_{NP}(^M$the $^Mgreen/large/old/tall \, ^H$building).

A further test is the insertion of the adverb *very* before the adjective, as a modifier in an adjective phrase:

(5c) [The building is $_{AjP}(^M$ very ^{H} *green/large/old/tall*)].

This test, however, applies to GRADABLE but not to NON-GRADABLE adjectives. Gradable adjectives are those referring to qualities that can vary along a continuous scale, such as size, age, weight, etc.: *large/small; old/young; heavy/light*. Non-gradable adjectives refer to 'all-or-none' qualities, like sex and nationality: *male, Austrian, chemical, wooden*. But adjectives move rather easily from one sub-class to another, often with a subtle change of meaning. *Wooden* meaning 'made of wood' is non-gradable, but when we say *His performance of Hamlet was very wooden*, we refer to a gradable metaphorical quality ('behaving as if made of wood'). As Table 3.4 shows, gradable adjectives can be modified by DEGREE adverbs like *very, extremely, utterly, rather*. They can also have comparative and superlative forms: The shorter and more common gradable adjectives take -*er* and -*est* suffixes, while the longer and less common ones are modified by a separate comparative or superlative adverb: *more/most*. There are also a few irregular adjectives which have special comparative and superlative forms, like *good/better/best*.

Table 3.4

	SIMPLE	COMPARATIVE	SUPERLATIVE	DEGREE ADVERB
Gradable	funny beautiful good	funnier more beautiful better	funniest most beautiful best	very funny rather beautiful quite good
Non-gradable	male	*maler	*malest	*very male

Because of their meaning, non-gradable adjectives can only occur in the simple construction. Although we can talk of *a male wombat*, it is non-English to say **a maler wombat*, **the malest wombat*, or **a very male wombat*. To be more precise, we **could** say *He was really a very male wombat*, but then *male* would take on a subtly different meaning.[Now try Exercises 3c and 3d.]

3.2.4 Adverbs (Av)

We can distinguish three major types of ADVERB (Av), but there is considerable overlap between them. CIRCUMSTANCE ADVERBS add some kind of circumstantial information (of time, place, manner, etc.) to the idea expressed in the core of the clause:

(6) $[^S(\text{He})\ ^P(\text{sold})\ ^O(\text{the car})\ ^A(_{Av}hurriedly)\ ^A(_{Av}yesterday)]$.

(On the symbol A, see below.) DEGREE ADVERBS modify adjectives and other words in terms of gradability ($_{Av}fairly\ new$, etc. – see Table 3.4); and SENTENCE ADVERBS, which apply to the whole clause or sentence, express an attitude to it, or a connection between it and another clause or sentence:

(7) $[^A(_{Av}So)\ ^S(\text{the whole thing})\ ^P(\text{was})\ ^A(_{Av}frankly)\ ^C(\text{too awful}$ for words)].

(a) FUNCTION: the primary function of an adverb is as head of an adverb phrase. This implies that it can typically be preceded and/or followed by a modifier, which is frequently itself a degree adverb:

(8) [She spoke $_{AvP}^A(_{Av}^H frankly)$].

(9) [She spoke $_{AvP}^A(_{Av}^M very\ _{Av}^H frankly\ _{Av}^M indeed)$].

(10) [She spoke $_{AvP}^A(_{Av}^M too\ _{Av}^H frankly\ _{PP}^M(\text{for comfort}))$].

This leads to a second function, especially of degree adverbs: an adverb can act as modifier in an adjective phrase, or in an adverb phrase as in (9) and (10).

As head of an AvP, an adverb very often stands on its own as an ADVERBIAL element (A) in clause structure (see 5.1.3). In this function, it is typical of adverbs that they can be omitted from the clause, or moved to a different position in the clause, without making it ungrammatical. This is illustrated by (6) and (7). Both of these sentences can be simplified by omission of adverbs: *He sold the car; The whole thing was too awful for words*. Also, both sentences can be rearranged by moving the adverbs to different positions: *Yesterday he hurriedly sold the car; So frankly, the whole thing was too awful for words*.

(b) FORM: (i) The examples we have given illustrate that most adverbs are formed by the addition of *-ly* to an adjective. (ii) In addition, a few adverbs resemble adjectives, in having comparative and superlative forms: *fast, faster, fastest; well, better, best;* etc. [Now try Exercise 3e.]

(c) MEANING: Adverbs can express many different types of meaning, especially as adverbials in the clause. We can only give the most important categories; and to distinguish them, it is useful to use a QUESTION TEST; for example, *home* answers the question *Where... to?* in the following exchange (see also Table 3.5 overleaf):

(11) *Where* did he go *to*? He went *home*.

Table 3.5

Adverb type	Eliciting question	Examples
Manner	*How?*	*well, nicely, cleverly*
Place	*Where?*	*here, there, somewhere*
Direction	*Where to/from?*	*up, back, forward, home*
Time – *when*	*When?*	*then, once, tonight, soon*
Duration	*How long?*	*long, briefly, always*
Frequency	*How often?*	*always, weekly, often*
Degree	*To what degree?*	*rather, quite, much, hardly*

Sentence adverbs, like *fortunately, probably, actually* and *however*, do not answer questions. But they can be divided into two main categories:

Attitude *fortunately, actually, oddly, perhaps, surely*
Connective *so, yet, however, therefore, secondly, though.*

For example, in (12) *fortunately* is an attitude adverb, while in (13) *however* is a connective adverb:

(12) $[^A(_{Av}Fortunately)$ $^S(elephants)$ $^P(cannot\ fly)]$.

(13) $[^S(Some\ of\ them)$ $^P(can\ run)$ $^A(pretty\ fast),$ $^A(_{Av}however)]$.[1]

[Now try Exercises 3f and 3g.]

3.3   Closed word classes

Luckily the closed word classes do not need so much individual attention as the open classes. They have relatively few members, so we can, in the last resort, identify each of them by listing their members. The best way to deal with them, however, is to consider their function within the higher units; in this way, you will gradually grow familiar with these small but important classes of words in the next two chapters, as we deal with phrases and clauses. All closed class words tend to occur at or towards the beginning of the larger units of which they are parts; in this respect they are **markers** of the units they introduce.

Now here is a brief definition of the closed classes, and a fairly full listing of their members.

---

[1] There is some overlap between adverbs of different classes. For example, in *She answered the question sensibly*, *sensibly* is a manner adverb; but in *She sensibly answered the question*, *sensibly* is an adverb of attitude.

3.3.1 Determiners (d)

DETERMINERS introduce noun phrases, and function as modifiers. Unlike adjective modifiers, however, they are sometimes obligatory. If the head of an NP is a singular count noun, then some determiner has to be added:

(14a) *$[(^H_N Dog) \, (^{Mv}_V bit) \, (^H_N man)]$.

(14b) $[(^M_d the \, ^H_N dog) \, (^{Mv}_V bit) \, (^M_d a \, ^H_N man)]$.

The ARTICLES *the* and *a* are the most common determiners.

Determiners: *the, a/an; this, that, these, those; all, some, any, no, every, each, either, neither, one, several, enough, such; many, much, more, most; (a) few, fewer, fewest; (a) little, less, least; what, which, whatever, whichever, half.*

3.3.2 Pronouns (pn)

PRONOUNS are words which are in a sense 'dummy' Ns or NPs, because they have a generalised or unspecific meaning. Because they are normally obligatory elements of noun phrases, we regard them as acting as **head** of such phrases, though they are limited in terms of what modifiers can be added to them. For example, we cannot say *a strange it* or *the old everybody*.

Pronouns: *I, me, my, mine, myself; we, us, ourselves, our, ours; you, yourself, yourselves, your, yours; he, him, himself, his; she, her, herself, hers; it, itself, its; they, them, themselves, their, theirs; this, that, these, those; all, some, any, none, each, either, neither, one, oneself, several, enough; everybody, everyone, everything; somebody, someone, something; anybody, anyone, anything; nobody, no one, nothing; many, much, more, most; (a) few, fewer, fewest; (a) little, less, least; who, whom, whose; what, which; whoever, whichever, whatever; each other, one another.*

You can see that there is a large overlap between determiners and pronouns; *this, that, all, some, which* are among those forms which can belong to either category: for example,

(15) $[^S(This \, wine) \, ^P(is) \, ^C(very \, sweet)]$.
       (*This* is a determiner)

(16) $[^S(This) \, ^P(is) \, ^C(a \, very \, sweet \, wine)]$.
       (*This* is a pronoun)

Similarly, in $^M some \, ^H girls$, *some* is a determiner, whereas in $^H some \, ^M(of \, the \, girls)$ (where *some* is modified by a prepositional phrase), *some* is a pronoun.

3.3.3 Enumerators (e)

These words include CARDINAL NUMBERS (*one, two, three, . . .*);
ORDINAL NUMBERS (*first, second, third. . .*), and a few GENERAL
ORDINALS (*next, last, other, further*, etc.).

3.3.4 Prepositions (p)

PREPOSITIONS introduce prepositional phrases, and express relations of
possession, place, time, etc.: PP($_p$*of the world*). PP($_p$*by it*), PP($_p$*on the
coldest night of the year*). What follows the preposition in the PP has
the structure of an NP.

Prepositions: *about*‡, *above*‡, *across*‡, *after*‡, *against, along*‡, *alongside*‡,
amid, among, around‡, *as, at, before*‡, *behind*‡, *below*‡, *beneath*‡,
beside, besides‡, *between*‡, *beyond*‡, *by*‡, *despite, down*‡, *during,* .
for, from, in‡, *inside*‡, *into, of, off*‡, *on*‡, *opposite*‡, *outside*‡, *over*‡,
past‡, *round*‡, *since*‡, *than, through*‡, *throughout*‡, *till, to, toward* {*s*},
under‡, *underneath*‡, *until, up*‡, *via, with, within*‡, *without*‡.

There is large overlap between prepositions and adverbs, particularly
adverbs of place or direction:

(17)   [^{S}(I) ^{P}(looked) ^{A}($_p$*up the chimney*)].

(18)   [^{S}(I) ^{P}(looked) ^{A}($_{Av}$*up*)].

In (17) *up* is a preposition, while in (18) *up* is an adverb. All the forms
marked ‡ in the above list can also be adverbs.

3.3.5 Conjunctions (cj)

CONJUNCTIONS, like prepositions, are introductory linking words; but
they often introduce clauses rather than phrases. In fact they subdivide
into two main classes, SUBORDINATING conjunctions and COORDINAT-
ING conjunctions:

Subordinating: *after, although, as, because, before, but, if, how,
however, like, once, since, than, that, till, unless, until, when, whenever,
wherever, whereas, whereby, whereupon, while; in that, so that, in order
that, except that; as far as, as soon as; rather than, as if, as though, in
case.*

Coordinating: *and, or, but, nor, neither.*

As the list shows, many of the subordinating conjunctions are written
as more than one word. In addition, in both categories, there are a
number of CORRELATIVE CONJUNCTIONS: that is, two conjunctions

occur together, one preceding one construction, and another preceding the other:

Subordinating   *if. . . then, although. . . yet*, etc.
Coordinating   *both. . .and, either. . . or, neither. . . nor.*

3.3.6   Operator-verbs (v)

As already explained, these constitute a closed class of verbs which can function as auxiliaries in the verb phrase (see 2.5.3). They fall into two main categories:

MODAL VERBS: *can, will, may, shall; could, would, might, should; must, ought to.*

	Vo	Vs	Ved	Ving	Ven
PRIMARY VERBS:	**be**, *am, are*	*is*	*was, were*	*being*	*been*
	have	*has*	*had*	*having*	*had*
	do	*does*	*did*	*doing*	*done*

The MODAL VERBS are best thought of as invariable, though for some purposes *could, would, might* and *should* can be regarded as the past-tense forms of *can, will, may* and *shall*. The PRIMARY VERBS are the three most important verbs in English, and we shall refer to them by their Vo form: **be, have** and **do**. They are very irregular, and are in fact the only English verbs, apart from the modals, that have an irregular Vs form. Another important thing about them is that they can each function **either** as auxiliaries, **or** as main verbs.

3.3.7   Interjections (ij)

INTERJECTIONS are rather peripheral to language: 'words' like *ugh, phew, oh, ah* and *ouch* are (linguistically) somewhat primitive expressions of feeling, only loosely integrated into the linguistic system. We can include here, too, swear words (*damn*, etc.), greetings (*hello*) and other signalling words like *goodbye, yes, no, okay*, etc.

3.3.8   Particles

There is a distinction to be made, among closed class words, between words which have a function in phrases (e.g. determiners are modifiers in noun phrases) and words which are simply 'markers' (e.g. prepositions are introductory markers in prepositional phrases). For the latter, which include prepositions, conjunctions and interjections, we shall use the time-honoured grammatical word PARTICLE, which literally means 'little part'. We can say that prepositions and conjunctions are 'little parts' of sentences in that they do not enter into the structure of phrases: they are rather like arithmetical signs +, -, x, etc. - which is not to say, of course, that they are devoid of meaning.

To illustrate the use of particles, we represent the structure of the clause *But gee, am I hungry* as follows:

(19)   [$_{cj}$But $_{ij}$gee, $_{VP}^{P}(_{v}^{Mv}$am) $_{NP}^{S}(_{pn}^{H}$I) $_{AjP}^{C}(_{Aj}^{H}$hungry)].

Or in tree diagram form (see Figure 3.1).

Figure 3.1

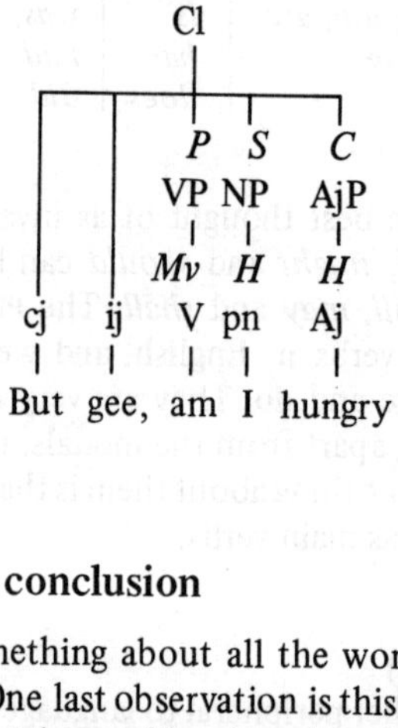

3.4   Summary and conclusion

We have now said something about all the word classes which will be used in this grammar. One last observation is this: some words are unique in function, and cannot be readily classed with any other words - for example, the *to* which precedes a verb (*to work, to have*) and the negative word *not*. For these words we do not need any special label; we can simply make use of these words in their normal written form: to, not.

The word classes we have now distinguished are:

Open classes: noun (N), verb (i.e. full-verb) (V), adjective (Aj) and adverb (Av).

Closed classes: determiner (d), pronoun (pn), enumerators (e), preposition (p), conjunction (cj), operator-verb (v) and interjection (ij).

[Now try Exercise 3h.]

Exercises

Exercise 3a (answers on p. 202)

1. Which of the following nouns are **count nouns** (having a plural), and which are **mass nouns**?

   weed, gold, rigidity, laugh, rubbish, employer, music.

2. Many nouns (like *hair*) are capable of acting as both count nouns and mass nouns, but with some difference of meaning. Explain such differences of meaning in the following:

   paper, wood, grass, cake, coffee, success, kindness, motorway.

3. Some English nouns have irregular plural forms (e.g. the plural of *man* is *men*, not the regular **mans*). Find two examples of each of the following kinds of irregular plural: (a) plurals involving change of vowel; (b) plurals ending in *-i*; (c) plurals ending in *-a*; (d) plurals which have the same form as the singular.

Exercise 3b (answers on p. 202)

1. List the Vo, Vs, Ved, Ving and Ven forms for the following verbs: *take, receive, begin, hang, sleep.*

2. Find ten irregular verbs, and list their five forms. (Do not attempt the verb *to be* at this stage.)

Exercise 3c (answers on p. 202)

Which of the following adjectives are gradable?

a *kind* thought	*criminal* law	a *male* pig
dirty water	a *Japanese* wrestler	a *chauvinist* pig
a *unique* painting	*careful* speech	an *absolute* pig

Be prepared to explain how you arrived at the answer.

Exercise 3d

Some adjectives are capable of being **gradable** or **non-gradable** with some difference of meaning: for example, in *an odd expression, odd* is gradable; while in *an odd number, odd* is non-gradable. Provide pairs of phrases, like these, which exemplify the gradable and non-gradable use of these adjectives: *human, guilty, musical, economic, magnetic, moral, correct, foreign.* Discuss how the two uses of each adjective differ in meaning.

Exercise 3e (answers on p. 203)

Many adverbs are derived from adjectives by the addition of *-ly*. Some adverbs, however, do not add the *-ly*, but have exactly the same form as adjectives. Which is the adjective and which is the adverb in the following? Why?

1. The *early*[1] train arrived *early*[2],
2. I have *long*[1] hated *long*[2] skirts.
3. She's not just a *pretty*[1] face, she's also *pretty*[2] good at grammar.
4. A *daily*[1] newspaper is one that's printed *daily*[2].
5. That's *right*[1], turn *right*[2] at the next stile.
6. The arrow fell a *short*[1] distance *short*[2] of the target.
7. When your health is *better*[1], you'll play *better*[2].
8. I tried *hard*[1], but the exercise was too *hard*[2].

Exercise 3f   (answers on p. 203)

Here are some further examples of word forms which can belong to more than one word class. Identify the word classes of the repeated words in the following.

1. His fur *coat*[1] was *coated*[2] with ice.
2. Herman is more *German*[1] than any of the *Germans*[2] I've met.
3. He *left*[1] her alone on the *left*[2] bank of the Seine.
4. There's no point in *drying*[1] your clothes if they're already *dry*[2].
5. Arabella *pointed*[1] at me, and made a very *pointed*[2] remark.
6. She drew the curtains to make the room *lighter*[1], then *lighted*[2] her cigarette with a *lighter*[3].
7. After he had *drunk*[1] the whisky, the *drunk*[2] was very *drunk*[3] indeed.
8. The *referee*[1] who *refereed*[2] the *match*[1] *matched*[2] the toughness of the players.

Exercise 3g   (answers on p. 203)

Now that you have studied the open word classes, we can return to nonsense words such as those which occur in *Jabberwocky*. Identify the nouns, verbs, adjectives and adverbs in the following:

> And then, whozing huffily, with cruppets in his spod, podulously priddling across the vomity, vipped Podshaw, that gleerful glup, brandling bindily a groon and flupless whampet. Magistly, mimsiness and manity gumbled on Podshaw's blunk gooves.

Exercise 3h   (answers on p. 203)

1. Here is a sentence which contains just one instance of each of the eleven word classes introduced in this chapter. Match the words to the word classes:

   But alas, the two ugly sisters had gone home without her.

2. Find another example (preferably a better one!) of a sentence which, like the one above, contains just one member of each of the eleven word classes.

4

Phrases

Now that we have investigated word classes in English, it is quite a simple matter to explain PHRASE CLASSES. This will mean taking a further look at the closed classes of words (such as determiners) which play an important role in phrases, and elaborating on the classes of phrase already introduced in 2.5.3.

4.1 Classes of phrase

We shall recognise six classes of phrase. Of these, NOUN PHRASES (NP), ADJECTIVE PHRASES (AjP) and ADVERB PHRASES (AvP) all have the same basic structure:

$$(\{M^n\} \, H \, \{M^n\})$$

The superscript 'n' means that there can be one or more than one modifier (M). These phrases must have a head (H), but the modifiers are optional $(\{ \ \})$. In 2.5.3 we showed modifiers only in front of the head, but now we shall have two kinds of modifiers: PREMODIFIERS precede the head, while POSTMODIFIERS follow the head:

(1) $_{NP}(^M\text{awful }^H\text{weather})$: (*awful* is a premodifier)

(2) $_{NP}(^H\text{something }^M\text{awful})$: (*awful* is a postmodifier)

Of the remaining three types of phrase, both PREPOSITIONAL PHRASES (PP) and GENITIVE PHRASES (GP) may be thought of as NPs with an extra particle or marker added to them:

(3)   the bride $_{PP}(_p \text{ of } ^M_d \text{ the } ^H_N \text{ heir } ^M_{Aj} \text{ apparent})$

      = **prepositional phrase**

(4)   GP $(^M_d \text{ the } ^H_N \text{ heir } ^M_{Aj} \text{ apparent}-\text{'s})$ bride

      = **genitive phrase**

The difference between them is that the preposition is added to the front of the PP, whereas the genitive marker ('*s*) is added to the end of the GP. Also the genitive marker, spelt '*s* or ', behaves more like a suffix than a separate word. Although the genitive phrase is one of the oddest constructions in English, the point to which we draw attention in (3) and (4) is its similarity, in spite of the difference of ordering, to a PP.

Finally the VERB PHRASE (VP) is a law unto itself, having a rather different structure from those of other phrases, and having a special pivotal role in the clause. We shall discuss it last, and so let it lead us on to the treatment of clauses in Chapter 5.

4.2   Main and subordinate phrases

The idea of main and subordinate clauses may be familiar, but here we introduce the same distinction for phrases. A MAIN PHRASE is one which is a direct constituent of a clause, i.e. which is not part of another phrase, while SUBORDINATE PHRASES are those which are part of other phrases. This is a new idea which must now be explained.

4.2.1   Subordinate phrases

In 2.2 we presented the rank hierarchy of units, and stated that a unit (e.g. a clause) higher in the scale consists of one or more of the next lower units (e.g. a phrase). This statement was correct, but may have misled by what it did **not** say. Now we have to add to it the possibility that a unit is not **directly** divisible into units of the next lower rank, but may contain as its elements units of the same, or even of a higher rank. This is the phenomenon of SUBORDINATION – and it is important because it allows us to make sentences as complex as we like.

Returning to (3) above, note that *the bride of the heir apparent* is a phrase (actually an NP), and that it contains another phrase (a PP) as a postmodifier within it: *of the heir apparent*. Similarly, in (4) *the heir apparent's bride* is an NP containing another phrase, the GP *the heir apparent's*, as a premodifier. We can represent these cases of subordination in terms of bracketing as follows:

(3a) $_{NP}$(the bride $_{PP}^{M}$(of the heir apparent))

(4a) $_{NP}$ ($_{GP}^{M}$(the heir apparent's) bride).

Wherever we have two sets of round brackets like these, one within the other, the inner brackets enclose a subordinate phrase. Consider now:

(5)   [$_{NP}^{S}$(The heir apparent) $_{VP}^{P}$(should have been) $_{PP}^{A}$(of royal blood)].

The heir apparent is here functioning as an element of clause structure, i.e. as subject. It is therefore a main phrase. We can tell this at a glance, because the round brackets are immediately within the square brackets of the clause. In simple bracketing notation, then, the following are indicators of main and subordinate phrases:

Main phrase	**Subordinate phrase**
[... (Ph) ...]	(... (Ph) ...)

In terms of tree diagrams, the following configurations indicate main and subordinate phrases respectively:

Main: Cl | Ph   **Subordinate:** Ph | Ph

Of course, where there is a subordinate phrase, it will always be directly or indirectly a part of a main phrase:

(6) $[^S_{NP}$ (The bride $^M_{PP}$ (of the heir apparent)) (was) (there)].

Here, *of the heir apparent* is a subordinate phrase and *the bride of the heir apparent* is the main phrase which includes it.

Once we have allowed the possibility of phrases within phrases, there is nothing to stop subordinate phrases themselves containing further subordinate phrases, and so on:

(7)   (his book (on gastronomy (in the Dark Ages)))

(8)   (my review (of his book (on gastronomy (in the Dark Ages))))

(9)   (his reply (to my review (of his book (on gastronomy (in the Dark Ages))))).

Subordination of phrases is one of the chief sources of complexity in grammar, particularly in NPs (see pp.61-2, 137). In the form of a tree diagram, sentence (7) looks as in Figure 4.1 overleaf.

4.2.2 Subordinate clauses
While on this subject, we should mention that subordinate **clauses** work on the same principle, as we shall see more fully in Chapter 6. This time subordination is indicated by a nesting of square brackets:

(10)   [Joe thinks [that Ann loves him]].

(11)   [Ann thinks [that Joe thinks [that she loves him]]].

(12)   [Joe thinks [that Ann thinks [that he thinks [that she loves him]]]].

Figure 4.1

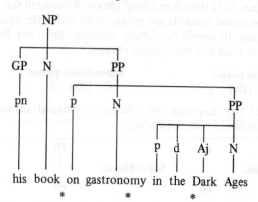

Taking the matter just one stage further, we must allow for the possibility of the subordination of one unit (say a clause) within a unit of **lower** rank (say a phrase) – see further 6.5. In such a case the bracketing will show square brackets inside round brackets:

(13) (the house [that Jack built])

(14) (the malt [that lay (in the house [that Jack built])]).

The clause *that Jack built* here is called a RELATIVE CLAUSE, and is part of an NP (see 6.2.3). These points will be taken up later. [Now try Exercise 4a.]

4.3 Noun phrases and related phrase classes

Like words, phrases can be classified partly by their external FUNCTION and partly by their internal FORM. By 'form', here, we mean the way the STRUCTURE of the phrase is made up of words and other constituents. Typically, in a phrase composed of head and modifiers, premodifiers tend to be single words and postmodifiers tend to be phrases or clauses. Although the genitive phrase (as we saw in 4.2) is an important exception, the structure of the NP illustrates this tendency.

4.3.1 The noun phrase (NP)

FUNCTION. In the clause, NPs act as subject (*S*), as object (*O*), or as complement (*C*):

(15) [$^S_{NP}$(The house) ^{P}(was) ^{C}(quite empty)]. NP = *S*

(16) [^{S}(We) ^{P}(have bought) $^O_{NP}$(the house)]. NP = *O*

(17) $[^S(\text{This})\ ^P(\text{must be})\ ^C_{\text{NP}}(\text{the house})]$.   NP = C (see 3.2.3)

Some kinds of NPs (e.g. some NPs of time) can act as adverbials (A):

(18) $[^S(\text{We})\ ^P(\text{walked})\ ^A_{\text{NP}}(\text{five miles})\ ^A_{\text{NP}}(\text{last week})]$.   NP = A

(On adverbials, see 3.2.4 and 5.1.3.)
     Subordinate NPs can act as modifiers in other NPs:

(19) $(^H_{\text{N}}\text{man}\ ^M_{\text{NP}}(\text{the hunter}))$

(20) $(^M_{\text{N}}\text{champion}\ ^H_{\text{N}}\text{unicyclist}\ ^M_{\text{NP}}(^H_{\text{N}}\text{Wilbur J. Beanstalk}))$.[1]   NP = M

This construction, in which one NP is 'defined' by another, is called
APPOSITION.
     STRUCTURE. The structures of NPs are very diverse, but the chief
elements are these:
     (a)   The HEAD of an NP may be:

(i)   a **noun**: (the $^H doll$), (dear $^H Margaret$), etc.

(ii)   a **pronoun**: $(^H it)$, $(^H herself)$, $(^H everyone$ (in the street)), etc.

(iii)   (less usually) an **adjective** (the $^H absurd$), an **enumerator** (all
        $^H fifteen$), or a **genitive phrase** $(^H(John's))$.

Two of the less usual possibilities are illustrated in:

(21) $[^S_{\text{NP}}(\text{The}\ ^H_{\text{Aj}}greedy)\ (\text{will take})\ ^O_{\text{NP}}(\text{all}\ ^H_e three)]$.

But in such cases there is usually a noun which semantically is understood to be the head: e.g. [(*The greedy people*) (*will take*) (*all three
loaves*)].

     (b)   The PREMODIFIERS of an NP may be:

(i)   **Determiners:** $(^M this$ morning), $(^M what^M a$ girl), etc.

(ii)   **Enumerators:** $(^M two$ eggs), (the $^M third$ man), etc.

(iii)   **Adjectives:** $(^M red$ shoes), $(^M older$ music), etc.

(iv)   **Nouns:** (a $^M garden$ fence), (a $^M gold$ ring), $(^M London$ pubs), etc.

(v)   **Genitive phrases:** $(^M(Fred's)$ whisky), $(^M(someone\ else's)$
        problems), etc.

---

[1] Multi-word names like *New York, Oxford Street*, and *Wilbur J. Beanstalk* count
grammatically as a single unit, and so we may treat the whole name as constitut-
ing the *H* of a phrase.

(vi) **Adverbs** (in initial position): (^{M}*quite* a noise).

(vii) Some less clear-cut categories, such as adjective phrases ($_{AjP}^{M}$ (*awfully bad*) weather); other phrases ($_{PP}^{M}$ (*round the clock*) service); compound words of various kinds (a *slow-witted* bumpkin); Ven and Ving forms of verbs (*grated* cheese), (a *running* total).

This last set of premodifiers is so miscellaneous that we cannot hope to deal with it thoroughly. There is often doubt as to whether, for example, a modifier is a phrase or compound word, and whether a word ending in *-ed* or *-ing* is a verb or an adjective derived from a verb. For parsing purposes, we may have to take some rather arbitrary decisions; for example, we can let hyphenation determine whether something is to be treated as a single word, and we can make some *ad hoc* bracketing distinctions in order to resolve ambiguities such as:

(22) NP(a (metal cutting) blade)/NP(a metal (cutting blade)).

(c) The POSTMODIFIERS of an NP may be:

(i) **Prepositional phrases**: (the best day $_{PP}^{M}$ (*of my life*)).

(ii) **Relative clauses**: (a quality ^{M} [*which I admire*]).

(iii) Various other types of modifier, including ADVERBS (the girl $_{Av}^{M}$*upstairs*), ADJECTIVES (something $_{Aj}^{M}$*nasty* (in the woodshed)), NOUN PHRASES in apposition (the bandicoot, $_{NP}^{M}$(*a tiny marsupial*)), and other types of clause (see 6.3).

Because of these various kinds of modifier, it is possible for an NP to reach considerable complexity. With premodification alone, such phrases as (23) are possible, though rare:

(23) ($_{Av}^{M}$absolutely $_{d}^{M}$the $_{e}^{M}$last $_{e}^{M}$two $_{Aj}^{M}$unsold $_{Aj}^{M}$ripe $_{Aj}^{M}$juicy $_{N}^{H}$peaches).

In postmodification there is in principle no limit to the length of NPs. The occurrence of subordinate PPs as postmodifiers is very common, and it is important to distinguish cases like:

(24) (the girl PP(by the table PP(with the carved legs)))

(25) (the girl PP(by the table) PP(with the sunburnt legs)).

In (24) one PP postmodifies *girl*, and the other PP is subordinate to it, postmodifying *table*. In (25), however, both PPs postmodify *girl*. [Now try Exercises 4b and 4c.]

4.3.2 Pronouns (pn) and determiners (d)

Pronouns and determiners are two closed word classes in the NP which have similar subdivisions:

PRONOUNS function as H

Personal pronouns: *I, we, you, he, she, it, they, me, us, them, myself, yourself, himself, herself,* etc.

Demonstrative pronouns: *this, that, these, those.*

Quantifier pronouns:

(a) General: *all, some, any, none, several,* etc.

(b) Compound: *everybody, someone, anything, nobody,* etc.

(c) Gradable: *many, much, more, most, few, fewer, little, least,* etc.

Wh- pronouns: *who, whom, whose, what, which, whichever,* etc.

DETERMINERS function as M

Articles: *the, a/an*

Demonstrative determiners: **same as pronouns.**

Quantifier determiners:

(a) General: *all, some, any, no, every,* etc.

(b) Gradable: **same as pronouns.**

Wh- Determiners: *what, which, whatever, whichever.*

Notice that, for example, the demonstratives and the gradable quantifiers are the same for both pronouns and determiners. Nevertheless, we shall treat these as separate word classes; the simple rule is that words from these classes which function as **heads** are **pronouns**, and those which function as **modifiers** are **determiners**. This rule has one exception: the so-called POSSESSIVE PRONOUNS *my, your, their, whose,* etc., occur as modifiers, as in *my sister, your book,* etc. But strictly, these are cases of subordination, the possessive pronoun acting as head of a genitive phrase: $(^M_{GP}(^H_{pn}your)$ $^M_{Aj}$favourite ^H_Nbook), $(^M_{GP}(^H_{pn}$ her) ^M_Ndislike $^M_{PP}$ (of J.R.)).

Since, as observed in 4.3.1, a GP can function as the head of an NP, the same applies to a possessive pronoun: as the head of GP, it can indirectly act as the head of an NP. Compare the functions of *your* (at M) and *yours* (at H) in (26) and (27):

(26) $[^S(^H_{pn}$Those) $^P_{VP}$(are) $^C_{NP}$ $(^M_{GP}$(your) ^H_Nbooks)] .

(27) $[^S(^M_d$ Those ^H_Nbooks) $^P_{VP}$(are) $^C_{NP}$ $(^H_{GP}$(yours))] .

These sentences, by the way, also show the difference between *those* as a pronoun and *those* as a determiner. [Now try Exercises 4d and 4e.]

4.3.3 Prepositional phrases (PP)

FUNCTION. In the clause, PPs act as adverbials (A):

(28) $[^A_{PP}$(By Monday) (we) (had arrived) $^A_{PP}$(by train) $^A_{PP}$(in Omsk)].

The adverbial PPs have various meanings (see 5.1.3). Thus in (28) the three PPs are adverbials of time–*when*, means, and place, answering the questions *When?*, *How?* and *Where?* In NPs, AjPs, AvPs and PPs subordinate PPs act as postmodifiers (see 4.3.1, 4.4).

STRUCTURE. We have already noted in 2.5.3 that PPs have exactly the same structures as NPs, except that they are introduced by a preposition; i.e. PP = pNP. Normally prepositions are inseparable from the head (and modifiers) which follow them. There are, however, various circumstances in which a preposition can be separated from its following NP.
Compare:

(29) (problems $[^A_{PP}$(with which) $^S_{NP}$(one) $^P_{VP}$(must live)])

(30) (problems $[_{NP}$(which) $^S_{NP}$ (one) $^P_{VP}$(must live) $_p$(with)]).

In (29) *with which* is a PP, but in (30) the preposition has been left 'stranded' at the end of the clause, and the pronoun *which* which follows it in (29) has turned itself into a separate NP.

Another way in which prepositions may separate themselves from the following NP is in idioms like *look at, look for, approve of, deal with*, etc. We may compare two apparently similar sentences:

(31) Professor Dumbello lives in a tower.

(32) Professor Dumbello indulges in wild parties.

In (31) the PP clearly has an adverbial function (*Where does Professor Dumbello live? In a tower*). But in (32) *in* seems more closely connected with *indulges*, so that *indulges-in* can be almost regarded as an idiomatic verb compound. Thus while the clause structure of (31) is *S P A*, that of (32) might be transcribed as *S P p O*, the preposition being a 'rogue' constituent of clause structure, in the manner of particles discussed in 3.3.8.

Idioms like *look at, care for, indulge in*, etc., are sometimes called PREPOSITIONAL VERBS, and the NPs which follow them PREPOSITIONAL OBJECTS. Mention should also be made of another type of verb idiom very common in English: that of PHRASAL VERBS like *make up, take off, hang about.* But in these cases, the second word *up, off, about,* etc., is an **adverb** rather than a **preposition** (see 3.3.4).[1]

4.3.4 The genitive phrase (GP)

We have already given some attention to this construction, and need do little more than summarise what has already been said.

FUNCTION. GPs function either as premodifiers (M) or as heads (H) in NPs.

STRUCTURE. GPs are just like NPs except that they end with the particle *'s* (') (i.e. GP = NP's), which is not, however, always separately pronounced. Some possessive pronouns are irregular, in that they function as GPs, but do not end in *'s* - e.g. *my, mine.*

4.4 The adjective phrase and the adverb phrase

Compared with NPs, AjPs and AvPs tend to have a simple structure. Although they consist of the same elements ($\{M^n\}H\,\{M^n\}$), in practice they often consist of only a head, and it is unusual for them to have more than one premodifier and one postmodifier.

4.4.1 The adjective phrase (AjP)

FUNCTION. In the clause, AjPs function as complement (C):

(33a) [This coffee is $\underset{\text{AjP}}{\overset{C}{(\text{hot})}}$].

(33b) [Adolphus drinks his coffee $\underset{\text{AjP}}{\overset{C}{(hot)}}$].

In the phrase, AjPs can function as premodifiers in NPs:

(34) ($\underset{\text{d}}{\overset{M}{}}$a $\underset{\text{AjP}}{\overset{M}{}}$(*very large*) $\underset{\text{N}}{\overset{H}{}}$slice $\underset{\text{PP}}{\overset{M}{}}$(of bread)).

STRUCTURE. The head of an adjective phrase is an adjective, which may be simple (*big*), comparative (*bigger*), or superlative (*biggest*) (see 3.2.3).

Premodifiers are always adverbs: typically, adverbs of degree (*extremely, rather, too, very*). Some, especially *very* and *too*, can be

---

[1] Phrasal verbs and prepositional verbs constitute an important but rather problematic area of English grammer. See Cowie and Mackin (1975), especially the Introduction. This discussion illustrates the principle that in grammar we are often trying to weigh up the merits of alternative solutions; there is no such thing as a 'correct' analysis of sentences like (32), but we may be able to argue for one analysis being better than another.

reduplicated (*very very very tall*). Postmodifiers can be either adverbs (*indeed, enough*) or PPs:

(35) $(^M_{Av}$very $^H_{Aj}$tall $^M_{Av}$indeed) $(^H_{Aj}$nice $^M_{Av}$ enough)

(36) $(^M_{Av}$rather $^M_{Av}$too $^H_{Aj}$hot $^M_{PP}$(for comfort)).

We also find certain kinds of clauses as postmodifiers: *younger* [*than I thought*], *too hot* [*for me to drink*], etc.

4.4.2 The adverb phrase (AvP)

FUNCTION. AvPs function in the clause as adverbials (*A*). (See 5.1.3.)

STRUCTURE. The head of an adverb phrase is an adverb (Av). Otherwise, the structure of AvPs is the same as that of AjPs:

(37) $(^H_{Av}$often) $(^M_{Av}$rather $^M_{Av}$too $^H_{Av}$quickly $^M_{PP}$(for comfort))

$(^M_{Av}$more $^H_{Av}$quickly $^M_{PP}$(than last year)).

4.5 The verb phrase (VP)

FUNCTION. The VP always acts as predicator (*P*) in the clause. Although we shall need to distinguish in 5.3 between **finite** and **nonfinite clauses**, at present we restrict ourselves to finite clauses, which means that we concentrate on the fullest kind of VP, the FINITE VERB PHRASE.

STRUCTURE. We have already outlined (in 2.5.3) the structure of the VP in terms of two kinds of element: the **main verb** (*Mv*) and **auxiliaries** (*Aux*). The auxiliaries are optional, and precede the main verb. At the most general level the structure of the VP is: {*Aux*} {*Aux*} {*Aux*} {*Aux*} *Mv*. But this is not by any means the whole story. In practice one can distinguish sixteen different kinds of VP, and, moreover, four different functions performed by the auxiliaries themselves (see Table 4.1).

In this table, we have replaced the general label *Aux* by some more specific function labels: *Mod, Perf, Prog* and *Pass. Mod* is always filled by one of the modals (m) (3.3.6). *Perf* is always filled by the primary verb *have* (hv), and *Prog* is always filled by the primary verb *be*; similarly, the *Pass* position is always filled by *be,* and the main verb position (*Mv*) can be filled either by a full verb (V), or by one of the primary verbs (be, hv, do). We can now explain the structure of the VP in more detail as: ({*Mod*} {*Perf*} {*Prog*} {*Pass*} *Mv*). The terms 'modal',

Table 4.1

S NP	P VP					
	MODALITY	PERFECT ASPECT	PROGRESSIVE ASPECT	PASSIVE VOICE	MAIN VERB	
M H	Mod	Perf	Prog	Pass	Mv	
d N	m	hv	be	be	V	
					shook	1
	might				shake	2
		had			shaken	3
			was		shaking	4
				was	shaken	5
	might	have			shaken	6
	might		be		shaking	7
the branch						
	might			be	shaken	8
		had	been		shaking	9
		had		been	shaken	10
			was	being	shaken	11
	might	have	been		shaking	12
	might	have		been	shaken	13
	might		be	being	shaken	14
		had	been	being	shaken	15
	might	have	been	being	shaken	16

NOTE: where there is **no** passive voice auxiliary, the verb phrase is in the ACTIVE VOICE.

'perfect', 'progressive' and 'passive' relate to the kinds of meaning expressed by the elements they label.

The formula just given explains that the elements of the VP can only occur in a strict order; for example, *could have worked* and *had been waiting* are grammatical combinations, but **have could worked* and **been had waiting* are not. However, there is still something to be explained: namely, that each auxiliary determines the FORM of the verb which follows it, e.g. *has worked* occurs, but **has working* does not. To explore this further, we have to return to the description of verb forms.

4.5.1 Verb forms

In Table 4.2 (p.68), the tables of verb forms given in 3.3.2 and 3.3.6 are expanded, so as to apply not only to full-verbs but also to operator-verbs (i.e. to modals and primary verbs). We also make a distinction here between FINITE and NON-FINITE forms. In the FINITE VERB PHRASE, the first word is always a FINITE VERB FORM.

In Table 4.2 we have now labelled an additional verb form, in addition to Vo, Vs, Ved, Ving and Ven. This new form is the INFINITIVE form (Vi) of the verb, but it differs from Vo only in the verb *be*. To all intents and purposes, then, the infinitive is the form

Table 4.2

			FINITE FORMS			NON-FINITE FORMS		
			TENSE			INFINITIVE	PARTICIPLES	
			PRESENT		PAST		PAST	PRESENT
			3rd person singular Vs:	other Vo:	Ved:	Vi:	Ven:	Ving:
Full-verbs	Regular		reaches	reach	reached	reach	reached	reaching
	Irregular		writes sinks puts	write sink put	wrote sank put	write sink put	written sunk put	writing sinking putting
Operator-verbs	Primary verbs	(do) (hv) (be)	does has is	do have am/are	did had was/were	do have be	done had been	doing having being
	Modals	(m)	may (must)		might (used to)	—— ——	—— ——	—— ——

of the verb which has no ending, just like Vo. The rules for combining verbs in the verb phrase can now be expressed as in Table 4.3.

Thus if we want to construct a VP with the structure *Perf Mv,* the rules of Table 4.3 say that the *Mv* must be a Ven: e.g. *has taken.* If we want to construct more complex phrases such as *Mod Prog Mv* or *Mod Pass Mv,* the rule will work as shown in Figure 4.2.

The non-initial parts of any VP are always non-finite (Vi, Ving, or Ven). This means that there is a quite different way of describing the structure of the VP, this time not in terms of *Aux* and *Mv,* but in terms of finite and non-finite verbs:

$$F\{Nf\}\{Nf\}\{Nf\}\{Nf\}$$

where F = finite, and Nf = non-finite.

Table 4.3

	Function	Class of verb	Form of following verb
Optional elements:	Modal (*Mod*)	MODAL VERB (m)	INFINITIVE (Vi)
	Perfect aspect (*Perf*)	HAVE (hv)	-EN PARTICIPLE (Ven)
	Progressive aspect (*Prog*)	BE (be)	-ING PARTICIPLE (Ving)
	Passive voice (*Pass*)	BE (be)	-EN PARTICIPLE (Ven)
Obligatory:	Main verb (*Mv*)	Verb (V)	(there is none)

Figure 4.2

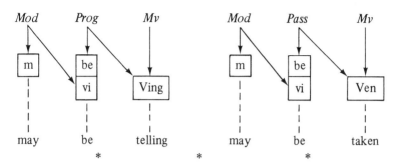

The English VP, in fact, cannot all be described by means of one set of labels: it is an unusual structure of interlocking patterns. However, these intricacies do not have to bother us in the procedure of parsing a sentence. For most purposes, it will be sufficient to label phrases by means of the function labels *Aux* and *Mv,* and the form labels v (or m (modal), be, hv, do) and V. For example:

$$\text{VP}(^{Mv}_{V}\text{eats}) \quad \text{VP}(^{Aux}_{be}\text{is } ^{Mv}_{V}\text{playing}) \quad \text{VP}(^{Aux}_{m}\text{ must } ^{Mv}_{V}\text{go})$$

$$\text{VP}(^{Aux}_{m}\text{ should } ^{Aux}_{be}\text{be } ^{Mv}_{V}\text{working}) \quad \text{VP}(^{Aux}_{m}\text{must } ^{Aux}_{be}\text{be } ^{Aux}_{be}\text{being}$$

$$^{Mv}_{V}\text{ done}).$$

4.5.2 The 'dummy operator' do
One important detail of the VP has still to be dealt with: the special role of the auxiliary *do.*

Earlier we identified the small closed class of verb (3.1) as **operator-verbs** (v). This name is especially appropriate, because these verbs in their finite form (normally as first auxiliary) are used in various 'operations' such as making a clause negative or interrogative. Consider **negation:**

(38) She *can sing.*

(38a) She *can – not sing.*   (She *can't sing*)

(39) She *is singing.*

(39a) She *is not singing.*   (She *isn't singing*)

(40) It *has been sung.*

(40a) It *has not been sung.*   (It *hasn't been sung*)

To form the negative, we simply add the particle *not* (or its reduced version *n't*) after the first word of the VP, which is a finite operator. But what about this case:

(41)　She *sang.*

(41a) *She *sang not.*

(41b) She *did not sing.*　(She *didn't sing*)

In (41a) we cannot add *not* after the finite operator, because there is no operator-verb in the VP: there is only the full-verb *sang*. So the negative rule just stated cannot work, unless we can find an operator-verb. The DUMMY OPERATOR *do* comes to the rescue: it is the verb that takes the role of operator where there is no other verb to do so, as in (41b). Notice that the verb *be* acts as an operator even when it functions as a *Mv*:

Bunter *is* my friend → Bunter *is not* my friend.

The same sometimes applies, in some varieties of English, to *have* as main verb: *He hasn't any ideas.* But nowadays people frequently use the operator *do* in such cases: *He doesn't have any ideas.* [Now try Exercise 4f.]

4.6　Summary

The following, then, are the **formal** structures of the six types of phrase:

A.　**Noun phrases** (NP): $\{M^n\}\, H\, \{M^n\}$
　　where H (head) may be: N, pn, Aj, e, or GP
　　　　　M before H (premodifiers) may be: d, e, Aj, N, GP, etc.
　　　　　M after H (postmodifiers) may be : PP, NP, Av, Aj, relative
　　　　　clause, etc.

B.　**Prepositional phrases** (PP): p $\{M^n\}\, H\, \{M^n\}$
　　where p is a preposition, and
　　　　　$M, H,$ and M are exactly as in noun phrases.

C.　**Genitive phrases** (GP): $\{M^n\}\, H\, \{M^n\}$'s
　　where 's is the genitive particle, and
　　　　　$M, H,$ and M are as in noun phrases (complex postmodifiers,
　　　　　however, are rare in GPs).

D.　**Adjective phrases** (AjP): $\{M^n\}\, H\, \{M^n\}$
　　where H (head) is an Aj
　　　　　M before H (premodifiers) are normally Av
　　　　　M after H (postmodifiers) are PP, Av, and some clauses.

E. **Adverb phrases** (AvP): $\{M^n\}\ H\ \{M^n\}$
   where H (head) is an Av, and
   M is as in AjPs.

F. **Verb phrases** (VP): $\{Aux\}\ \{Aux\}\ \{Aux\}\ \{Aux\}\ Mv$
   where all *Aux* are v (operator-verbs), and
   Mv is either v (operator-verb) or V (full-verb).

The **functions** of these phrase classes in the **clause** can be summarised as shown in Figure 4.3. The arrow X ——→ Y is to be interpreted: 'X may be a Y'. We turn in Chapter 5 to a more detailed description of how phrases behave in clauses.

Figure 4.3

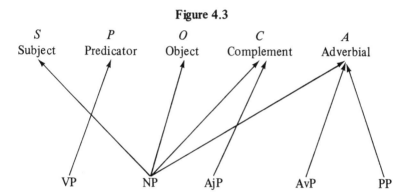

Exercises

Exercise 4a   (answers on p. 203)
Which phrases, in the following, are **main** and which are **subordinate**?

1. [(Mary) (had) (a little lamb)].
2. [(The fleece (of the little lamb)) (was) (as white (as snow))].
3. [(Everyone (in town)) (admires) (the whiteness (of the fleece (of (Mary's) little lamb)))].

Exercise 4b   (answers on p. 203)
Examples (24) and (25) on p.62 illustrate a possible ambiguity of prepositional phrases. To which of the examples (p. 72) do these descriptions apply:

(a)   Two PPs postmodify the same head (. . .*H* (PP) (PP)).
(b)   One PP is subordinate to another PP (. . .*H* (p. . .*H* (PP)).
(c)   The interpretation is ambiguous between (a) and (b).

1.   (her interest in the coins of Roman Britain)
2.   (the leader of the revolution in October)
3.   (the courage of a stag at bay)
4.   (a battle of words in Parliament)
5.   (the fall of Rome in 1527)
6.   (the highest rate of inflation in Europe)
7.   (a father of ten children with a criminal record).

Exercise 4c   (answers on p. 203)
The following are NPs in which the order of premodifiers is scrambled:

1.   sisters, two, Cinderella's, ugly
2.   jade, idol, carved, green, a, small
3.   designs, interlocking, Chinese, intricate, old, those, all
4.   old, disgusting, Victorian, a, drawings, few, quite
5.   brilliant, new, Moldwarp's, hypothesis, geological
6.   cylindrical, second, Morgan's, steam, condenser, revolutionary
7.   a, tower, church, Gothic, grey, ancient
8.   first, hundred, tourists, the, foreign, all, almost
9.   responsibilities, moral, new, his, heavy
10. life, hectic, my, social, London.

A.   Unscramble the words into their correct grammatical order. (In some cases there may be more than one possible order.)
B.   In doing A, you have exercised your ability, as a speaker of English, to apply rules for ordering premodifiers in an NP. Try to formulate these rules. First, work out the order in which these classes normally occur if they are combined: N, e, GP, Aj, d, Av. Second, if there is more than one member of the same class in the same NP, are there any principles for deciding in which order to put them?

Exercise 4d   (answers on p. 204)
In the following examples, give **function labels** and **form labels** for each of the words and phrases which are elements of each NP. For example, the NP *the new factory here in Lancaster* may be analysed:

$$(_{d}^{M}\text{the }_{Aj}^{M}\text{new }_{N}^{H}\text{factory }_{Av}^{M}\text{here }_{PP}^{M}(\text{in Lancaster})).$$

1.   she
2.   the skeleton in the cupboard
3.   that strange feeling
4.   half the people present
5.   Stanley's historic meeting with Livingstone at Ujiji
6.   all those utterly fruitless afternoon meetings of the committee last year.

Exercise 4e   (answers on p. 205)

The most important category of pronouns is that of the **personal pronouns**. In Table 4.4 the personal pronouns are arranged according to distinctions traditionally known as **person** (first, second, third), **number** (singular, plural), **case** (subject, object, genitive, etc.)[1] and **gender** (masculine, feminine, neuter). Often these distinctions are **neutralised**, which means that the same form has to go in two different boxes (e.g. this is true of boxes 3 and 11). Complete the table by filling in the numbered gaps.

Table 4.4

Person		First		Second		Third				
Number→	FUNCTION	Sing.	Plur.	Sing.	Plur.	Singular			Plural	
Gender→						Masc.	Fem.	Neut.		
Case↓										
Subject	H	1	2	3	4	5	she	7	8	
Object	H	9	us	11	12	him	14	15	16	
Reflexive	H	17	18	yourself	yourselves	21	22	23	themselves	
Genitive	M	my	26	27	28	29	30	its	32	
	H	mine	34	35	36	37	38	–	40	

Exercise 4f (preliminary consideration of constructions to be re-examined later)

Examine these sets of sentences in which the VPs are italicised, and then describe as well as you can: (i) the rules for forming constructions b–f below, and (ii) the circumstances under which the **dummy auxiliary** *do* is used in English:

a. **Ordinary Declaratives**

   She *is working.*
   They *had eaten* them.
   She *works* hard.
   They *made* a mistake.

b. **Negative Sentences**

   She *is not working.*
   They *had not eaten* them.
   She *does not work* hard.
   They *did not make* a mistake.

c. **Questions**

   Is she *working?*
   Had they *eaten* them?
   Does she *work* hard?
   Did they *make* a mistake?

d. **Emphatic Sentences**

   Yes, she *IS working.*
   Yes, they *HAD eaten* them.
   Yes, she *DOES work* hard.
   Yes, they *DID make* a mistake.

---

[1] The **object** form of the pronoun is not limited to pronouns functioning as object. In what other functions is the object form used? (See further section 11.4.)

74   ENGLISH GRAMMAR FOR TODAY

e. Tag Questions

She's *working*, *isn't* she?

They'd *eaten* them, *hadn't* they?

She *works* hard, *doesn't* she?

They *made* a mistake, *didn't* they?

f. Comparative Clauses

She's *working* harder than Bill *is*.

They'd *eaten* more than we *had*.

She *works* harder than I *do*.

They *made* more mistakes than we *did*.

5
Clauses

5.1 Elements of the clause

We have recognised five principal elements of the clause, and it is now time to explain them more carefully. They are shown in (1) in order of the degree to which they are 'central' to clause structure:

(1) CLAUSE ELEMENTS   *Label*

    Predicator   *P*
    Subject   *S*
    Object   *O*
    Complement   *C*
    Adverbial   *A*

These five clause elements are illustrated in (2):

(2) [^{S}(Many people) ^{P}(are painting) ^{O}(their houses) ^{C}(white) ^{A}(these days)].

This example also gives the typical ordering of these elements.

5.1.1 Predicator (P) and subject (S)

The PREDICATOR is the only element which is a verb phrase. The SUBJECT normally precedes the predicator, and there is CONCORD between the subject and predicator as regards NUMBER and PERSON (see Exercise 4e, p. 73). Number concord is illustrated in:

(3) [^{S}(Many gentlemen) ^{P}(prefer) blondes].   (**plural** *S*, **plural** *P*)
(4) [^{S}(This gentleman) ^{P}(prefers) brunettes].   (**singular** *S*, **singular** *P*)

It is often possible to use a **substitution test**, substituting one of the **subject personal pronouns** (see p. 73) (*I, we, he, she, they*) for the phrase in subject position. This is a very useful test, since apart from *you* and *it* personal pronouns have distinctive forms when they act as subject: *He prefers her, She prefers him*.

We should emphasise the need to use several tests when identifying clause elements. Consider the sentences in (5) and (6):

(5)   [^{A}(In the box) ^{P}(are) ^{S}(six skulls)].
(6)   [^{S}(The box) ^{P}(contains) ^{O}(six skulls)].

The criteria of position and meaning (2.5.2) do not help to identify S and O here, but we can still rely on tests of concord and pronoun substitution (cf. *They are in the box; It contains six skulls*).

5.1.2   Object (O) and complement (C)

The OBJECT is very closely tied to the predicator in terms of meaning, and typically denotes the person or thing most intimately affected by the action or state, etc., denoted by the P. The COMPLEMENT can look superficially like an object (both can be NPs), but in terms of meaning it provides a definition or characterisation of the S or O. Objects and complements normally follow the P:

(7)   [^{S}(Meg) ^{P}(dislikes) ^{O}(Gus)].
(8)   [^{S}(Gus) ^{P}(is) ^{C}(a scoundrel)].

If there are both an O and a C in the clause, then normally the C follows the O:

(9)   [^{S}(Meg) ^{P}(called) ^{O}(Gus) ^{C}(a scoundrel)].

In (9) as in (8), *a scoundrel* characterises *Gus* – in Meg's opinion, anyway.

5.1.3   Adverbials (A)

ADVERBIALS fill out the clause by adding extra circumstantial information of various kinds, ranging from time and location to the speaker's attitude. Of the clause elements that we have examined, they are the least closely integrated into clause structure – and this goes especially for sentence adverbials.

The first point about adverbials is that there is no fixed number of them in a clause; in this they are rather like modifiers in the NP. The more common adverbial types are listed in Table 5.1, together with typical questions which elicit them.

The clause in (10) has four adverbials:

(10)   [^{A}(Actually), ^{S}(he) ^{P}(works) ^{A}(at home) ^{A}(very rarely) ^{A}(these days)].

Its variants (10a) and (10b) show that adverbials are generally much more mobile in the clause than the other clause elements we have met:

(10a) [^{S}(He) ^{A}(very rarely) ^{P}(works) ^{A}(at home) ^{A}(these days), ^{A}(actually)].

(10b) [^{A}(These days) ^{S}(he) ^{A}(very rarely) ^{A}(actually) ^{P}(works) ^{A}(at home)].

So mobile are certain adverbials that they can be placed in the middle of the P, interrupting its elements, as in (11), where we use a new symbol (⌐⎯⎯⌐) to link the interrupted elements of the phrase:

(11) [^{S}(Crabs) ^{P}(are ^{A}(now) being served)].
(Cf. *Crabs are being served now.*)

Adverbials are also **optional** in most clause types. They can normally be omitted from the clause, as in (12):

(12) [He works *at home very rarely*], [He works *at home*], [He works].

[Now try Exercises 5a and 5b.]

Table 5.1

Adverbial type	Eliciting question	Example
Place	*Where?*	*(on a box)*
Direction	*Where to/from?*	*(to/from York)*
Time – *when*	*When?*	*(on Sunday)*
Duration	*How long?*	*(for a month)*
Frequency	*How often?*	*(once a week), (every day)*
Manner	*How? In what manner?*	*(quickly), (with confidence)*
Agency	*By whom?*	*(by a tall dark stranger)*
Goal	*To/for whom?*	*(to Mary), (for himself)*
Reason	*Why?*	*(because of her mother)*
Condition	*In what circumstances?*	*[if you do the dishes]*
Degree	*How much? How far?*	*(completely), (to some extent)*
Sentence adverbial	*(expresses attitude, connection, etc.)*	*(in fact), (consequently)*

5.2 Complex sentences

So far we have dealt only with SIMPLE SENTENCES consisting of a single MAIN CLAUSE (MCl), which is precisely a clause that can stand alone as a simple sentence (since this is the **only** element in the sentence, no function label is necessary):

(13) Se MCl[I'll scratch your back].

But the majority of English sentences that you are likely to meet in texts are COMPLEX SENTENCES, i.e. sentences which contain additional clauses.

There are two ways in which additional clauses can occur in a complex sentence. Two or more clauses can be COORDINATED, that is, they can be linked as units of equal status:

(14) $_\text{Se}$ $_\text{MCl}$[You scratch my back] and $_\text{MCl}$[I'll scratch yours].

Or there may be one or more SUBORDINATE CLAUSES (SCl), i.e. clauses which are grammatically SUBORDINATED because they are part of another clause. A subordinate clause is either an element in another clause, in this example A:

(15) $_\text{Se}$ $_\text{MCl}$[^A_SCl[If you scratch my back] ^S_NP(I) ^P_VP('ll scratch)
      ^O_NP(yours)].

or else a postmodifier (M) in a phrase within a clause:

(16) $_\text{Se}$ $_\text{MCl}$[(The ^H_Nperson ^M_SCl[whose back I scratch]) should scratch mine].

Complex sentences can also result from a combination of coordination and subordination of clauses, for example:

(17) $_\text{Se}$ $_\text{MCl}$[^{S}[$_\text{SCl}$[That the earth is round] and
      $_\text{SCl}$[that it can thus be circumnavigated]] was once a surprising fact].

We shall be dealing with **subordination** and **coordination**, and with classes of **subordinate clauses**, in the next chapter. The remainder of this chapter, apart from 5.3, will be concerned primarily with classes of **main clause**.

5.3   Finite and non-finite clauses

So far we have dealt only with FINITE VERB PHRASES, containing a finite verb, which is a verb showing TENSE (past or present) and SUBJECT CONCORD (for person and number), and is either the OPERATOR (the first auxiliary verb in the VP) or the MAIN VERB if there is no operator (see 4.5.1).

But there are also many NON-FINITE VERB PHRASES, containing **no** finite verb. Table 5.2 shows that in a non-finite VP all the verbs must be Vi, Ving or Ven. (Modal verbs have no non-finite forms.) Examples of finite and non-finite VPs (see 4.5.1) are shown in Table 5.2. The particle

Table 5.2

FINITE VP	*Structure*	NON-FINITE VP	*Structure*
ate	$\frac{Mv}{Ved}$	eating	$\frac{Mv}{Ving}$
will eat	$\frac{Aux\ Mv}{m\ \ \ Vi}$	to eat	to $\frac{Mv}{Vi}$
is eaten	$\frac{Aux\ Mv}{Vs\ \ Ven}$	be eaten	$\frac{Aux\ Mv}{Vi\ \ Ven}$
have been eating	$\frac{Aux\ Aux\ Mv}{Vo\ \ Ven\ Ving}$	having been eaten	$\frac{Aux\ Aux\ Mv}{Ving\ Ven\ Ven}$

to is always followed by Vi, and it can be considered an optional part of the Vi form. In fact, it is the usual practice in English to quote verbs in the TO-INFINITIVE (*to* Vi) form: *to be, to create, to bludgeon*.

The clauses we have dealt with so far have been FINITE CLAUSES, in which P has been a finite VP. But there are also many NON-FINITE CLAUSES, i.e. clauses in which P is a non-finite VP. Examples of finite and non-finite subordinate clauses are:

(18) $\Big\{$ [It would be best $_{SCl}$[if you $_{VP}^{P}$($_{Ved}^{Mv}$ told) everyone]]. [**finite** SCl].

(19) $\Big($ [The best thing would be $_{SCl}$[for you $_{VP}^{P}$($_{Vi}^{Mv}$ to tell) everyone]]. [**non-finite** SCl]

(20) $\Big\{$ [$_{SCl}$[That Spock $_{VP}^{P}$($_{Vs}^{Mv}$ has) pointed ears] is intriguing]. [**finite** SCl]

(21) $\Big($ [$_{SCl}$[Spock's $_{VP}^{P}$($_{Ving}^{Mv}$ having) pointed ears] is intriguing]. [**non-finite** SCl]

(22) $\Big($ [$_{SCl}$[As the job $_{VP}^{P}$($_{Ved}^{Mv}$ was) finished] , we went home early] . [**finite** SCl]

(23) $\Big\{$ [$_{SCl}$[The job $_{VP}^{P}$($_{Ving}^{Mv}$ being) finished] , we went home early] . [**non-finite** SCl] .

The finite subordinate clauses have finite verbs in the Ved, Vs and Ved forms respectively, while the non-finite subordinate clauses have non-finite verbs in the Vi, Ving and Ving forms respectively. Almost all non-finite clauses are subordinate clauses.

5.4 Declarative, interrogative and imperative clauses

Now we turn to main clauses, of which there are three major forms in English. The DECLARATIVE MOOD is generally used to make statements. It is the most basic form of the clause, and the clauses we have been using as examples have almost all been declaratives:

(24) Jim will post these letters.

The INTERROGATIVE MOOD is most commonly used to ask questions:

(25) Will Jim post these letters?
(26) Who will post these letters?

Finally, the IMPERATIVE MOOD is most commonly used to give orders or make requests:

(27) Post these letters.

5.4.1 The interrogative
There are two kinds of interrogatives. The YES–NO INTERROGATIVE, e.g. (25) above, asks for a *yes/no* answer. It is always the **finite operator** that carries this contrast between 'yes' and 'no' – not only negation (see 4.5.2), but also strong, positive affirmation:

(28) Jim won't post these letters.
(29) Jim **will** post these letters.   (**will** carries the emphasis)

In forming *yes-no* interrogatives we place the **finite operator** in the prominent position before S in the clause:

(30) *Has* ^{S}(she) *typed* that letter?   (P = v. . .V)
(31) *Hasn't* ^{S}(she) *typed* that letter?   (P = v. . .V)

As with negation in 4.5.2, if there is no operator in the declarative, then the corresponding interrogative uses **dummy auxiliary** *do*, followed by an infinitive.

(32) [^{S}(He) ^P_Vscratched my back].   (P = V)
(33) [$_V$Did ^{S}(he) $_V$scratch my back]?   (P = v. . .V)

It is *do* (ved = *did*) that is finite, and thus expresses present and past tense. Also notice that in the interrogative, the verb phrase is split into two parts, rather as the verb phrase is split when an adverbial is shifted into it (see p. 77):

(34) [^{S}(He) ^{P}(is ^{A}(always) making) ^{O}(things) ^{C}(difficult)].
(35) [$_V$Is ^{S}(he) ^{A}(really) (V making) ^{O}(things) ^{C}(so difficult)]?

The second kind of interrogative is the WH- INTERROGATIVE, e.g. (26) above, which asks about one of the clause elements S, O, C or A (or sometimes about a phrase element) using a WH- WORD:

WH- DETERMINERS: *what, which*
WH- PRONOUNS: *who, who(m), whose, which, what*
WH- ADVERBS: *where, when, why, how*

Note that *how* counts as a *wh-* word in spite of its spelling.

Because a *wh-* interrogative is an interrogative, the finite operator is normally placed before S, and then, because the *wh-* word is the focus of attention, it is placed before the operator:

(36) [^{O}(What) $_v$did ^{S}(she) ^{P}(say)]?

(37) [^{A}(Where) $_v$has ^{S}(she) ^{P}(hidden) ^{O}(it)]?

(38) [^{O}(^{M}Whose ^{H}book) $_v$was ^{S}(she) ^{P}(reading)]?

(39) [^{A}(^{M}How ^{H}hard) $_v$will ^{S}(she) ^{P}(be working)]?

In those cases where the *wh-* word is in the S element, however, one rule cancels out the other, so that we finish up with the normal, declarative, order:

(40) [^{S}(Who) ^{P}(ate) ^{O}(that sandwich)]?
     [^{S}(Which window) ^{P}(was broken)]?

5.4.2 The imperative

While the declarative and interrogative both have an S (which for the latter **may** be an interrogative pronoun) and a finite P, the imperative has a non-finite P and no S.

We can think of the imperative as being derived from a declarative by deletion of ^{S}(*you*) and of the VP operator *will*:

(41) [^{S}(You) ^{P}(will write) a thousand lines].

(42) [^{P}(Write) a thousand lines].

In the imperative, the first verb in the VP is thus a Vi. How do we know that it is not Vo, which is identical to Vi for all verbs except *be*? There are two reasons. First, when we have the verb *be* in an imperative, it takes the Vi form, not the Vo form:

(43) Be quiet! NOT: *Are quiet!

Second, if it were Vo, P would be finite, and therefore a contrast in tense between present (Vo) and past (Ved) would be possible. But there is no such contrast:

(44) Run to the shop. BUT NOT: *Ran to the shop.

So the verb must be Vi. In fact, this is always a good TEST FOR FINITE-NESS of a VP. If the VP is finite, it can show subject concord and an alternation in tense between Vo/Vs and Ved, while if it is non-finite it does not. Since Vo = Vi for all but one verb, and Ved = Ven for very many verbs, it is often a good idea to test P for finiteness.

5.5　Active and passive clauses

We have already met the active and passive voice in the verb phrase (4.5); now we must consider them in the clause. The ACTIVE VOICE is the basic, unmarked form of the clause:

(45)　$[^S$(She) ^{P}(has eaten) ^{O}(my porridge)].
(46)　$[^S$(She) ^{P}(has not made) ^{O}(me) ^{O}(a cup of tea)].
(47)　$[^S$(She) ^{P}(was sleeping) $^A_{PP}$(in this bed)].

The PASSIVE VOICE is the more marked form of the clause in which the S corresponds in meaning to an O (or very occasionally an A) of a corresponding active clause. So parallel to (45)-(47), we have the corresponding passives:

(48)　$[^S$(My porridge) ^{P}(has been eaten)].
(49)　$\begin{cases} [^S$(A cup of tea) ^{P}(was not made) ^{A}(for me)]. \\ [^S$(I) ^{P}(was not made) ^{O}(a cup of tea)]. \end{cases}$
(50)　$[^S_{NP}$(This bed) ^{P}(has been slept) $(_p$in)].

The S of the corresponding active becomes an optional A of AGENCY in the passive, nearly always a PP marked with the preposition by:

(51)　$[^S$(This bed) ^{P}(has been slept) $(_p$in) $^A_{PP}(_pby\ Goldilocks)]$.

5.6　More on clause structure

Having defined the clause elements P, S, O, C, A, we must now introduce some extra details of clause structure.

There are two kinds of object (O), and two kinds of complement (C). A DIRECT OBJECT (Od) is the most usual kind of object, and an IN-DIRECT OBJECT (Oi), when it occurs, comes between the predicator and the direct object. The Oi is normally optional, and can very often be replaced by an A element, a PP introduced by to or for, coming after the Od:

$\begin{cases} (52)\ \ [^S$(Tom) ^{P}(showed) $^{Oi}_{NP}$(me) ^{Od}(his etchings)]. \\ (52a)\ [^S$(Tom) ^{P}(showed) ^{Od}(his etchings) $^A_{PP}$(to me)]. \end{cases}$

$\begin{cases} (53)\ \ [^S$(Milly) ^{P}(built) $^{Oi}_{NP}$(her brother) ^{Od}(a sandcastle)]. \\ (53a)\ [before ^{S}(Milly) ^{P}(built) ^{Od}(a sandcastle) $^A_{pp}$(for her brother)]. \end{cases}$

Occasionally, the Oi occurs alone after the P, as in the joke:

(54) Waiter, do you serve ^{Od}(crabs)?
      Sit down, sir. We serve ^{Oi}(anybody).

The ambiguity of Od and Oi allowed the waiter to misinterpret the customer's question. But unless there is a need to distinguish them, we shall use O for both Oi and Od.

There are also two kinds of complement, SUBJECT COMPLEMENT and OBJECT COMPLEMENT. When we wish to distinguish them, we can symbolise them Cs and Co. The subject complement characterises or describes the subject, whereas the object complement characterises or describes the direct object:

(55) [^{S}(Joe Walcott) ^{P}(was) ^{Cs}(a great boxer)].
(56) [^{S}(Everyone) ^{P}(considered) ^{O}(Joe Walcott) ^{Co}(a great boxer)].

Once again, the difference between the two subclasses can be usually recognised by their position, as well as by their meaning. The Cs normally follows P (which typically contains the copula verb *to be*), and the Co normally follows Od. A clause normally contains only one complement, either Cs or Co.

To complete the list of what may occur in a clause, we must finally mention some 'peripheral' elements. First, two closed classes of words, conjunctions and interjections (see 3.3.5, 3.3.7):

(57) $_{ij}$*Ugh*, it's a coffee-cream again!
(58) $_{cj}$*And* so it went on.

We treat these simply as particles (see 3.3.8). Second, a NP may occur as a VOCATIVE (Voc), a phrase which identifies the person addressed:

(59) Come into the garden, $^{Voc}_{NP}$(Maud).

(60) $^{Voc}_{NP}$(Dearest Reggie), I am waiting for you, $^{Voc}_{NP}$(you little monster).

Vocatives are optional, and mobile, and are therefore more like adverbials than any other type of constituent. Notice the difference in role between the vocative in imperative clauses, and the subject in declarative clauses:

(61) $^{Voc}_{NP}$(Jock), pay attention.

      (Cf. $^S_{NP}$(*Jock*) *pays attention*.)

Only the vocative can be omitted or moved to the end of the clause.
[Now try Exercise 5c.]

5.7   Clause patterns

Adverbials (*A*) and peripheral elements (cj, ij and *Voc*) tend to be optional parts of the clause. When we have stripped away the optional elements of each clause, we are left with a nucleus which may be called its CLAUSE PATTERN. For example:

(62) But gee, Alice, *you must be kidding me* now, baby.

The clause has the structure [cj ij *Voc S P O A Voc*]. But once we have thrown away the optional elements, we are left with a nucleus [*S P O*], the clause pattern. When illustrating clause patterns, it is convenient to use a **main clause** in the **declarative mood**, in the **active voice** (see 5.4, 5.5), and with the **unmarked** (or most neutral) word order. *S* and *P* are always obligatory, but whether *O*, *C* and *A* are obligatory chiefly depends on the main verb. For example:

(63)

*The chef stuffed.	*[S P]	The chef stuffed a chicken	[S P O]
The chef talked.	[S P]	*The chef talked a story	*[S P O]
*The chef seemed.	*[S P]	The chef seemed hungry	[S P C]
The chef served lunch	[S P O]	The chef served me lunch.	[S P Oi Od]

We can arrange the principal clause elements in a hierarchy: *P, S, Od, Oi, C, A*. Then, using *P* as a reference point, the further down the hierarchy we move, the more likely the clause function is to be optional, and the more free is its position in the clause. So *S* is generally obligatory in declaratives, but *A* is obligatory with only a small number of verbs such as *put*; the position of *S* is relatively fixed, but the position of *A* is rather free.

The most common clause patterns for English are shown in Table 5.3, together with an example of each, and a list of some of the verbs that take that pattern. These clause patterns can always be extended with additional optional clause elements: particularly *A*, and sometimes *C* and *O*. For instance, we could extend the [*S P O A*] and [*S P Oi Od*] patterns, using the examples in Table 5.3:

(64) He always put it there in the evening [*S A P O A A*]
(65) Actually, he sold her the book cheap, too, darling. [*A S P Oi Od C A Voc*]

Among the verbs listed in Table 5.3 for each clause pattern there is a great deal of overlap, for many verbs can occur in more than one pattern, often with a noticeable or even extreme change in meaning. For instance, the verb *keep* occurs in all the patterns in (66):

Table 5.3 *The major clause patterns for English*

[*S P*]: [He walks]. Verbs: *walk, die, work, come, run, sleep, dream, eat, look, behave*, and many more	[*S P Od*]: [He caught it]. Verbs: *catch, hit, kiss, find, pull, work, run, dream, eat, look, behave*, and many more
[*S P Oi*]: [She served him]. Verbs: *serve, tell*, and a few others; this is in fact an uncommon clause pattern in English	[*S P Oi Od*]: [She sold him the book]. Verbs: *sell, give, tell, send, buy, make*, and some others; this is an important but limited clause pattern in English
[*S P C*]: [He is kind/a nurse]. Verbs: *be, become, seem, look, appear*, and a few others; this is a limited but important clause pattern	[*S P Od C*]: [He proved her wrong/a liar]. Verbs: *prove, call, make, think*, and some others; this is a fairly limited clause pattern
[*S P A*]: [He is there].† [She thinks about it]. Verbs: *be, stand, lean, live, reside, know, think, talk, grieve, worry*, and a few others	[*S P Od A*]: [He put it there].† [She tells him about it]. Verbs: *put, place, keep, tell, inform, worry*, and a few others

† With the *S P A* and *S P O A* patterns, different verbs require different obligatory adverbials.

*   *   *

(66) [*S P O*]:   Gladys keeps a pet python.
  [*S P O C*]:   Gladys is keeping Archie happy.
  [*S P O A*]:   Gladys keeps her pet python in the bath.
  [*S P Oi Od*]:   Gladys is keeping Archie a piece of pie.
  [*S P C*]:   Gladys is keeping very fit.
  [*S P A*]:   The piece of pie is keeping well.

The verbs of English are, by and large, remarkably flexible in the clause patterns which they govern, and though it often takes some imagination to think of plausible examples, users of the language are constantly putting the verbs to new uses. For these reasons it is often safer to specify what clause patterns a given verb **cannot** take. [Now try Exercises 5d and 5e.]

5.7.1 Passive clause patterns

It is a general rule that a clause pattern with an object can be changed into a passive clause pattern, with the same main verb, in which this object functions as subject. Thus each clause pattern on the **right-hand side** of Table 5.3 above can be converted into a passive pattern which fits into the corresponding position on the **left-hand side**:

(67) $[S\ P\ O] \rightarrow [S\ P]$
[(Jim) (caught) (the ball)] $\rightarrow$ [(The ball) (was caught) {by Jim}].

(68) $[S\ P\ Oi\ Od] \rightarrow [S\ P\ Oi]$
[(He) (sold) (me) (the car)] $\rightarrow$ [(The car) (was sold) (me) {by him}].

(69) $[S\ P\ O\ C] \rightarrow [S\ P\ C]$
[(They) (made) (her) (captain)] $\rightarrow$ [(She) (was made) (captain) {by them}].

(70) $[S\ P\ O\ A] \rightarrow [S\ P\ A]$
[(Sid) (put) (the pepper) (in my soup)] $\rightarrow$ [(The pepper) (was put) (in my soup) {by Sid}].

For the $[S\ P\ Oi]$ and $[S\ P\ Oi\ Od]$ patterns, there is also a more common passive version, in which the Oi becomes the subject: for example, *He was served by her, I was sold the car*. Each passive pattern has an optional PP of agency (*by him*, etc.).

5.8 The structure of non-finite clauses

Corresponding to the three non-finite forms of the verb (Vi, Ving, Ven) there are three types of clause, in which those forms occur as the first (or only) element of the predicator. We call these types of clause INFINITIVE CLAUSE (Cli), -ING CLAUSE (Cling) and -EN CLAUSE (Clen) respectively. Even though they lack a finite verb, such constructions are analysed as clauses, because they can be analysed into *P, S, O, C, A,* etc., just like finite clauses:

(71) **Infinitive clause:** [$_{cj}$for $_{NP}^{S}$(you) $_{VP}^{P}$(to tell) $_{NP}^{O}$(everyone)] $[S\ P\ O]$

(72) **-ING clause:** [^{S}(Spock's)$_{p}^{P}$(having) ^{O}(pointed ears)] $[S\ P\ O]$

(73) **-EN clause:** [^{S}(The job) ^{P}(finished)] $[S\ P]$

There are one or two details, apart from the verb, which distinguish non-finite from finite clauses. For example, in infinitive clauses like (71) a conjunction *for* normally precedes the subject, and the infinitive particle *to* normally precedes the VP. In *-ing* clauses like (72) the subject is often a genitive form, like *Spock's* above (but see 11.4.3). But it is more significant that, in other respects, these non-finite clauses have almost the same structural possibilities as finite clauses: they can, for instance, be classified in terms of the clause patterns in Table 5.3. One point about non-finite clauses, however, is that the S is frequently omitted:

(74) [The best thing would be $_{Cli}[^{P}$(to tell) ^{O}(everyone)]].
(75) [$_{Cling}[^{P}$(Having) ^{O}(pointed ears)] is a characteristic of Vulcans].
(76) [$_{Clen}[^{P}$(Educated) ^{A}(at Eton)], he published his translation of Homer at the age of 16].

The $-en$ clauses are passive in meaning, and have passive clause patterns.

5.9 Parsing a simple sentence

We now have all the grammatical resources we need to parse a simple English sentence. For this purpose, we return to our sentence which contains all word classes (p. 56):

(77) But alas, the two ugly sisters had gone home without her.

There is no single right way to parse a sentence, but generally it pays to work down the rank scale (2.2), starting with the sentence and working down to the words of which it is composed. At each rank, we suggest, you:

(i)   identify the **elements** of structure (usually units of the next rank down),
(ii)   then identify the grammatical **function** of each element,
(iii) and finally, identify the **class** of units that fills each of these functions.

Step (iii) gives us a new set of units to begin the whole cycle of steps (i), (ii) and (iii) on all over again (see Figure 5.1).

Figure 5.1

Identify: (i)   Immediate constituents
               (ii)   Grammatical functions of these constituents
               (iii) Class of units filling these functions

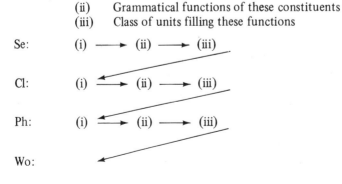

Because a tree diagram brings out the nature of grammatical analysis visually, we shall build up a tree diagram (or rather, build one down!) for (77) above, step by step.

Se: (i)   There is only one VP, (*had gone*), so there should be only one clause (see Figure 5.2).

Figure 5.2

Se

[But alas, the two ugly sisters had gone home without her].

Se: (ii)   Because we have a single clause in a complete sentence, it must be a main clause. We do not use a function label: none is needed (see 5.2).

Se: (iii)   This is a main clause (MCl) (see Figure 5.3).

Figure 5.3

Se

MCl

[But alas, the two ugly sisters had gone home without her].

We now have a clause to parse:

Cl: (i)   We bracket the constituent phrases. Note that *but* is a conjunction (cj), and therefore does not count as a phrase (see 3.3.8). The same applies to the interjection (ij) *alas*. (See Figure 5.4.)

Cl: (ii)   We identify the clause elements (see 5.1, 5.6 if in doubt). (See Figure 5.5.) Note that *but* and *alas* do not have function labels, because they are grammatical particles (see 3.3.8).

Cl: (iii)   Now identify the class of phrase filling each function (see Chapter 4). (See Figure 5.6.) Note that *but* and *alas* are labelled at this stage because, although they are not phrases, they are clause constituents.

Figure 5.4

Se
|
MCl
|

[But alas, (the two ugly sisters) (had gone) (home) (without her)].

Figure 5.5

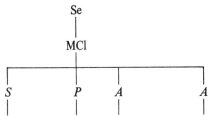

[But alas, (the two ugly sisters) (had gone) (home) (without her)].

Figure 5.6

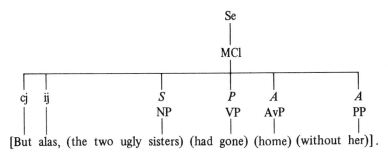

[But alas, (the two ugly sisters) (had gone) (home) (without her)].

We now have four phrases to parse:

Ph: (i) This step is vacuous in this case, since all the elements of the phrases are words, and these are already identified for us by our writing system. But later, when we parse phrases with subordinated phrases in them, this step will be a necessary one.

Ph: (ii)   Now identify the phrase elements (see Chapter 4). This is fairly easy, but remember the VP (see 4.5) and prepositions (see 4.3.3). The brackets become superfluous at this stage, so we omit them (see Figure 5.7).

Figure 5.7

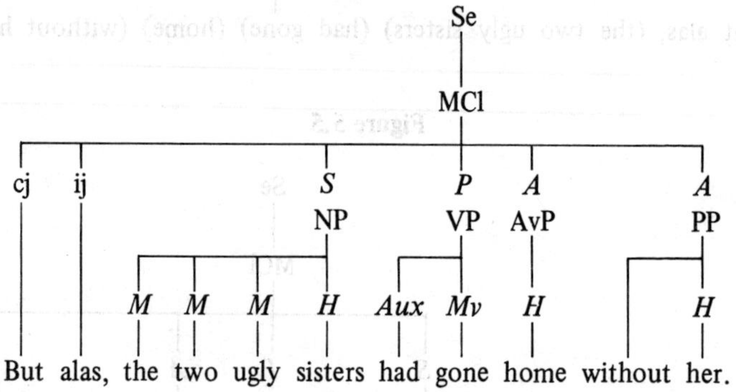

```
                              Se
                               |
                             MCl
   ┌──────┬───────────────────┬──────────┬──────────────┐
   cj    ij                   S          P     A         A
                             NP          VP   AvP        PP
                        ┌───┬───┬───┐  ┌───┬───┐ |     ┌──┐
                        M   M   M   H  Aux  Mv  H        H
   |      |      |     |   |    |  |   |    |   |        |
  But   alas,   the  two ugly sisters had gone home without her.
```

Ph: (iii)   Identify the class of the words filling each phrase function (see Chapter 3). Remember that we have already identified the class of *but* and *alas*, and remember the preposition *without*, which does not receive a function label because it is a particle (see Figure 5.8).

Figure 5.8

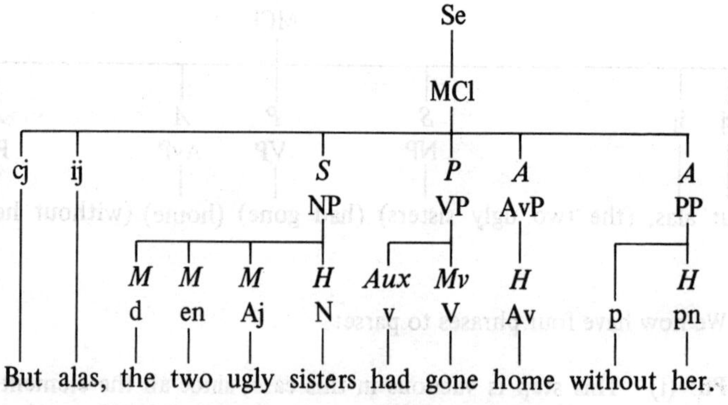

```
                              Se
                               |
                             MCl
   ┌──────┬───────────────────┬──────────┬──────────────┐
   cj    ij                   S          P     A         A
                             NP          VP   AvP        PP
                        ┌───┬───┬───┐  ┌───┬───┐ |     ┌──┐
                        M   M   M   H  Aux  Mv  H        H
                        d   en  Aj  N   v    V  Av      p  pn
   |      |      |     |   |    |  |   |    |   |        |
  But   alas,   the  two ugly sisters had gone home without her.
```

We have now parsed the sentence as fully as we can do without parsing words into their grammatical constituents. [Now try Exercise 5f.]

5.10 Summary

In this chapter we have distinguished:

(a) In addition to the clause elements *P* (predicator), *S* (subject), *O* (object), *C* (complement) and *A* (adverbial), the **peripheral** elements *Voc* (vocative), cj (conjunction) and ij (interjection); also *Od* (direct object) and *Oi* (indirect object), *Cs* (subject complement) and *Co* (object complement).

(b) Main clauses (MCl); and subordinate clauses (SCl), which are parts of other clauses.

(c) Declarative, interrogative and imperative as categories of MCl.

(d) Clause patterns [*S P*], [*S P O*], [*S P Oi*], [*S P Oi Od*], [*S P C*], [*S P O C*], [*S P A*] and [*S P O A*].

(e) Three kinds of non-finite clause: infinitive (Cli), -*ing* (Cling), and -*en* (Clen) clauses.

Exercises

Exercise 5a   (answers on p. 205)
Identify the *clause structures* (in terms of *P, S, O, C, A*) of the following:

1. [(My wife) (always) (has) (a good cry) (over a wedding)] .
2. [(That story about live alligators in the canal) (has been denied)] .
3. [(All of them) (were worrying) (about their own problems)] .
4. [(The police) (caught) (the thief) (red-handed)] .
5. [(We) ('ll rehearse) (Reggie's act) (once again)] .
6. [(On wages policy), (the leader of the opposition) (is being) (extremely cautious)] .
7. [(No doubt) (they) (will tell) (us) (the same old story) (tomorrow)] .

Exercise 5b   (answers on p. 205)
Now identify the *phrase classes* of the clause elements in the above sentences.

Exercise 5c   (answers on p. 205)
Distinguish the clause structures of these pairs:

1. The porter called me a taxi.
   The porter called me a blackguard.
2. Max was ogling a girl with red hair.
   Max was ogling a girl with brazen audacity.
3. Lesley sounds an interesting girl.
   Lesley knows an interesting girl.

4.   He found his secretary a reliable typewriter.
      He found his secretary a reliable typist.
5.   Most of us are working this evening.
      Most of us are dreading this evening.

Exercise 5d   (answers on p. 205)
Identify the *clause patterns* (see Table 5.3, p. 85) of the sentences in
Exercise 5a, by deleting optional adverbials.

Exercise 5e   (answers on p. 205)
Grammatical ambiguities play a part in some (often rather feeble) jokes.
Explain how the following jokes exploit ambiguities of clause structure
and/or word meaning:

1.   'The police are looking for a man with one eye.'
      'Typical inefficiency!'
2.   'How do you get down from an elephant?'
      'You don't – you get down from a duck.'
3.   'You've been working in the garden for hours. What are you grow-
      ing?'
      'Tired.'
4.   'Job cursed the day he was born.'
      'They must have grown up early in those days.'

Exercise 5f   (answers on p. 206)
Parse fully the following sentences, by drawing tree diagrams as recom-
mended in 5.9:

1.   [(No man) (is) (an island)].
2.   [(You) (have been eating) (too many green olives) (recently)].
3.   [(Dad) ('s given) (the carol singers) (a cheque (for a thousand
      pounds))].

(In labelling constituents of the verb phrase, restrict yourself to *Aux*,
Mv, v and V.)

6

Subordination and coordination

After three chapters on the grammatical units of word, phrase and clause, you may now be expecting a chapter on the highest unit of all on our grammatical rank scale (2.2), the SENTENCE. In fact, the sentence does not have a structure like that of lower units: *sentence* is simply a name for the largest stretch of language we normally consider in grammar, and which normally consists either of (a) a **single** clause, in which case it is known as a SIMPLE SENTENCE; or of (b) **more than one** clause, in which case it is known as a COMPLEX SENTENCE. In the complex sentence the clauses may be related to one another by SUBORDINATION or by COORDINATION (see 5.2).

Subordination, as we have seen (4.2), is not necessarily a relation between two clauses; it may be a relation between two phrases, or two words. The same applies to coordination (see 6.7). But to begin with, we limit our attention to subordinate and coordinate CLAUSES:

(1) [You pull out the plug]. [I'll scream]. (Two simple sentences.)
(2) [You pull out the plug] and [I'll scream]. (Two coordinate main clauses in one sentence.)
(3) [[If you pull out the plug], I'll scream]. (One subordinate clause and one main clause within one and the same sentence.)

The bracketing of (2) and (3) reveals a crucial difference between the two relations: a subordinate clause is always **part** of another clause, while a coordinate clause is joined with another clause (or clauses) of the **same status**, i.e. at the same level of the tree. This becomes clearer in tree diagrams (see Figures 6.1 and 6.2 overleaf).

We shall deal with subordinate clauses first, and return to coordination in 6.7. Thus by the end of the chapter we shall have dealt with the various ways in which sentences can be composed of clauses.

6.1 Subordinate clauses (SCl)

Like other kinds of grammatical construction, subordinate clauses are

93

Figure 6.1

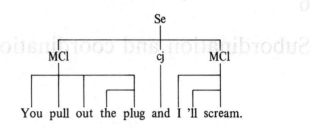

Figure 6.2

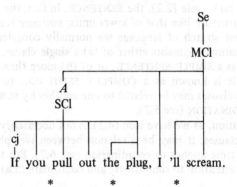

*   *   *

recognised in part by their function, and in part by their internal structure.

6.1.1 Function

We can classify subordinate clauses by their ability to function within larger units, especially within clauses. For example, the subordinate clause *what this country needs* functions as *S*, *O* and *C* in the following:

(4)   [[*What this country needs*] is a good ten-cent cigar].
(5)   [As a politician, you should know [*what this country needs*]].
(6)   [A decrease in taxation is exactly [*what this country needs*]].

We can therefore say that *what this country needs* in (4)–(6) is a NOUN CLAUSE (NCl), with a function similar to that of a NOUN PHRASE (NP). On the other hand, in (7) the clause *while we were arguing* is an AD-VERBIAL CLAUSE (ACl) with an ADVERBIAL function in the clause:

(7)   [The burglar slunk away [while we were arguing]] .

We can tell that the function of the clause is adverbial because it has the characteristics of adverbials as discussed in 5.1.3:

(a)   It is optional (cf. *The burglar slunk away*).
(b)   It is mobile (cf. *While we were arguing, the burglar slunk away*).
(c)   It answers the question *When did the burglar slink away?*, and thus shows itself to be an adverbial in terms of meaning.

In these respects, *while we were arguing* is like an adverbial phrase, such as *during our argument*:

(8)   The burglar slunk away (*during our argument*).

6.1.2 Structure
In their internal structure, subordinate clauses are divisible into the clause elements *S, P, O, C, A*. If they were not, there would be no justification for calling them clauses at all. For instance, *What this country needs*, which is an *S* in (4), must itself be broken down into the elements *O, S, P*:

(4a) $[^S[^O$(What) ^{S}(this country) ^{P}(needs)] ^{P}(is) ^{C}(a good ten-cent cigar)] .

But in addition, subordinate clauses usually have some marker or other to help indicate their subordinate status. There are three types of marking:

(i)   A SUBORDINATING CONJUNCTION : e.g. *if, when, that, because, although*.
(ii)   A WH- CLAUSE ELEMENT : e.g. *what, who, whoever, which girl, what time, how*. A *wh-* element is a phrase which contains or consists of a *wh-* word (cf. 4.3.2).
(iii) A NON-FINITE PREDICATOR (see 5.8). As mentioned in the last chapter, non-finite clauses (Cli, Cling, Clen) are those which have Vi, Ving or Ven as the first verb of their predicator. They rarely occur as main clauses.

Examples are:

(i)   [Martha will look chic^A $[_{cj}if$ ^{S}(she) ^{P}(wears) ^{O}(those clothes)]] .
(ii)   [Martha will look chic ^{A} $[^O$(*whatever*) ^{S}(she) ^{P}(wears)]] .
(iii) [Martha will look chic ^{A} $[^P$(*wearing*) ^{O}(those clothes)]] .

Wh- elements, like subordinating conjunctions, generally come at the beginning of the clause. What distinguishes a *wh-* element from a conjunction is that it is one of the major elements in a clause, such as *S, O* or *A*. In addition, it has a special interrogative or relative function.

Remember also that, as with *wearing those clothes*, in (iii), a non-finite clause often has no subject. Therefore, we can usually identify a subordinate clause by its very first word, which is likely to be a marker of types (i), (ii) or (iii) above.

But there are two difficulties to mention. The first is that there is an overlap between conjunctions and *wh-* words. *When, where* and *if*, for example, belong to both categories. The second is that there are certain types of clause, especially common in informal English, which have no introductory marker at all. We shall call these ZERO clauses, because they have no overt sign of their subordination to another clause. Let us now examine the various classes of subordinate clause, concentrating first on finite clauses. [Now try Exercise 6a.]

6.2   Finite subordinate clauses

6.2.1   Noun clauses (NCl)

The main types of finite NCl are these:

A.   THAT- **clauses** begin with the cj *that*:

(9) $[^S[$*That ghosts exist*$]_{}$(is) (hardly controversial)].
(10)   [(Seamus) (believes) $^O[$*that ghosts vanish at sunrise*]].

B.   **Zero THAT-clauses** are just like *that* clauses, except that *that* itself is omitted. A test for a zero *that-* clause is therefore whether we can insert the cj *that* at the beginning of the clause:

(11)   [(I) (told) (Jake) $^O[$the earth is round]].
(12)   [(I) (told) (Jake) $^O[$*that* the earth is round]].

C.   WH- **clauses** begin with a *wh-* element which may function within them as *S, O, C, A*, etc.:

(13) $[^S[^S(Who)$ (stole) (the teaspoon)] (is) (a mystery)].
(14)   [(Hamish) (asked) (me) $^{Od}[^A(how)$ (I) (grow) (my carrots)]].
(15)   [(You) (can ask) $^{Od}[^{Od}(whichever$ girl) (you) (like)] (to the party)].

Just as *that* noun clauses often have the role of indirect or reported statements (see p. 164), so *wh-* noun clauses often have the role of indirect or reported questions. We can thus compare (11), an example of an indirect statement, with (16), which is an indirect *yes-no* question:

(16)   [(I) (asked) (Jake) $[_{cj}$*if/whether* the earth was round]].

6.2.2 Adverbial clauses (ACl)

Like adverbs and phrases which act as adverbials, ADVERBIAL CLAUSES can be classified semantically according to what questions they answer. Table 6.1 shows some major types. Examples of these types are:

(17) [They went ^{A} [*wherever they could find work*]]. (**place**)
(18) [I lent her my savings ^{A} [*because she was short of money*]]. (**reason**)
(19) [^{A} [*When the weather improves*] , we are going on holiday]. (**time**)
(20) [I lent him some money ^{A} [*so that he could buy himself a meal*]].
(**purpose**)
(21) [^{A} [*If you follow the instructions carefully*] , nobody will be hurt].
(**condition**)
(22) [^{A} [*Although no goals were scored*], it was an exciting game].
(**contrast**).

Table 6.1

Adverbial clause of	Eliciting question	Subordinating conjunctions
Place	*Where?*	*where, wherever*
Time†	*When?*	*when, before, after, as, while, until, since, whenever*
Manner/ comparison	*How?*	*as, as if, as though*
Reason	*Why?*	*because, as, since*
Purpose	*Why?*	*so that, in order that*
Condition	—	*if, unless*
Contrast	—	*although, though*

† Adverbial clauses have meanings which are not often found in other adverbials, and vice versa. This is why the table of meanings here is somewhat different from those in 3.2.4 and 5.1.3. For example, we have found it convenient to combine the meanings of time–*when*, duration and frequency in one category of adverbial clauses of time.

Again we have to beware of overlapping uses of conjunctions. For example, *as* has a number of different meanings, and *since* can express either time or reason:

(23) [[*Since* I lost my glasses yesterday] , I haven't been able to do any work].

This sentence is ambiguous between the two interpretations.

All these ACls are introduced by a conjunction. There are also WH-ADVERBIAL CLAUSES and ZERO ADVERBIAL CLAUSES, but these are less common, and tend to function as sentence adverbials – (24) and (26) illustrate the *wh-* type, and (25) the zero type:

(24)   [^{A}[*However hard I try*], I always fail the test].
(25)   [Wombats, ^{A}[*I understand*], are virtually tailless].
(26)   [They breed copiously, ^{A}[*which is a pity*]].

The ACl in (26) is very similar to a relative clause (see 6.2.3), and such clauses are sometimes called 'sentential relative clauses'.

6.2.3   Relative clauses (RCl)

RELATIVE CLAUSES function as postmodifiers in a noun phrase or pre-positional phrase, and are thus only indirectly part of another clause (see 4.2.2, 6.5.2). Finite relative clauses typically begin with a RELATIVE PRONOUN, so called because it **relates** the clause to the word, normally a noun or pronoun, which is the head of the NP:

(27)   [Do you know $^O_{NP}(^H_{pn}$anyone $^M_{RCl}$[*who* can lend me a typewriter])]?

(28)   [Do you have $^O_{NP}$(a ^H_Ntypewriter $^M_{RCl}$[*which* you can lend me])]?

In (27) and (28) the arrow shows the relation between the relative pronoun and the head of the NP.

Like noun clauses, relative clauses can be introduced by a *wh-* word, as in (27) and (28), or by *that*, or by zero. We may thus distinguish WH-RELATIVE CLAUSES, (27), (28), from THAT RELATIVE CLAUSES, (27a), (28a), and ZERO RELATIVE CLAUSES, (28b). The last two types are illustrated by:

(27a)   [Do you know (anyone [*that* can lend me a typewriter])]?
(28a)   [Do you have (a typewriter [*that* you can lend me])]?
(28b)   [Do you have (a typewriter [you can lend me])]?

The word *that* in (27a) and (28a), however, is different from the *that* which introduces noun clauses: it is a relative pronoun, like *who* and *which* in (27) and (28), rather than a conjunction. To see this, notice that the words *who, which* and *that* in these sentences have a NP-like function of *S* or *O* in the RCl itself:

   . . . $(^H_{pn}$anyone $^M_{RCl}$[^{S}(*that/who*) ^{P}(can lend) ^{Oi}(me) ^{Od}(a type-writer)])

   . . . (a ^H_Ntypewriter $^M_{RCl}$[^{Od}(*that/which*) ^{S}(you) ^{P}(can lend) ^{Oi}(me)]).

By the way, in standard English only in the second case can the pronoun be omitted: a zero relative clause cannot normally be formed by deleting a relative pronoun functioning as S:

(27b) *[Do you know (anyone [can lend me a typewriter])]?[1]

In addition to relative pronouns (*who, whom, which, whose, that*) there are relative adverbs (*where, when, that*), which also introduce relative clauses:

(29) (the house [^{A}(*where*) ^{S}(I) ^{P}(spent) ^{O}(my childhood)])
(30) (the year [^{A}(*when/that*) ^{S}(I) ^{P}(was born)]).

Two other possibilities, for a RCl introduced by an adverbial, are a zero RCl in which the relative adverb is omitted, and a *that* RCl in which *that* functions as an adverb:

(30a) (the year [^{S}(I) ^{P}(was born)])
(30b) (the year [^{A}(that) ^{S}(I) ^{P}(was born)]).

Yet a further possibility is the use of a prepositional phrase in which the relative pronoun acts as head:

(30c) (the year [$^A_{PP}$(in *which*) ^{S}(I) ^{P}(was born)])

(31) (the children [$^A_{PP}$(with *whom*) ^{S}(I) ^{P}(used to play)]).

Even this does not exhaust the number of structural variations on sentences like (30). It is possible to leave the preposition 'stranded' at the end of the clause, and to place the relative pronoun in its customary front position, or else to omit it:

(30d) (the year [^{O}(that) ^{S}(I) ^{P}(was born) $_P$in])
(31a) (the children [^{S}(I) ^{P}(used to play) $_P$with]).

[Now try Exercise 6b.]

6.2.4 Comparative clauses (CCl)

COMPARATIVE CLAUSES are like RCls in that they have a postmodifying function. Unlike RCls, however, they may postmodify not only nouns, but also adjectives and adverbs. The most common and most typical comparative clause is easy to recognise, because it follows a comparative form such as *more, less, bigger*, and is introduced by the conjunction *than*:

(32) [In this country, we eat $^O_{NP}$(more food $^M_{CCl}$[$_{cj}$*than we can grow*])].

(33) [He's $^C_{AjP}$(less noisy [$_{cj}$*than his sister was at that age*])].

---

[1] In some people's speech sentences like (27b) do occur.

(34) [You must have been working $_{AvP}^{A}$(harder $_{CCl}^{M}$[$_{cj}$*than I thought*]))].

(35) [He's scored $_{NP}^{O}$(more goals $_{CCl}^{M}$[$_{cj}$*than* ^{S}(*I*) ^{P}(*'ve had*) ^{O}(*hot dinners*))]).

As we can see from (35), a CCl can be a full clause; but more often it has one or more 'missing' elements. We shall have more to say about these omissions in 7.3. Under this same heading of 'comparative clause' may be included a range of clauses of degree, introduced by such constructions as *as. . .as, so. . .as, so. . .that*:

(36) [She went ($_{Av}$*as* $_{Av}$quickly $_{CCl}$[$_{cj}$*as she could possibly run*])].
(37) [Ben is not ($_{Av}$*so* $_{Aj}$stupid $_{CCl}$[$_{cj}$*as some people think*])].
(38) [It was ($_{Av}$*so* $_{Aj}$hot $_{CCl}$[$_{cj}$*that the rails buckled*])].

6.2.5 Prepositional clauses (PCl)

PREPOSITIONAL CLAUSES, like prepositional phrases, begin with a preposition. Just as PPs are like NPs (2.5.3, 4.3.3), so PCls are like NCls. In symbolic form, we may represent this parallel as follows: p + NP = PP; p + NCl = PCl. In finite prepositional clauses the preposition is followed by a *wh-* element:

(39) [The butler was astonished $_{PCl}^{A}$[at what he saw]].

(40) [We have $_{NP}^{O}$(little ^{H}evidence $_{PCl}^{M}$[of who committed the murder])].

The function of a PCl, as these examples illustrate, is the same as that of a PP: it can be either an adverbial, or a postmodifier.

6.3 The functions of subordinate clauses

Table 6.2 provides a summary of the functions of the subordinate clauses illustrated in 6.2.1–6.2.5. On the right of this table, we have listed the

Table 6.2

DIRECTLY SUBORDINATE CLAUSES *(i.e. clauses which are elements of clauses)*

Noun clauses (see 6.2.1)	function as	S, O, C	Compare: NP
Adverbial clauses (see 6.2.2)	function as	A	Compare: AvP
Prepositional clauses (see 6.2.5)	function as	A	Compare: PP

INDIRECTLY SUBORDINATE CLAUSES *(i.e. clauses which are elements of phrases)*

Relative clauses (6.2.3)	function as	M in NP	Compare: Aj, PP
Comparative clauses (6.2.4)	function as	M in NP, AjP or AvP	Compare: Av, PP
Prepositional clauses (6.2.5)	function as	M in NP, AjP or AvP	Compare: PP

elements which are closest in their function to the clause classes listed on the left. In the middle of the table are given the most common functions of each class. We should mention, in conclusion, that there are some less common functions of subordinate clauses which have not been illustrated. Consider this example:

(41) $[^S_{NP}$(The report $^M_{NCl}$[that elephants were stampeding on the South Downs]) ^{P}(proved) ^{C}(totally incorrect)].

After certain nouns such as *report* in (41) we can have a NCl, as well as a RCl as postmodifier in an NP. The *that* clause in (41) can be mistaken for a RCl; but one way to distinguish it from a RCl is to note that in it *that* does not have the function of a relative pronoun: *that* cannot, for instance, be replaced by *which*: **the report [which elephants. . .]* The following sentence, in fact, is ambiguous between the two interpretations:

(42) [He received (a message [*that* she had left him])].

If [*that she had left him*] in (42) is a relative clause, the NP means 'a message *which* she had left him'; but if it is a NCl, the meaning is: 'a message *to the effect that* she had left him'.

A further type of NCl function, that of postmodifier in an adjective phrase, is illustrated in (43):

(43) $[^S$(I) ^{P}(am) ^{C}(afraid $^M_{NCl}$[the Yorkshire pudding has collapsed])].

And the same function may be filled by a PCl:

(44) $[^S$(Our team) ^{P}(is) ^{C}(ready $^M_{PCl}$[for whatever our opponents may do])].

6.4 Non-finite subordinate clauses

In the last chapter (5.8) we introduced non-finite clauses, and divided them into three classes according to the form of the predicator: **infinitive clauses** (Cli), -ING **clauses** (Cling), and -EN **clauses** (Clen). We now show how these categories combine with the functional classification of subordinate clauses given in 6.2.1–6.2.5. For example, an -ING **clause** can be further classified as a NCl, as an ACl, as a RCl, as a CCl, or as a PCl. We can easily combine the labels for these classifications to make composite labels; e.g. NCling means '-ING **noun clause**', AClen means '-EN **adverbial clause**'. In looking at the following list of examples, remember that, usually, non-finite clauses do not have a subject.

6.4.1   Non-finite noun clauses

A.   INFINITIVE NOUN CLAUSES (NCli):

(45)   [They advised him $_{NCli}$[^{P}(to resign) ^{O}(his job) ^{A}(immediately)]].

(46)   [I want $_{NCli}^{Od}$[^{S}(all of you) ^{P}(to listen) ^{A}(carefully)]].

B.   -ING NOUN CLAUSE (NCling):

(47)   [$_{NCling}^S$[^{P}(Seeing) ^{O}(a ghost) ^{A}(in your bedroom)] is a serious matter].

(48)   [We saw $_{NCling}^O$[^{S}(them) ^{P}(being threatened) ^{A}(by the gang)]].

6.4.2   Non-finite adverbial clauses

A.   INFINITIVE ADVERBIAL CLAUSE (ACli):

(49)   [People work overtime $_{ACli}^A$[$_{cj}$in order ^{P}(to earn) ^{O}(extra money)]].

(50)   [$_{ACli}^A$[^{P}(To escape) ^{O}(detection)], he wore an indigo hairpiece].

We can often insert the conjunction *in order* before the infinitive in an ACli. This indicates that the clause's meaning is that of an adverbial of purpose.

B.   -ING ADVERBIAL CLAUSE (ACling):

(51)   [$_{ACling}^A$[Not ^{P}(knowing) ^{O}(Hitler's intentions)], the allies signed the agreement].

(52)   [The committee adjourned at 9 p.m., $_{ACling}^A$[^{S}(all further business) ^{P}(being postponed) ^{A}(until the next meeting)]].

C.   -EN ADVERBIAL CLAUSE (AClen):

(53)   [$_{AClen}^A$[^{A}(Heavily) ^{P}(disguised) ^{A}(as human beings)], they frequented the quayside bars].

(54)   ['Marbles' Kneesmith, $_{AClen}^A$[^{S}(his head) ^{P}(covered)], was hustled from the courtroom].

6.4.3   Non-finite relative clauses

A.   INFINITIVE RELATIVE CLAUSE (RCli):

(55)   NP(the best car $_{RCli}^M$[$_{cj}$for ^{S}(you) ^{P}(to buy)])

(56)   NP(some tools $_{RCli}^M$[^{A}(with which) ^{P}(to do) ^{O}(the job) ^{A}(properly)]).

B.   -ING RELATIVE CLAUSE (RCling):

(57) [We talked $_{PP}$(to the peasants $_{RCling}^{M}$ [^{P}(working) ^{A}(in the rice-fields)])].

C.   -EN RELATIVE CLAUSE (RClen):

(58) $_{NP}$(The information $_{RClen}^{M}$ [^{P}(given) ^{Oi}(us) ^{A} (at the post office)]).

6.4.4 Non-finite comparative clauses

These are less common:

(59) [She is (more likely to act $_{CCli}^{M}$ [*than to think*])].

(60) [He is (better at sleeping $_{CCling}^{M}$ [*than doing a job*])].

6.4.5 Non-finite prepositional clauses

The -*ing* clause (PCling) occurs in this category:

(61) They escaped $_{PCling}^{A}$ [$_{P}$by ^{P}(climbing) ^{A}(through a window)].

[Now try Exercise 6c.]

6.5   Direct and indirect subordination

When we introduced the rank scale of grammatical units (2.2) we assumed that the elements of a unit are always units of the next lower rank: for example, that clauses are composed directly of phrases. But we have now seen that this need not be so: a unit can be an element (a) of another unit of the same rank (e.g. an adverbial clause as an element of another clause), or (b) of another unit of lower rank (e.g. a relative clause as an element of a noun phrase). Subordination of type (a) may be called DI-RECT SUBORDINATION, and subordination of type (b) INDIRECT SUB-ORDINATION. We summarise these types, together with the kind of bracketing associated with them, in Figure 6.3. The arrow here means 'can be part of'. The broken arrow — — —→ indicates that subordination within the word does take place, but that it is not such a general phenomenon as subordination within phrases and within clauses. There follows here a summary of the various types of subordination, the most important of which we have already dealt with. (See Figure 6.3 overleaf.)

6.5.1 Direct subordination

A.   **Clause-within-clause** [[Cl]] : e.g. NCl as *S, O*; ACl as *A*.

B.   **Phrase-within-phrase** ((Ph)): e.g. PP as *M* of an NP or of another PP.

Figure 6.3

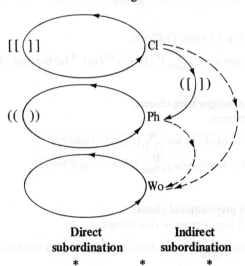

Direct	Indirect
subordination	subordination

*   *   *

C.   **Word-within-word**: e.g. *tea-pot*, *writing-paper*, *rock-hard*, *fast-talk-ing*. In COMPOUND WORDS, like these, one word (e.g. the noun *tea*) occurs as part of another word (e.g. *teapot*).

6.5.2   Indirect subordination

A.   **Clause-within-phrase** ([Cl]): e.g. RCl as *M* in an NP or a PP.

B.   **Phrase-within-word**: e.g. some compound words contain pre-positional phrases – *lilies-(of-the-valley)*; *master-(at arms)*, *mother-(in-law)*.

C.   **Clause-within-word**: this is a doubtful category, but we might argue that an expression like *batter-pudding-hurling-contest* is a single word, in which the sequence ^{O}(batter pudding)^P (hurling) has the structure of an *-ing* clause.

It is generally agreed that the principle of subordination (also called **embedding**) is essential to grammar, but there is disagreement on how exactly subordination is to be applied to particular constructions. It is common, for example, to regard a PP as a phrase containing a prep-osition followed by a subordinate noun phrase, as in (I):

(I)   PP($_p$in NP(the house))
(II)   PP($_p$in the house).

But we have preferred the simpler analysis (II). Although (I) is the better analysis from some points of view, it tends to make the PP appear more complex than it actually is. Similarly, it is possible to regard a genitive phrase as a NP subordinated within a word (a determiner) but, again, we have preferred an analysis which involves less subordination.

Whatever solutions one chooses to particular problems, an important point is that subordination can be replicated so as to make a sentence as complicated as we wish:

(62)   NP(GP(GP(GP(GP(Cholmondeley's) wife's) father's) oldest friend's) farm).

In theory, there is no end to the possibilities of subordination within subordination – a fact which recalls the couplet:

> Great fleas have little fleas upon their backs to bite 'em.
> And little fleas have lesser fleas, and so *ad infinitum*.

6.6   Skeleton analysis

Because subordination introduces so much potential complexity into the structure of sentences, it is useful to have a simplified notation for showing the layers of structure. This will be called SKELETON ANALYSIS. Tree diagrams, although they show structure clearly, tend to be bulky (see Figure 6.4).

Figure 6.4

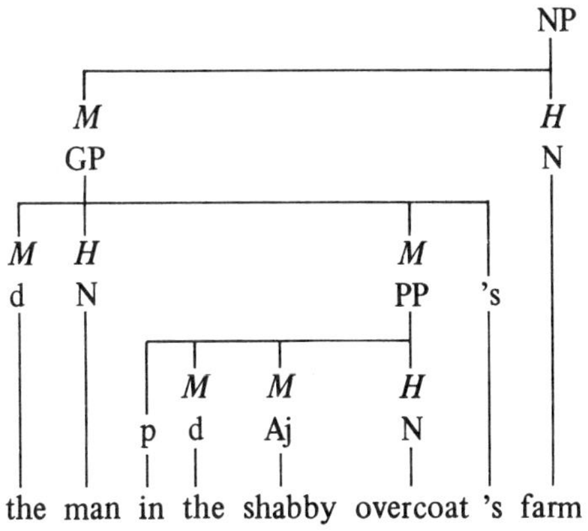

Thus it is convenient to summarise a structure like that shown in Figure 6.4 by placing a single line under a symbol, to indicate that whatever constituents occur underneath that line are the elements of the constituent named above it. For example, (63) shows the same NP as Figure 6.4:

(63) (M _____ H)
      ($M\,H\,M$ _____ -'s)
      (p $M\,M\,H$)

In skeleton analysis we need to use only the function labels. A further example is the following analysis of the phrase *my uncle's farm in the north of Scotland*:

(64) (M _____ $H\,M$ _____)
      ($M\,H$ -'s) (p $M\,H\,M$)
      (p H)

6.6.1 Skeleton clause analysis

In a similar way we can use **skeleton clause analysis** to show the structure of a sentence in terms of main and subordinate clauses. The sentences:

(65) [^{S}[$_{cj}$That ^{S}(the earth) ^{P}(is) ^{C}(flat)] ^{P}(is) ^{C}(obvious) ^{A}(to everyone)] .

(66) [^{S}(Few people) ^{P}(realise) ^{O}[$_{cj}$that ^{S}(jackasses) ^{P}(can fly)]] .

can be analysed:

(65a) [S _____ $P\,C\,A$]
       [cj $S\,P\,C$]
(66a) [$S\,P\,O$ ___]
       [cj $S\,P$]

But skeleton analysis is most useful when we are analysing more complex sentences containing a number of subordinate clauses:

(67) [Politicians always like [to think [that [what they want] is [what the country needs]]]]

Skeleton analysis:

[$S\,A\,P\,O$ _____]
  [$P\,O$ _____]
   [cj S _____ $P\,C$]
    [$O\,S\,P$] [$O\,S\,P$]

A further device of abbreviation is to use double underlining as a means of representing INDIRECT subordination. Suppose we are analysing a sentence containing a relative clause:

(68) [A miser is a person _{RCl}[who never pays a gas-bill _{AClen}[unless threatened with prosecution]]].

(a)   [*S P C*   ]   (b)   [*S P C*   ]
          (*M H M*   )   [*S A P O A*   ]
             [*S A P O A*   ]   [cj *P A*]
                  [cj *P A*]

The skeleton analyses (a) and (b) are both methods of showing the structure of sentence (68); but whereas (a) shows the structure of the phrase of which the relative clause is a constituent, (b) omits this level, and simply shows the clause structures. The double underlining for indirect subordination is a way of saying 'I am taking this short cut to save writing out structures which are in any case irrelevant to my purpose.' [Now try Exercise 6d.]

6.7 Coordination

COORDINATION, like subordination, is a way of making a sentence as complex as we like. Through coordination (typically signalled by the conjunctions *and, or,* or *but*), clauses, phrases or words (or indeed parts of these) can be conjoined to form a more complex construction which is, nevertheless, of the same rank and kind. In Figure 6.1 (p. 94) we showed how this worked in the case of coordinate main clauses. Here are examples of the coordination of subordinate clauses (Figure 6.5), the coordination of phrases (actually NPs) (Figure 6.6) and the coordination of words (actually adjectives) (Figure 6.7).

Figure 6.5

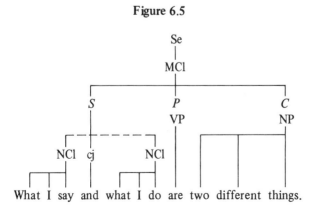

What I say and what I do are two different things.

Figure 6.6

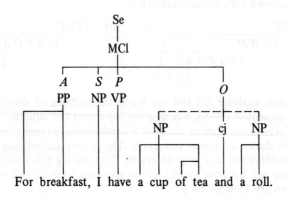

For breakfast, I have a cup of tea and a roll.

Figure 6.7

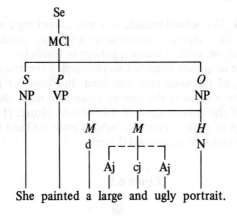

She painted a large and ugly portrait.

Again, however, it is convenient to save space and effort by using skeleton analysis for most purposes. In skeleton analysis and in labelled bracketing, we use ANGLE BRACKETS to enclose the two or more elements, or COORDINATES, as we shall call them, of a coordinate construction. Examples (69)–(71) repeat the structures of Figures 6.5, 6.6 and 6.7:

(69) [^{S}⟨$_{NCl}$[What I say] $_{cj}$and $_{NCl}$[what I do]⟩^{P}(are) ^{C}(two different things)].

(70) [For breakfast, I have ^{O}⟨$_{NP}$(a cup of tea) $_{cj}$and $_{NP}$ (a roll)⟩].

(71) [She painted ^{O}(a $^M\langle_A$ large $_{cj}$and $_A$ugly$\rangle$ ^{H}portrait)].

In skeleton analyses it is convenient to use the '+' sign to indicate the coordinating conjunction:

(72) Paul is a grouch, but I rather like him. $\langle[S\ P\ C] + [S\ A\ P\ O]\rangle$
(73) You can pay *by cheque or in cash.* $\langle\langle(p\ H) + (p\ H)\rangle\rangle$

There can be ambiguity as to what is being coordinated; for example, *He was wearing old shoes and trousers* may or may not imply that the trousers are old. The two analyses are:

(a) $^O\langle_{NP}$(old shoes) $_{cj}$and $_{NP}$(trousers)$\rangle$
(b) $^O_{NP}$(old $^H\langle$shoes $_{cj}$and trousers$\rangle$).

6.7.1   Omitting conjunctions
There may be more than two members of a coordinate construction:

(74) The primary colours are $\langle$red and green and blue. . . .$\rangle$

But in such cases it is usual for the conjunction to be used only once, before the last coordinate:

(75) Eggs can be $\langle$boiled, fried, poached, or scrambled$\rangle$.

Also, conjunctions can be omitted altogether. This may be called UN-
LINKED COORDINATION:

(76) $\langle$You're not a man, you're a mouse$\rangle$.

To represent unlinked coordination, we may use a comma in the skeleton analysis; thus (76) is analysed: $\langle[S\ P\ \text{not}\ C], [S\ P\ C]\rangle$.

6.8   Summary and conclusion

In this chapter we have introduced a classification of subordinate clauses:

noun clause (NCl);   **adverbial clause** (ACl);   **relative clause** (RCl);
comparative clause (CCl);   **prepositional clause** (PCl).

The abbreviations for these may be combined with the abbreviations for non-finite clauses (Cli, Cling, Clen - see 5.8) to form composite labels such as: NCling (-ING **noun clause**); ACli (**infinitive adverbial clause**); RClen (-EN **relative clause**).

The angle brackets ⟨⟩ are used to enclose coordinate constructions, whether the coordinates (members) are clauses, phrases, words, etc.

We have introduced a method of analysis, **skeleton analysis**, which can be used to summarise a structure which it would be tedious to analyse in full. Skeleton analysis makes use of:

(i) Ordinary function labels such as $S P O C A, M H$, etc.
(ii) Underlining to indicate subordination.
(iii) Double underlining to indicate indirect subordination.
(iv) Angle brackets ⟨⟩ to enclose a coordinate construction, '+' to indicate linked coordination, and a comma to indicate unlinked coordination.

We now have the means to analyse the most complex sentences, and it will be fitting to end this chapter with an example of parsing (of a sentence from P. G. Wodehouse, *The Code of the Woosters*) which involves a variety of structures, including both subordination and coordination of clauses. First, here is the sentence in its original printed form:

> She laughed – a bit louder than I could have wished in my frail state of health, but then she is always a woman who tends to bring plaster falling from the ceiling when amused.

Now here is a version with labelled bracketing:

$\langle_{MCl}[^{S}_{NP}(^{H}_{pn}She) ^{P}_{VP}(^{Mv}_{V}laughed) ^{A}_{AvP}(^{M}_{Av}a bit)^1 ^{H}_{Av}louder ^{M}_{CCl}[_{cj}than$
$^{S}_{NP}(^{H}_{pn}I) ^{P}_{VP}(^{Aux}_{v}could ^{Aux}_{v}have ^{Mv}_{V}wished) ^{A}_{PP}(_{p}in ^{M}_{GP}(^{H}_{pn}my) ^{M}_{Aj}frail$
$^{H}_{N}state ^{M}_{PP}(_{p}of ^{H}_{N}health\rangle)]]]_{cj}but _{MCl}[^{A}_{AvP}(^{H}_{Av}then) ^{S}_{NP}(^{H}_{pn}she)$
$^{P}_{VP}(^{Mv}_{v}is) ^{A}_{AvP}(^{H}_{Av}always) _{NP}(^{M}_{d}a ^{H}_{N}woman _{RCl}[^{S}_{NP}(^{H}_{pn}who)$
$^{P}_{VP}(^{Mv}_{V}tends) _{Cli}[^{P}_{VP}(to ^{Mv}_{V}bring) _{NP}(^{H}_{N}plaster) _{Cling}[^{C}_{VP}(^{Mv}_{V}falling)$
$^{A}_{PP}(_{p}from ^{M}_{d}the ^{H}_{N}ceiling)]]] ^{A}_{Clen}[_{cj}when ^{P}_{VP}(^{Mv}amused)]]]\rangle$

Finally, here is a skeleton clause analysis of the same sentence:

$$\langle [S \underline{P \underline{A}}] + [A S P A \underline{\underline{C}}] \rangle$$
$$[_{cj} S P A] [\underline{S P O} \underline{A}]$$
$$[\underline{\underline{P O C}}][_{cj}\underline{P}]$$
$$[\underline{\underline{P A}}]$$

[Now try Exercise 6e.]

---

¹ We analyse *a bit* as a degree adverb, i.e. as a single word. Other analyses would be possible.

Exercises

Exercise 6a   (answers on p. 207)
Draw tree diagrams (complete with form and function labels) of sentences (5) and (7) on pp. 94, 95 respectively.

Exercise 6b   (answers on p. 208)
Each of the following sentences contains one subordinate clause. For each clause, (i) describe its structure in terms of cj, *S, P, O, C, A* ; (ii) say whether it is a noun clause (NCl), an adverbial clause (ACl), or a relative clause (RCl); (iii) in the case of each adverbial clause, identify its meaning as time, condition, contrast, etc.

1.   [When we asked her], she sang an old Patagonian lyric.
2.   She sang out of tune, [so that everyone would go away].
3.   I have forgotten [who gave us this present].
4.   The person [who gave us this present] was my great uncle Cedric.
5.   Steinhacker had a large room [in which he kept gigantic frogs for his experiments].
6.   [Why you bought that elephant gun] I cannot imagine.
7.   [Although Paul is sometimes a grouch], I rather like him.
8.   They tell me [he eats voraciously].
9.   The snails [he eats voraciously] are expensive.

Exercise 6c   (answers on p. 208)
Identify the non-finite clauses bracketed in the following sentences as Cli, Cling, Clen, and say what function they have (e.g. *S, O, A, M*):

1.   I regret [speaking to you so rudely].
2.   I am very sorry [to have caused you offence].
3.   [For Max to pay his gas-bill on time] would be very surprising.
4.   I saw [Spurs beaten by Villa] last Saturday.
5.   [Having remarkably strong teeth], Batman soon severed the ropes confining him.
6.   I have several important things [to say to her].
7.   [Duncan having retired for the night], Lady Macbeth put her sinister plan into effect.
8.   [Always haunted by guilty memories], he lurked at the scene of his crime.

Exercise 6d   (answers on p. 208)
The following sentences are grammatically ambiguous. Show the ambiguities by giving two different skeleton analyses for each sentence. In each case, add a comment to explain how the ambiguity arises.

1.   I regret criticising her bitterly.
2.   I clearly remembered the time when I looked at my watch.

3. I told him that I had written the essay before he gave the lecture.
4. To speak the truth frankly is an unsafe policy.

For the following, three different skeleton analyses can be given:

5. The combatants agreed to sign a peace treaty in Geneva last week.
6. We must ask the farmer who owns the fields where we can camp.
7. I found the dog smoking a cigar.

Exercise 6e   (answers on p. 209)

Here are some further ambiguities, this time involving coordination.
Again, distinguish the different interpretations of the same sentence by
different skeleton analyses, using angle brackets ⟨ ⟩ to enclose coordinate
structures.

1. I love Danish butter and cheese.
2. Their officers always wear pink berets and moustaches.
3. She has passed her exams in French, German and English literature.
4. The manuscript is very old and difficult to read.
5. That evening we stayed indoors, reading and writing letters.
6. I was taught by the man who taught Mabel and the woman who
    taught you and Fred.
7. The neighbourhood is infested with stray cats and dogs of question-
    able parentage.
8. Mountjoy was a great lover and ardent student of English language
    and literature.

7

Basic and derived structures

Chapters 2 to 6 have outlined a method of parsing English sentences. In this final chapter of Part B, we concentrate on some difficulties you are likely to meet when you apply this parsing method to sentences you meet in texts. As we do this, we shall sketch in an extra dimension to the study of grammar: that is, the study of what we may call BASIC and DERIVED structures. This will enable us to deal with a range of grammatical patterns which do not fit neatly into the view of grammar so far presented. But first, let us take stock of what has been done up to now.

7.1 Constituent structure grammar

In Chapter 2 (p. 23) we defined grammar, roughly, as a set of 'rules for constructing and for analysing sentences'. So far, we have been primarily interested in 'analysing' rather than 'constructing': essentially, we have been aiming at a parsing of sentences, and have been mainly concerned with the kinds of rules which enable us to identify the constituents of sentences, and their structures. For example:

(a) 'The structure of an NP is $\{M^n\} H \{M^n\}$' (specifying the structure of a class of constituent).

(b) 'An O can be an NP or an NCl' (saying what classes of constituent can fill a given functional slot).

(c) 'A subordinate clause can be either finite or non-finite' (specifying the subclasses of a constitutent).

Such rules can be used in analysis, but if they were formulated precisely enough, they could also be used for **constructing** or **generating** grammatical sentences by rule. For example, we could use such rules to construct a sentence like *The question may arise*. But we could not use them to construct sentences such as:

(1)   *The ask may arise.

(2)   *The question arise may.

Why not? Because each of these sentences violates one of the rules of English grammar. In (1) *ask* is a V, not a N, and cannot therefore be used as head of a noun phrase. In (2) *may* is a modal auxiliary, and like all auxiliaries, can only occur **before** the main verb, not after it. Thus the rules that have been presented in a rather passive sense, as a means of analysis, can also be thought of in a more active, productive sense, as a MODEL of the English speaker's knowledge of grammar, whether it is used to analyse sentences, to produce them, or to judge whether sentences are grammatical or not.

The model we have presented may be called a CONSTITUENT STRUCTURE model of grammar, and it works pretty well. But there are some aspects of English grammar which it fails to explain. Some of them have been glimpsed already. Our response to them is not to throw away the whole model, but rather to see how the model can be improved or extended to cope with them. The tree diagrams of constituent structure grammar provide a two-dimensional view, and what we aim to do now is to make that grammar three-dimensional, by introducing the notion of BASIC and DERIVED structures. For this, we call on a further kind of grammatical rule, called a TRANSFORMATION.[1] This is the kind of rule which relates two different constituent structures. [Now try Exercise 7a.]

7.2   Basic and derived structures

It is often said that English has a fairly fixed word order, but that exceptional orders are allowed. Actually, when people discuss English word order, they almost invariably refer to what would be more correctly called 'phrase order' – the order of elements in the clause (the order of words in phrases being more or less fixed). And in this connection we have already assumed a neutral, basic order of clause elements – *S, P, O, C, A* – which is that of the normal declarative clause. We have already implied, however, that some other clause types – e.g. questions, relative clauses – can be explained as systematic deviations from this expected order. Here are some more examples:

(3) ⎰ [(I) (adore) (cocktails)] .   BASIC ORDER   *S P O*
(3a) ⎱ [(Cocktails) (I) (adore)] .   DERIVED ORDER   *O S P*

---

[1] The concept of transformational rules has been developed in recent technical studies of English grammar (see, for example, Akmajian and Heny, 1975). Our aim is to make very informal use of this concept as a means of explaining significant relations between sentence structures.

$\Bigg\{$
(4)   [(He) (looks) (an old fogey)].   BASIC ORDER   *S P C*

(4a)   [(What an old fogey) (he) (looks)].   DERIVED ORDER   *C S P*

$\Bigg\{$
(5)   [(The rain) (came) (down)].   BASIC ORDER   *S P A*

(5a)   [(Down) (came) (the rain)].   DERIVED ORDER   *A P S*

(5b)   [(Down) (it) (came)].   DERIVED ORDER   *A S P*

We can now compose rough-and-ready rules to explain such variations of order (see Table 7.1). These rules can be called 'transformations' because they change one clause structure into another. The advantage of such rules is that they allow us to keep the idea of a 'basic' or 'neutral' ordering – an ordering that will be used unless there is some reason for doing otherwise – and at the same time account for acceptable departures from this order. We have already adopted such an approach, for example, in explaining questions (in 5.4.1), and relative clauses (in 6.2.3). Since constituent structure can be displayed in a two-dimensional tree diagram, Figure 7.1 shows how transformations give an extra, third dimension to grammar. This diagram shows the relation between (3) and (3a) by means of the 'fronting' rule – Rule 1.

Table 7.1

RULE	BASIC STRUCTURE	becomes	DERIVED STRUCTURE	under these conditions
Rule 1 'Fronting'	*S P O/C/A*	→	*O/C/A S P*[†]	(a) in MCls, to give emphasis (b) when the shifted element is a *wh-* element like *what, which*, etc.
Rule 2 'S–P inversion'	*A S P*	→	*A P S*	In MCls, where *A* is an adverbial of place, where *S* is not a pronoun (cf. (5b)) and where *P* contains a *Mv* of position or motion

[†]*'O/C/A'* means 'either *O* or *C* or *A*'.

Figure 7.1

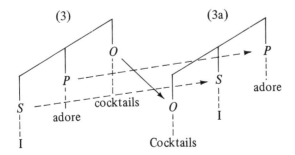

Transformations are either OPTIONAL or OBLIGATORY. Rule 1(a) is optional because either order is grammatical:

(6) $[^S$(They) ^{P}(call) ^{O}(me) ^{C}(the Texas Ranger)].

(6a) $[^C$(The Texas Ranger) ^{S}(they) ^{P}(call) ^{O}(me)].

Rule 1(b), on the other hand, is obligatory, because only the derived order is possible:

(7)   *I can't see $[^S$(I) ^{P}(am doing) ^{O}(what)].

(7a) I can't see $[^O$(what) ^{S}(I) ^{P}(am doing)].

In such cases we obviously cannot say that the basic order is the more likely or expected one; nevertheless, in the context of English as a whole, the *S P O* order is usual.

Another way of expressing the same thing is to say that the *S P O/C/A* order is the **unmarked** order – i.e. the neutral order that is used when there is no reason to use some other order – whereas the *O/C/A S P* order is **marked**. The derived, or marked, form is often, but not necessarily, the less frequent one, and the one which is stylistically more noticeable.

7.3 'Missing' elements

7.3.1 Omission of relative pronouns

Another phenomenon of grammar that we have encountered, and which the constituent structure model does not explain, is the existence of 'ghost' elements which do not occur in a given sentence, but are nevertheless 'understood' as part of the meaning of that sentence:

(8)   The stories [(which) (he) (invented)] were incredible. [*O S P*]

(8a) The stories [(he) (invented)] were incredible. [*S P*]

In accordance with Rule 1(b), the relative clause in (8) has its object (the relative pronoun *which*) in front position. But in (8a), which is like (8) in all other respects, this object is omitted. We would like to say, all the same, that the object in a sense 'is there' in (8a), because *invent* is a verb which cannot normally occur without an object: **He invented* is ungrammatical. But how can we say that the pronoun 'is not there' on the one hand, and 'is there' on the other? A way to make sense of this riddle is to treat (8a) as a derived structure, and to say that a rule of RELATIVE PRONOUN OMISSION converts (8) into (8a):

Rule 3: 'A relative pronoun preceding the subject can be omitted.'[1]

7.3.2 Omission in comparative clauses

Like relative clauses, comparative clauses can be lacking in one or more of their elements:

(9)   [Bill is taller [$_{cj}$than ^{S}(he) ^{P}(seems)]] .
      (Cf. [^{S}(He) ^{P}(seems) ^{C}(tall)].)

But unlike the relative clause case, there is no option in this case of a clause in which the 'missing' element actually occurs:

(9a) *[Bill is taller [than he seems tall]] .

So this is an example where the omission is obligatory. But usually the omissions in the comparative clause are optional:

(10a) [Ann can knit mittens faster [than Pam can knit mittens]] .
       [cj S P O]
(10b) [Ann can knit mittens faster [than Pam can]] .   [cj S Aux]
(10c) [Ann can knit mittens faster (than Pam)] .   (PP)

In (10c) so much of the basic structure of the clause has been omitted that what remains is merely a prepositional phrase (*than* behaves here like a preposition). So omission can actually affect the rank of a constituent. In (10b) the auxiliary remains, but the rest of the clause is missing. This illustrates ELLIPSIS (see 12.4), the type of omission which avoids repetition of words and structures used elsewhere in the context (in this case, in the MCl). The construction of (10b) is derived rather than basic because, contrary to basic constituent structure rules, an *Aux* here occurs without its *Mv*.

7.3.3 Omission in coordinate constructions

We have already observed how coordination of words and phrases often implies ellipsis:

(11) [(⟨ *Molly* and *her sister* ⟩) (are) (still) (at school)] .

---

[1] This rule in fact only applies to 'restricting' relative clauses, which are not separated from the rest of the sentence by commas or other punctuation marks. Compare (8) with *The stories, which he invented, were incredible*. Here *which* could not be omitted.

(11) has a meaning which can be spelled out as:

(11a)   [(Molly) (is) (still) (at school)] and [(her sister) (is) (still) (at school)].

Here again the notions of basic and derived structure are helpful. A sentence containing two coordinated phrases (here NPs) can be regarded as deriving from a sentence with two coordinated clauses. The same is true of coordinated words:

(12)   [(The butler) (was ⟨ *amazed* and *delighted* ⟩) (by what he saw)].

means the same as:

(12a)   [(The butler) (was *amazed*) (by what he saw)] and [(the butler) (was *delighted*) (by what he saw)].

We can easily think of (11) and (12) as being derived, by ellipsis, from the more complex sentences (11a) and (12a). But there is no difficulty in parsing them as they stand, once we allow coordinated words and phrases like ⟨ *Molly and her sister* ⟩. Less straightforward, however, are types of coordination where the coordinate parts are not whole constituents. For instance:

(13)   [(She) ⟨ (*got*) (*out of bed*) and (*went*) (*to the phone*) ⟩].

Here the elements coordinated are whole clauses except for the subject: S ⟨ P A + P A ⟩. Still more tricky is:

(14)   [(I'll ⟨ *phone*) (*the hotel*) and *order*) (*some lunch*) ⟩].

where the coordinate parts are not even composed of clause elements: S Aux ⟨ Mv O + Mv O ⟩. Such examples as (13) and (14) exemplify

Figure 7.2

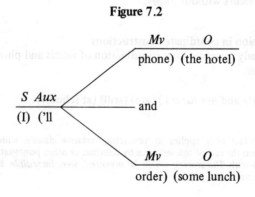

BRANCHING COORDINATION, and Figure 7.2, in which the coordinate structures branch out of a shared part of the clause, shows why this is an appropriate name.

There is no easy way of deciding, in such cases, whether the sentence consists of one or two clauses. Perhaps it is most sensible to say that if the two coordinate parts have different main verbs, they are different clauses. On this basis, both (13) and (14) are complex sentences, each containing coordinate clauses.

These and the preceding examples can be explained by a rule of COORDINATION REDUCTION, very roughly as follows:

> Rule 4: 'Two or more coordinate clauses can be reduced in length by the omission of any words and structures which are mere repetitions of what is in one of the clauses.'

7.3.4 Tag questions

There are a number of conditions under which elliptical clauses such as that of (10b) occur. They occur, for example, in replies to questions:

(15) Who would like some coffee? [*I would*]. [*S Aux*]

Perhaps the most interesting type of elliptical clause is the TAG QUESTION – an interrogative clause which is 'tagged' on to the end of a declarative clause, and which acts as a request for confirmation:

(16) [We must go now], [*mustn't we*]? [*Aux* not *S*]?
(17) [You aren't leaving], [*are you*]? [*Aux S*]?

Such questions, which are common in conversation, are a rather eccentric feature of English. They change according to the form of the declarative clause, whereas similar tags in other languages (e.g. French *n'est-ce pas,* Italian *non è vero*) are invariable. Tag questions are difficult from the parsing point of view, not just because of their elliptical form, but because their relation with the preceding clause seems to fit neither the pattern of coordination nor that of subordination. Perhaps it is better, if a decision must be made, to treat tags as cases of unlinked coordination (6.7.1):

(18) $_{MCl}$[You can drive], $_{MCl}$[can't you]?
(19) $_{MCl}$[He said that], $_{MCl}$[did he]?

7.4 Split constituents

We have already met constituents which are split into two parts by an 'intrusive' element:

(20) [^S(Their team) ^P(has ^A(often) beaten) ^O(our team)].

(21) [^P(Can ^S(you) drive) ^O(a car)]?

Such discontinuities spoil the neatness of the constituent structure model, requiring tree diagrams with criss-crossing branches, as Figure 7.3 shows.

Figure 7.3

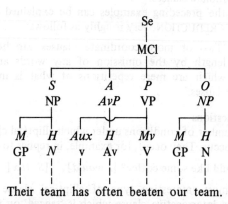

Once again, it helps to suppose that there is a simpler basic structure for these sentences, and that the splitting of phrases arises in derived structure. This is a reasonable supposition, since the language has clause structures in which these same elements may occur in a different order, without splitting:

(20a) [^S(Their team) ^P(has beaten) ^O(our team) ^A(often)].

(21a) [^S(You) ^P(can drive) ^O(a car)].

So to account for (20) and (21), we can postulate (a) a rule which moves adverbials from final position to earlier positions in the clause, and (b) a rule which inverts the subject and finite operator. Here again, the point of introducing the notions of basic structure and derived structure is to enable us to make generalisations, i.e. to state rules, about aspects of English grammar which would otherwise seem baffling. [Now try Exercises 7b and 7c.]

7.5 'Double analysis'

A final problem with a purely constituent structure model of grammar is that it sometimes leads to two conflicting analyses, neither of which is satisfactory on its own.

7.5.1   The passive reconsidered

A passive clause is a classic case of a structure which seems to require a double analysis:

(22) $[^S(\text{Fido})\ ^P(\text{bit})\ ^O(\text{the cat-burglar})\ ^A(\text{on the leg})]$.

(22a) $[^S(\text{The cat-burglar})\ ^P(\text{was bitten})\ ^A(\text{on the leg})\ ^A(\text{by Fido})]$.

The relation between these two sentences (and similar pairs) is obvious, and can be represented by a rule converting an active-type structure like (22) into a passive-type structure like (22a):

Rule 5   ('passive')
            (optional)

$$\boxed{\begin{matrix} S & \dots P & \dots O \\ NP_1 & Mv & NP_2 \end{matrix}} \longrightarrow \boxed{\begin{matrix} S & \dots P & \dots \left\{\begin{matrix} A \\ PP \end{matrix} = \text{by} + NP_1 \right\} \\ NP_2 & Pass\ Mv & \end{matrix}}$$

In words, this means that the object of the active clause becomes the subject of the passive clause, and the subject of the active clause becomes the AGENT of the passive clause, i.e. the adverbial introduced by the preposition *by*. Traditionally, *the cat-burglar* in (22a) has been called the 'grammatical' subject, but the 'logical' object of the clause. But how can an element be both S and O at the same time? In terms of a simple constituent structure model it cannot; but in terms of the distinction between basic and derived structure, it is perfectly sensible to say that *the cat-burglar* is O in basic structure, but S in the passive derived structure. In this way, transformations allow us to have our cake and eat it: to say that two apparently incompatible analyses are both correct.

7.5.2   Subject raising

Here is a slightly more complicated example of the same type. In English there is a common type of construction, called CATENATIVE ('chain-like'), where a sequence $NP_1 + VP_1 + \{NP_2\} + VP_2 \dots$ occurs, VP_2 being non-finite (see Table 7.2 overleaf).

Since there are two VPs, there must be two Ps, and therefore two clauses – a finite clause and a non-finite one. But the status of NP_2 is unclear: is it an O in the main clause, or a S in the non-finite clause?

For (23) and (24), the better of these two analyses is the latter:

(23a) $[^S(\text{John})\ ^P(\text{desired})\ ^O[^S(\text{his valet})\ ^P(\text{to warm})\ ^O(\text{his slippers})]]$.

Table 7.2

	NP$_1$	VP$_1$	NP$_2$	VP$_2$	NP$_3$, etc.
(23)	John	desired	his valet	to warm	his slippers.
(24)	I	'd like	you	to read	this letter.
(25)	They	required	all citizens	to vote	for the party.
(26)	Bob	considered	grammar	to be	a waste of time.
(27)	Tina	told	the secretary	to type	a letter.
(28)	She	asked	me	to phone	her.

The following arguments favour (23a):

(a)　The V in the main clause, *desire*, is the kind of verb which takes an *O* (e.g. *John desired a bath*).

(b)　We can change NP$_2$ + VP$_2$ + NP$_3$ into the passive without a change of meaning, thus suggesting that these three elements should be analysed as a clause, with the structure [*S P O*]:

(23b)　[John desired [his slippers to be warmed by his valet]].

(c)　NP$_2$ + VP$_2$ + NP$_3$ is logically equivalent to a finite NCl functioning as object:

(23c)　[John desired [that his valet should warm his slippers]].

On the other hand, for (27) and (28) the best analysis seems to be different:

(27a)　[^{S}(Tina) ^{P}(told) ^{Oi}(the secretary) ^{Od}[^{P}(to type) ^{O}(a letter)]].

The arguments in favour of (27a) are:

(d)　The V in the main clause takes the pattern [*S P Oi Od*] (e.g. *They told me a story*).

(e)　NP$_2$ behaves like the *O* of the main clause, in that it can become subject of a passive clause:

(27b)　[The secretary was told [to type a letter] by Tina].

(f)　In this case, unlike that of (23), it is only the VP$_2$ + NP$_3$ that is logically equivalent to a finite NC1:

(27c)　[Tina told the secretary [that she must type a letter]].

BUT NOT:

(27d)　*[Tina told [that the secretary must type a letter]].

So we have found that clauses which appear on the surface to have the same kind of structure, like (23) and (27), actually require different analyses. The main difficulty comes, however, when we look at sentences like (25) and (26). For some purposes (e.g. for argument (c) above) they are like (23):

(26a)   [Bob considered [that grammar is a waste of time]].

But for other purposes (e.g. argument (e)) they are like (27):

(26b)   [Grammar was considered [to be a waste of time] by Bob].

Thus we have to entertain conflicting analyses of the same sentence:

(26c)   [Bob considered [grammar to be a waste of time]].
(26d)   [Bob considered grammar [to be a waste of time]].

This dilemma, like that which arose with the subject of a passive clause, can be resolved if we allow both analyses to coexist – that of (26c) being the basic structure (the one which is appropriate 'logically speaking'), and (26d) the derived structure. To get from (26c) to (26d), we apply a rule which raises the subject of a subordinate clause and makes it the object of the main clause:

Rule 6   ('subject raising')

$$\left[{}^{S}_{NP_1}\ {}^{P}_{VP_1}\ {}^{O}_{SCli}{}[{}^{S}_{NP_2}\ {}^{P}_{VP_2}\cdots]]\right] \longrightarrow \left[{}^{S}_{NP_1}\ {}^{P}_{VP_1}\ {}^{O}_{NP_2}\ {}^{C}_{SCli}[{}^{P}_{VP_2}\cdots]]\right]^{1}$$

7.6   Back to parsing

Catenative constructions such as those of (23)–(28) above are among the most problematic constructions in English: they demonstrate more clearly than any of the examples so far the need for both basic and derived structures to be considered in the analysis of a sentence. But there is still a role for the 'two-dimensional' parsing of tree diagrams and labelled bracketing. It is very convenient to be able to break down sentences, or sequences of sentences in a text, into their visible or audible 'working parts'. For this purpose, it is a parsing of the derived structure that is required. We must have a serviceable method of analysing the sentence as it appears when written down on a page, but

---

[1]   The infinitive clause is here labelled as a complement, because of its close parallel to the object complement in sentences like *Bob considered grammar a waste of time*.

this method must be rather more flexible than that which was allowed for in Chapters 2-6; we must even be allowed to improvise to some extent in the way we represent the structure of sentences. Consider these examples of derived clause structures:

(29) [(You) (should (always) arrive) [before the boss does]].

(30) [(Why) (must (you) (always) find) (something [to grumble about])]?

The main clause in (29) may be labelled [SAPA], showing the split predicator by the horizontal bracket. The subordinate clause may be analysed as [cj S Aux], in a way which mixes clause elements (S) with phrase elements (Aux) (cf. 7.3.3, 7.3.4), showing that ellipsis has deprived this clause of its main verb. In (30) the main clause has two 'intrusive' elements which split the predicator [ASAPO], and the subordinate clause has a stranded preposition: [to P p]. All these notations correctly render the structures of their clauses, even though none of them strictly conforms to the constituent structure model, whereby a clause is analysed exhaustively at each rank.

7.6.1 An alternative analysis of catenative constructions

Returning to catenative constructions, we may find ourselves puzzling laboriously over the reasons for choosing between three alternative analyses for what appears to be the same type of construction. For (24), (26) and (28) it can be argued that the following different parsings of derived structure are to be given:

(24) [S P O   ]
          [S P O]

(26) [S P Od C   ]
             [P C]

(28) [S P Oi Od]
            [P O]

(24) I'd like you to read this letter.

(26) Bob considers grammar to be a waste of time.

(28) She asked me to phone her.

Moreover, the boundaries between these three analyses are sometimes unclear. It may be better to replace this analysis in terms of subordination by another type of analysis which has been widely adopted. This is to relax the 'one-clause–one-predicator' rule, and to allow a single clause to contain more than one predicator, of which only the first can be finite. So in addition to the eight clause patterns listed in Table 5.3 (p.85), there also may be patterns such as the following:

[S P Pi . . .]   [S P O Pi . . .]
Mary wants to go.   Mary wants me to go.
[S P Ping . . .]   [S P O Ping . . .]
Mary stopped talking.   Mary stopped me talking.
[S P Pen . . .]   [S P O Pen . . .]
Mary got discussed.   Mary saw her friend attacked.

(Here *Pi*, *Ping*, and *Pen* stand respectively for infinitive, *-ing* and *-en* predicators.) In fact, by admitting clauses with more than one predicator, this analysis opens the door to clauses with as many predicators as we like:

(31) [Bert is going to have to try to get me to help him mend the sink].

has the structure [S P Pi Pi Pi O Pi O Pi O]. However, the convenience of this type of analysis may easily outweigh the descriptive problems that it raises, and we offer it as an alternative to the parsing exemplified by (24), (26) and (28) above:

(24) [S P O Pi O]

(26) [S P O Pi C]

(28) [S P O Pi O].

7.7 Style and transformations

From the examples given, it will be clear that the transformation from basic to derived structures leaves the content of a sentence largely unchanged. Hence many transformations – particularly those which move constituents around in the sentence – are primarily stylistic in function. For example, why should we prefer a passive sentence to an equivalent active one? The answer is suggested by the following, in which the final and communicatively most important elements (see 12.2.3) are italicised:

(32)   The heavy rains have destroyed *seventy houses.*

(32a) Seventy houses have been destroyed *by the heavy rains.*

(32b) Seventy houses have been *destroyed.*

One function of the passive, as in (32a), is to put the main emphasis on the 'logical subject' of the sentence, by moving it towards the end. Notice, in this connection, the different emphasis of (32) and (32a). Another function of the passive, quite the opposite of this, is to permit the 'logical subject' to be omitted altogether, as in (32b), which lacks the optional agent. Consequently (32), (32a) and (32b) are likely to have different communicative effects.

To conclude this chapter, we now illustrate a number of other cases of stylistic transformations. In all of them the effect of the change of structure in general is either to move an element to the front of the sentence ('fronting'), or to move it towards the end ('postponement'). The function of postponement is generally to move the element to a position where it will attract attention as new information, whereas the effect of fronting an element is generally to stress its connection with what has gone before in the text.

7.7.1   'Cleft sentences'
It is often possible to form a number of different 'CLEFT SENTENCES' from the same basic sentence:

(33)   John was wearing pink socks last night.

$$\rightarrow \begin{cases} \text{It was } John \text{ that was wearing pink socks last night.} & \text{[a]} \\ \text{It was } pink\ socks \text{ that John was wearing last night.} & \text{[b]} \\ \text{It was } last\ night \text{ that John was wearing pink socks.} & \text{[c]} \end{cases}$$

The following is a rough approximation to the rule for forming cleft sentences:

(i)   'Choose an element of the clause: it may be S, O, C or A, but not P.'

(ii)   'Move that element (which we may call X) into the initial position, then prefix to it the 'prop' subject it, and the verb to be.'

(iii)   'Introduce the rest of the clause by the relative pronoun that following X.'

Thus in (33) the following structures are derived:

$$[S\ P\ O\ A] \rightarrow \begin{cases} \text{[It be } S \text{ that } P\ O\ A] & \text{[a]} \\ \text{[It be } O \text{ that } S\ P\ A] & \text{[b]} \\ \text{[It be } A \text{ that } S\ P\ O] & \text{[c]} \end{cases}$$

The 'cleft sentence' derives its name from the fact that a single clause is 'cleft' into two separate clause-like parts. But it is generally analysed as a single clause with two predicators, rather than as two separate clauses.

7.7.2   'Existential sentences'
This type of clause resembles the 'cleft sentence' in that it is introduced by a special particle as subject, followed by the verb to be. The 'prop'

subject in this case is the so-called EXISTENTIAL particle *there*, introducing a proposition of existence:

(34) Nobody was around. → There was nobody around.

(35) A few people are getting promoted. → There are a few people getting promoted.

(36) A whole box has been stolen. → There has been a whole box stolen.

The following is a rough approximation to the rule we can use for deriving existential sentences from a straightforward declarative clause:

$$[S \text{ be } X] \rightarrow [\text{There be } S \, X]$$

where S is an indefinite NP, and X is anything which is added to complete the clause after the operator-verb BE.

7.7.3 Extraposition

This term is used for a construction in which a noun clause, usually one functioning as subject, is postponed to the end of the MCl, and is replaced in its basic position by the 'empty' subject *it* (cf. 6.2.1):

(37) [[What you say to them] doesn't matter]. → [It doesn't matter [what you say to them]].

(38) [[That the dispute has been settled] is encouraging]. → [It is encouraging [that the dispute has been settled]].

(39) [[To move his arm] causes him considerable pain]. → [It causes him considerable pain [to move his arm]].

The clause is usually the most complex constituent, and extraposition postpones it in accordance with the principle of 'end-weight' (see 12.2.3). So in this case it is the basic structure rather than the derived structure that is the marked one. The analysis of the changes in (37)–(39) is as follows:

(37) [S P] → [It P S]
     NCl   NCl

(38) [S $P C$] → [It $P C S$]
     NCl   NCl

(39) [S $P Oi Od$] → [It $P Oi Od S$]
     NCl   NCl

Three more types of stylistic transformation will be illustrated without comment.

7.7.4   Fronting of subordinate clause object

It is convenient to take the extraposition construction of 7.7.3 as the basic structure for this example of fronting:

(40)   It's a pleasure to teach her. → She's a pleasure to teach.

(41)   It's difficult to play a saxophone. → A saxophone is difficult to play.

(42)   It's fun to be with Margaret. → Margaret is fun to be with.

7.7.5   Substitution of PP for indirect object

(43)   Tim sent Freda a telegram. → Tim sent a telegram to Freda.

(44)   Moira knitted her mother a tea-cosy. → Moira knitted a tea-cosy for her mother.

(45)   Bill is finding his brother a job. → Bill is finding a job for his brother.

7.7.6   Postponement of postmodifier

(46)   The time to think of many things has come. → The time has come to think of many things.

(47)   A meeting of all the ratepayers was held. → A meeting was held of all the ratepayers.

(48)   I have less time than I used to have nowadays. → I have less time nowadays than I used to have.

[Now try Exercises 7d and 7e.]

7.8   Summary and conclusion

In this chapter we have been able only to touch on some of the more subtle and complex areas of English grammar. As far as parsing is concerned, these constructions require us to introduce some latitude into the notations for grammatical analysis introduced in earlier chapters.

We have reintroduced and extended the use of ⌐——⌐ for showing a split constituent, and have extended the practice of using named particles (e.g. *not, it, there*) in our labelling notation. We have also recognised the need for parsing with mixture of ranks (e.g. [*Aux S*] for tag questions) where ellipsis gives rise to 'defective' structures.

The introduction of stylistic transformations in 7.7 leads naturally into the application of grammar to the study of style and composition: topics which are developed later in the book.

Exercises

Exercise 7a   (answers on p. 210)
Explain why these are not grammatical sentences in English:

1. *The standing at the door girl was making.
2. *My has got a job interesting.
3. *He has very good reputation for.
4. *To own an oil-well.
5. *Has plenty of friends.

There may be circumstances in which 4 and 5 would be grammatical. Have you any comments on this?

Exercise 7b   (answers on p. 210)
Examine once again the groups of sentences given in Exercise 4f (p. 73). Formulate, as transformations, rules by which negatives, questions, emphatic sentences, tag questions and comparative clauses may be derived from the basic declarative structure. Add a special rule to deal with the auxiliary *do*. (You are not expected to formulate the rules in a particularly rigorous way, but of course the more precise you can make them the better. You may use either special symbols or ordinary words.)

Exercise 7c   (answers on p. 211)
Bracket the following sentences containing branching coordination, using angle brackets as in examples (13) and (14) on p. 118:

1. Every morning Pat gets into her car and drives to the office.
2. Have you been listening to the radio or watching television?
3. I bought a puppet for Linda and a teddy-bear for Malcolm.
4. At last the child went back to school and we had a rest.
5. Unfortunately Jack Sprat likes lean meat, but his wife doesn't.
6. With practice, your voice will grow more versatile, and your breathing more controlled.

Exercise 7d   (answers on p. 211)
1. Invent two more examples of each of the stylistic transformations introduced in 7.7.4, 7.7.5 and 7.7.6. Give both the basic and the derived structures.
2. Give as precise and general a description as you can of the relationship between the two structures.

Exercise 7e   (answers on p. 212)
Do a skeleton clause analysis (6.6.1) of the following sentences:

1. It was odd that, although Rose had often been to her Aunt's in Southford, she had never talked alone with her cousins before.
2. There was a sinister atmosphere about the deserted cottage, as if it was here that Gilpin had decided on his last, desperate course of action.

PART C
APPLICATIONS

8

Discourse analysis: speech and writing

8.1 Introductory

If you have worked through Part B of this book, you should by now be equipped to analyse the structure of English sentences. In this chapter and the next we aim to demonstrate how this knowledge of grammar can be applied to the analysis of DISCOURSE, or pieces of language which are bigger than a single sentence.

The term DISCOURSE applies to both spoken and written language (literary and non-literary), in fact to any sample of language used for any purpose. In Part B we used mostly invented sentences for analysis, and did not pay much attention to the context in which they might have occurred. This was necessary in order to focus on the sentence as a unit of language structure, but now we shall expand our horizons to look at chunks of language in actual use.

In 1.3.3 we briefly examined the categories of language use which affect language variation for all language users. These categories were TENOR, MODE and DOMAIN. The category of MODE is particularly important because it is related to the distinction between speech and writing. As we said in 1.3.3, mode 'has to do with the effects of the medium in which the language is transmitted'. The obvious distinction for English is between the auditory and visual medium, that is, between speech and writing.

In 1.1 we made the point that grammar is at least as much the study of speech as the study of writing. Writing is intrinsically no 'better' or 'worse' than speech, but each performs different functions in society, uses different forms, and exhibits different linguistic characteristics. In this chapter we shall compare speech and writing in detail, and our comparison will be illustrated by the analysis of spoken and written discourse.

8.2 Speech and writing: which comes first?

In 1.1 we said that the written language is 'secondary to its spoken form, which developed first'. However, it should not be secondary in our consideration, for as we shall see, written and spoken language have different functions, different forms and different linguistic characteristics.

In the history of the human race, spoken language certainly came before writing. We have no evidence of the existence of a writing system of any kind before about 3500 BC, whereas we assume that spoken language existed well before then. In the history of individual societies, spoken language also pre-dates written language, and many languages spoken today have no written form. For the individual, too, spoken language comes first, since children learn to speak before they learn to write.

However, in societies which do have writing systems (such as the Roman alphabet, used for English and many other languages), the written language is very important from a social and educational point of view. It would be impossible to imagine our own society functioning as we know it without the advantage that writing gives (see 8.3). Literacy is closely associated with civilisation and education. It is no wonder, then, that the written language usually has greater social prestige than the spoken language, and more official recognition. Speech is often evaluated socially according to its closeness to the written language, which explains why standard spoken English is probably closer to written English than is any other spoken variety. Written language is often viewed as more 'correct' than spoken language, and as more worthy of study. Also, from a legal point of view, written language takes precedence: a written contract, for example, is more binding than a verbal or spoken agreement. However, from a linguistic point of view we can only say that speech and writing are different; we cannot say that one is superior to the other.

8.3   Functions of writing and speech

The social prestige of written language is probably derived from the added functions which a written variety can fulfil for a society.

Writing has the advantage of relative permanence, which allows for record-keeping in a form independent of the memories of those who keep the records. It also allows for communication over a great distance (by letters, newspapers, etc.), and to large numbers simultaneously (by publications of all kinds). The invention of the tape-recorder, the telephone and the radio have helped to overcome the limitations of the spoken language regarding time, distance and numbers, but these are relatively recent developments in human history.

Another advantage of written language is that it is not only permanent, but also visible. An important consequence of this is that it can be carefully planned and revised by the writer in a way that spoken language cannot. And for the reader, written language can be processed at leisure, with parts of it re-read and others omitted at will. This characteristic of written language promoted the development of literature, and intellectual development in general. Written language makes possible the creation of literary works of art in ways comparable with the creation of paintings or sculpture. It also promotes intellectual development by overcoming the limitations of human memory and allowing the storage of visually accessible knowledge.

Speech, of course, retains functions which writing will never be able to fulfil, such as quick, direct communication with immediate feedback from the addressee. Speech is particularly important in integrating an individual into a social group, and those who cannot speak, even though they may be able to write (e.g. deaf people), often experience severe social isolation. Speech is used far more than writing: speech is an every-day activity for almost everyone, whereas writing may not be.

Thus speech and writing are complementary in function, and we cannot say that one is more important than the other. Ideally we need to be able to use both appropriately as members of an English-speaking (and writing) society.

8.4   The form of speech and writing

As well as being different in function, speech and writing differ in form as a result of the difference of medium. Features of speech which are absent in writing include rhythm, intonation and non-linguistic noises such as sighs and laughter. Since speech is typically used in a face-to-face situation, it can also be accompanied by non-verbal communication such as gestures and facial expression. None of these features can easily be conveyed by conventional writing systems, and those wishing to represent them have had to devise special transcription systems. Writing, on the other hand, has several features which speech lacks, including punc-tuation, paragraphing and the capitalisation of letters. Written language can be spoken probably more easily than spoken language can be written, but features of speech such as intonation have to be introduced by the speaker. Intonation can to some extent be conveyed by punctuation (especially commas, full stops and question-marks), but not completely. The intonation of the sentence *I'll take a taxi to the station* will differ according to whether the means of transport ('taxi') or the destination ('station') is the most important idea. This will be clear if you try read-ing the sentence aloud in different ways. The different meanings implied by differences of intonation would be difficult to convey in writing without changing the structure of the sentence.

8.5 Linguistic characteristics of speech and writing

Having compared the functions and forms of speech and writing, let us now compare their linguistic characteristics. For the sake of clarity we shall outline the characteristics of 'typical' speech compared with 'typical' writing, though (as we shall see) there is actually some overlap between the two.

INEXPLICITNESS. As we have said, speech is generally used in face-to-face situations, so that both the auditory and visual media are available. As a result, speech can be much less explicit than writing, because (a) extra information is conveyed by 'body language' (e.g. facial expressions, gestures); (b) the immediate physical environment can be referred to, e.g. by pointing to objects or people; (c) shared knowledge of the participants in a conversation makes explicitness unnecessary; and (d) in a conversation there is an opportunity for feedback from the hearer, so that the message can be clarified or repeated. Speech tends to make frequent use of pronouns such as *it*, *this* and *that*, all of which reflect its inexplicitness. Consider the following imaginary conversation (inadequately represented in writing):

A.   How did it go?
B.   Not too bad. I'm just glad it's over.
A.   Was it the last one?
B.   Yes, for the time being.

Unless we were participants in this conversation, we could only guess at what it might be about, e.g. an examination or a tooth extraction.

LACK OF CLEAR SENTENCE BOUNDARIES. Related to inexplicitness in speech is the absence of clearly defined units we can call sentences. In written language, a grammatical sentence as described in 2.2 is expected to begin with a capital letter and end with a full stop, and it is the accepted norm for people to write in sentences. The same applies to scripted speech, like that of radio news bulletins. But in spontaneous speech, sentences are often difficult to delimit: they may simply be unfinished, because the knowledge of the addressee makes completion unnecessary, or they may not be discernable as units at all. The following is an excerpt from an actual conversation (dashes represent pauses):

and he was saying that erm - you can go to a nightclub in Birmingham - and watch Tony Bennet for about thirty bob - something like this a night with Tony Bennet - have a nice meal in very plushy surroundings very nice warm pleasant -

(Quoted in Crystal (1980 b), transcription simplified)

Even with information about intonation, it is difficult to work out how the above could be divided into sentences. In particular, what is the status of the last group of words, *very nice warm pleasant*? We cannot give a definite answer to this question, but it has been suggested (by Crystal in the above-quoted article) that the clause may be a more appropriate unit for analysing speech than the sentence. In context, the absence of clear sentence boundaries does not mean that conversation is difficult to follow; it just shows that the conversation is organised in a different way from writing.

SIMPLE STRUCTURE. In general, speech is more simple in grammatical structure than writing. However, when we use terms like 'simple' and 'complex', we must be careful to explain what they mean. There is no one measure for complexity of structure, but the following measures, when combined, should be useful:

(a) *Clause structure*. How many elements do the clauses contain, and how many levels of subordination are there? A sentence with the structure [*S P O*], like (1), will be less complex than one with the structure [*A S P O O A*], like (2):

(1)   [John read a book]
(2)   [Last night John gave me a book [when he came home]].

But the second sentence not only has more clause elements, it also has more subordination, since there is a subordinate adverbial clause, *when he came home*. The following sentence has even more subordination:

(3)   [Last night John gave back the book [he had borrowed [when he had last seen me]]].

While the number of elements in the clause can be seen as 'horizontal' complexity, subordination can be seen as 'vertical' complexity.

(b) *Noun phrase structure*. How many modifiers do they contain (horizontal complexity), and how many subordinate phrases (vertical complexity)? A noun phrase such as *a book* is clearly less complex than *an interesting book about grammar on the table in the kitchen*. The second noun phrase is horizontally complex, consisting of two pre-modifiers, a head, and two postmodifiers. It is also vertically complex because the prepositional phrase *in the kitchen* is contained in another – *on the table in the kitchen* – and this structure as a whole constitutes one of the postmodifiers of *book*.

(c) *Where is vertical complexity located?* In clauses, subordination at the beginning ('left-branching') seems to make for more complexity than embedding at the end ('right-branching'). This can be illustrated by drawing abbreviated tree diagrams of the following two sentences (Figures 8.1 and 8.2):

(4)   [The man [who is a friend of the woman [who lives in the house
      [which used to belong to us]]] came to see us yesterday].
(5)   [Yesterday we saw the man [who is a friend of the woman [who
      lives in the house [which used to belong to us]]]].

Most people would probably agree that the second sentence is easier to
understand, and in that sense simpler. As we have shown, this can be
explained in terms of the location of complexity.

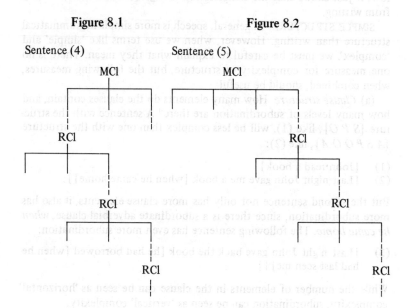

Figure 8.1   **Figure 8.2**

Sentence (4)   Sentence (5)

In noun phrases also, subordination towards the end of the phrase
tends to be less complex than subordination at the beginning. So the
noun phrase *my sister's husband's brother's friend* seems harder to understand than *the friend of the brother of the husband of my sister* (though
neither is simple).

We have thus outlined ways of measuring complexity in discourse. In
general, we can say that the greater the number of branches in the tree
diagram of a sentence, the more complex the sentence will be. Also,
naturally enough, there is a strong correlation between complexity and
length (measured in number of words). Speech is less complex than
writing because of the short time available to produce and process it.
Writing, on the other hand, can be re-drafted and re-read.

REPETITIVENESS. Because of the lack of permanence of speech, it is more repetitive than writing. Important information has to be repeated since the addressee cannot refer back to what has gone before. This is noticeable, for instance, in the amount of repetition that occurs in television commercials, and (for that matter) in normal conversation.

NORMAL NON-FLUENCY. This results from the unprepared nature of speech and refers to phenomena such as hesitation, unintended repetitions (e.g. *I I*. . .), false starts, fillers (e.g. *um, er*), GRAMMATICAL BLENDS and unfinished sentences. A blend occurs where a sentence 'swaps horses' (see 11.7), beginning in one way and ending in another; for example, in *Would you mind telling me what's the time*? the sentence begins as an indirect question, but ends as a direct question. This is slightly different from a 'false start', where a sentence is broken off mid-way as a result of a change of mind; for example, *You really ought - well do it your own way*. These phenomena are edited out in written language, which consequently appears more fluent. We may also note the apparent fluency of fictional speech that appears in literature.

MONITORING AND INTERACTION FEATURES. These appear in speech, as a result of its use in dialogue, with a physically present addressee, rather than in monologue. MONITORING features indicate the speaker's awareness of the addressee's presence and reactions, and include adverbs and adverbials such as *well, I mean, sort of, you know*. INTERACTION features invite the active participation of the addressee, as in questions, imperatives, second-person pronouns, etc. Writing, which is rarely used in dialogue, usually lacks these features.

INFORMALITY. The situations in which speech is used are generally less formal than those in which writing is used. Therefore, the linguistic characteristics of informality (see below in 9.2) generally appear in speech, while those reflecting formality appear in writing.

Table 8.1

	'TYPICAL' SPEECH	'TYPICAL' WRITING
1.	Inexplicitness	Explicitness
2.	Lack of clear sentence boundaries	Clear sentence boundaries
3.	Simple structure	More complex structure
4.	Repetitiveness	Non-repetitiveness
5.	Normal non-fluency	Fluency
6.	Monitoring features	No monitoring features
7.	Interaction features	No interaction features
8.	Features reflecting informality	Features reflecting formality

We can summarise the above discussion by listing the characteristics of 'typical' speech and writing (see Table 8.1, previous page).

However, although these are characteristics of 'typical' speech and writing, there is some overlap. For example, a less typical use of speech occurs on the telephone, where the visual medium is not available. The result is that the language needs to be more explicit. Also, although speech is generally unprepared, it may be prepared for a lecture or debate, and we may expect more fluency as a result. Sometimes speech is prepared word for word in advance, as in the script of a play or a television advertisement. This speech will also appear more fluent than normal. Conversely, writing can sometimes display the characteristics of speech, as in a personal letter, which may have monitoring and interaction features (e.g. *if you know what I mean*; *What do you think?*). Letters will also have features reflecting a lesser degree of formality than is typical for writing.

So instead of seeing written and spoken language as watertight sub-categories of mode, we have to recognise that there is some overlap, depending on the use of the language. We might think of mode of discourse as a continuum from 'typical' speech to 'typical' writing, with in-between examples. The continuum could be represented as below:

'Typical' speech

Conversation in a pub
Seminar
Telephone conversation
Personal letter
Job interview
Radio discussion
Television advertisement
Lecture
Sermon
Script of a play
Television news
Newspaper
Business letter

'Typical' writing This book

8.6 Analysis of spoken and written discourse

The above discussion should have provided the background necessary for an analysis of spoken and written discourse. For this purpose we shall use a transcript of part of an actual conversation about a summer holiday. We shall compare this with an imaginary version written in the form of a personal letter.

Since the following is a transcript of a conversation, there is no punctuation, but vertical lines indicate boundaries of the major units of intonation, and dashes indicate pauses. Laughter is indicated thus – *laughs* – and the material in brackets indicates the responses of the person who is not speaking at the time. You may wish to (a) try reading the transcript aloud, and (b) write it out in conventional orthography, using capital letters and punctuation. This may help to identify for you some of the features which characterise it as speech: these features will be discussed below.

(1)   TRANSCRIPT OF CONVERSATION

Line

B.	so what how did you map out your day | you had your	1
	breakfast in the kitchen |	2
A.	we had our breakfast | (*laughs*) in the kitchen | – and	3
	then we sort of did what we liked | and er got ready to	4
	go out | (m |) we usually went out quite soon after	5
	that | – erm the children were always up | at the crack of	6
	dawn | (m |) with the farmer | – and they went in the	7
	milking sheds | and helped him feed the pigs | and all	8
	this | you know we didn't see the children | – and er	9
	then we used to go out | we – we had super weather | –	10
	absolutely super | – and so we went to a beach | usually	11
	for er but by about four o'clock it we were hot and we	12
	had to come off the beach (m | m |) – so we'd generally	13
	go for a tea somewhere | just in case supper was delayed	14
	you know | (*laughs*) *laughs* and then we'd get back | and	15
	the children would go straight back on to the farm | . . .	16

(from Crystal and Davy, 1975, simplified transcription)

(2)   IMAGINARY LETTER VERSION

Line

Dear B,	1
I thought I would write and tell you about our	2
summer holiday, which we spent on a farm.	3
Every day, the children were up at the crack	4
of dawn with the farmer. They went to the milking	5
sheds with him and helped him feed the pigs, so that we	6
barely saw them at all.	7
Then we would have our breakfast in the	8
kitchen. After breakfast, we usually did what we liked	9
for a short while, and then went out.	10
We had absolutely super weather, and so we	11
usually went to a beach. But by about four o'clock we	12

> were hot and had to come off the beach. Then we'd   13
> generally go and have tea somewhere just in case supper   14
> was delayed. When we got back, the children would go   15
> straight back on the farm . . .   16

We shall analyse the above samples in terms of the characteristics listed, in Table 8.1, p. 139, as identifying 'typical' speech and 'typical' writing, and numbered 1-8. However, we should remember that while the conversation is close to 'typical' speech, the letter is some distance on the continuum (see previous section) from 'typical' writing.

1. The inexplicitness of (1) is reflected, for example, in *that* (line 6), which occurs at some distance from its presumed antecedent, *breakfast* (see 12.4). *Breakfast* is repeated for greater explicitness in (2), where there is no chance for the addressee to ask for immediate clarification. Also, *and all this* in (1) (lines 8-9) is a vague, inexplicit reference to the farmer's tasks; it is eliminated in (2). The time sequence is made more explicit in the structure of the discourse of (2) than it is in (1), where events at dawn are mentioned after the description of breakfast. Lack of chronological reference to events is more common in speech than in writing, though it can occur in the latter.

2. If you have attempted a conventional orthographic transcription of (1), you may have had difficulty in deciding where the sentence boundaries should be. For example, do the occurrences of *and* indicate coordinated clauses, or new sentences? This is difficult to resolve for (1), whereas sentences are clearly marked by capital letters and full stops in (2).

3. The clause structure of (2) is generally more complex than that of (1), especially in its greater use of subordination where (1) uses coordination. Examples of subordinated clauses in (2) are *which we spent on a farm* (line 3), *so that we barely saw them at all* (lines 6-7), and *when we got back* (line 15). The last is embedded at the beginning of the main clause, which is less typical of speech than being embedded at the end. The noun phrase structure of the two samples, however, seems to be about equally complex.

4. The repetitiveness of speech is reflected in (1) in the paraphrasing of *we usually went out quite soon after that* (line 5) to *then we used to go out* (line 10), and in the repetition of *the children* (lines 6 and 9), *super* (lines 10 and 11) and *beach* (lines 11 and 13). In (2) there is some repetition, but less than in (1), and no paraphrasing.

5. The non-fluency features in (1) are *er, erm, we - we* (line 10), *usually for er* (lines 11-12), and *it* (line 12). The latter two are false starts, where the speaker changed her mind about what she was going to say. These features do not appear in (2) (except possibly as the deletion of errors in the original handwriting).

6. The monitoring features in (1) are *sort of* (line 4), *you know* (lines 9 and 15). There are none in (2), where there is no physically present addressee.

7. An obvious interaction feature in (1) is B's question, which is missing in (2). In (1) we also find responses from B while A is speaking, in the form of *m* and laughs. In line 15 A's laughter is in direct response to B's.

8. The informality of both (1) and (2) is reflected in the simple (non-parenthetical) structure and non-technical, accessible vocabulary.

In all, we can say that although both (1) and (2) have the same speaker and addressee and cover the same topic, and although they are not too far apart on the continuum between 'typical' speech and 'typical' writing, (1) nevertheless exhibits more of the characteristics typical of speech, and (2) more of those typical of writing. One would expect to find even more characteristics of 'typical' writing in discourse which does not really have a spoken equivalent. See, for example, the legal discourse in Exercise 8 at the end of this chapter.

8.7 Conclusion

In this chapter we have exemplified the category of mode with special reference to spoken and written discourse. We hope to have shown that speech and writing are generally complementary, but that there can be some overlap in their linguistic characteristics, depending on what they are used for, and in what situation. In fact, the characteristics of spoken and written discourse can be better accounted for if we also consider the effect of the two other categories of use, TENOR and DOMAIN. These two categories will be dealt with in the next chapter.

Exercise

Exercise 8

Analyse the following samples of discourse as in 8.6, paying special attention to the linguistic characteristics which reflect mode.

a.   Carriage hereunder is subject to the rules and limitations relating to liability established by the Warsaw Convention unless such carriage is not 'international carriage' as defined by that Convention.

To the extent not in conflict with the foregoing carriage and other services performed by each carrier are subject to: (i) provisions contained in this ticket, (ii) applicable tariffs, (iii) carrier's conditions of carriage and related regulations which are made part hereof (and are available on application at the offices of the carrier), except in transportation between a place in the United States or Canada and any place outside thereof to which tariffs in force in those countries apply.

(From 'Conditions of Contract', Laker Airways ticket)

b. B. well I remember Dave rang me up about this business | (yes |) of changing to family grouping | - and erm - er you know | it depends on so many things | really | but I have this friend of ours who lives er erm over the other side of Reading | you know |

A. oh yes | -

B. she erm - she teaches somewhere over that side | I don't quite know where | - but she's terribly against it | (is she |) she's a far more experienced infant teacher than I am | you know | (yes |) I mean I've only been doing infant teaching for a short while | - but she won't have anything to do with it | because she says | that it puts too much strain on the teacher |

B. I'm sure it does | ...

(From Crystal and Davy, 1975, transcription simplified; conventions as explained for passage (1) on p. 141).

9

Discourse analysis: tenor and domain

9.1 Introductory

In the last chapter we looked closely at the effect of MODE on language, and we noticed in particular how speech and writing differ from one another. In this chapter we shall see how other kinds of language differ from one another. Just as we saw how people vary their language according to whether they are speaking or writing, we shall now see how they vary it according to factors such as who they are speaking to, in what situation, and what kind of activity the language is being used for.

This will involve us in investigating the effect of the categories of language use which we call TENOR and DOMAIN. Although we are considering the effect of each of the categories separately at first, we must recognise that they have a combined effect on any discourse. We shall illustrate this combined effect in 9.6.

In this chapter, as in the last, we shall be dealing with non-literary language. This is because the next chapter deals in particular with the analysis of literary discourse.

9.2 Tenor

In 1.3.3 we said that tenor 'has to do with the relationship between a speaker and the addressee(s) in a given situation, and is often characterised by greater or lesser formality'. To illustrate this, if the relationship between the speaker and addressee is distant and official, as in a legal document, the tenor will be FORMAL, whereas if it is close and intimate, as in a conversation between a husband and wife, the tenor will be INFORMAL. These two examples in fact represent extremes of formality, and it is more realistic to think of a scale or continuum, from the most formal at one extreme to the most informal at the other. The tenor of a conversation between a solicitor and a client, for example, would have an intermediate degree of formality.

Other scales relating to that of formality are those of POLITENESS and IMPERSONALITY, which, like formality, have an effect on the language used. If the speaker and addressee are not well known to one another, they will tend to use polite language. Impersonality will result when the roles of the speaker and addressee are in the background, as in written documents with no specific author or addressee.

In Table 9.1 we depict the three interrelated scales of use, with some typical linguistic contrasts listed in each case. The extent to which a situation is formal, impersonal, etc., will be reflected in the type of language used.

Table 9.1

FORMAL	INFORMAL
Complex sentences	Simple sentences
Polysyllabic, classical, vocabulary, e.g. *investigate, extinguish, decipher*	Monosyllabic, native vocabulary, especially phrasal verbs, e.g. *look into, put out, make out*

POLITE	FAMILIAR
Respectful terms of address, e.g. *Sir*	Intimate terms of address, if any, e.g. *John, love*
Indirect requests, e.g. *Would you be so kind as to...*	Direct imperatives, e.g. *Give me...*

IMPERSONAL	PERSONAL
Passive voice, e.g. *the terrorists were shot*	Active voice, e.g. *police shot the terrorists*
Third person noun phrases, e.g. *the reader, customers*	First and second person pronouns, e.g. *I, you*

9.3   Tenor and discourse

We shall now illustrate the general effect of tenor by the analysis of two samples of language from radio news broadcasts. The mode (spoken) and domain (journalism) of the two are identical, so in many ways we might expect the language to be fairly similar. However, the tenor of the two is a little different. Both samples of discourse come from BBC Radio news broadcasts on 25 July 1980, and both cover the same topic. However, the first is from *Newsbeat*, the Radio One news programme, and the second from *The World Tonight*, the Radio Four news programme. Radio One is aimed at a young audience primarily interested in popular music, while Radio Four is aimed at a wider age range of people with an interest in current affairs. Formality is associated with social distance, as we have seen (9.2), and the relationship between an unseen radio news broadcaster and an anonymous public is necessarily distant. The tenor of Radio Four news broadcasting is therefore formal. The tenor of Radio One news broadcasting, however, is less formal because of its central concern with popular music, and because of the important role played by the personalities of the disc jockeys. The DJs try to minimise social distance from their audience, encouraging correspondence and participation in competitions, etc. When Radio One shifts from its normal emphasis to news broadcasting, it has to maintain the relationship with its listeners in order to retain their attention: hence an informal tenor.

We shall analyse the samples of discourse which follow, to see whether their linguistic characteristics reflect the difference of tenor as outlined above:

(1) (From Radio One *Newsbeat*)

Fifty people may have died because of a negligence of two major oil companies, Gulf and Total. That's according to the official report of the explosion in Bantry Bay nineteen months ago when the tanker *Betelgeuse* exploded wrecking the oil terminal. Tonight Total, the owners of the tanker, completely rejected the report, but Gulf refused to comment. From Dublin, Philip Whitfield told us more about the enquiry's findings. . .

(2) (From Radio Four *The World Tonight*)

In the Irish Republic, pressure is building up on the government to take action following the publication of the report of the British judicial enquiry into the Bantry Bay oil tanker disaster last year, in which fifty people were killed. The report found that the tanker, the *Betelgeuse*, owned by the oil company Total, had not been properly maintained. It also found that one of the employees at the Bantry Bay terminal owned by Gulf was absent from his post and was not able to summon the rescue services which could have saved the lives of those who died. The report has started a considerable controversy, as Philip Whitfield reports from Dublin. . .

An important measure of formality is sentence complexity. As pointed out on pp. 137-8, complexity can be measured in terms of clause structure, noun phrase structure, and location of vertical complexity.

The clause structure of the sentences in the samples can be summarised as follows, with the sentences numbered in consecutive order:

(1)   Sentence 1: SPA

             Sentence 2: SPA

$$\text{cj}\ \overline{\overline{SPA}}$$

$$\overline{PO}$$

             Sentence 3: $A \langle SAPO + SPO \rangle$

$$\overline{P}$$

             Sentence 4: $ASPOO$

(2)   Sentence 1: $ASPAA$

$$\overline{POA^1}$$

$$\overline{ASP}$$

             Sentence 2: SPO

$$\text{cj}\ \overline{\overline{S}}\ \text{not}\ A\ P$$

$$\overline{PA}$$

             Sentence 3: $SAPO$

$$\text{cj}\ \overline{\overline{S}}\quad \langle PCA + P\ \text{not}\ C\ \rangle$$

$$\overline{PA}\qquad \overline{\overline{PO}}$$

$$\overline{\overline{SPO}}$$

$$\overline{\overline{SP}}$$

             Sentence 4: $SPOA$

$$\text{cj}\ \overline{SPA}$$

A glance at the above summaries should suffice to show that clause structure is generally more complex in sample (2) both horizontally and vertically, and from the point of view of location. This reflects its greater formality. Only sentence 2 in sample (1) approaches the complexity of clause structure in any of the sentences of sample (2).

As we said before, complexity can also be assessed according to the structure of the noun phrase. In (1), the most complex NP is *the official report of the explosion in Bantry Bay nineteen months ago when the tanker Betelgeuse exploded wrecking the oil terminal.* A labelled bracketing of this NP would look as follows:

NP(the official report $^{M}_{PP}$(of the explosion $^{M}_{PP}$(in Bantry Bay) $^{M}_{NP}$(nineteen months ago) $^{M}_{ACl}$[when the tanker Betelgeuse exploded $^{A}_{ACl}$[wrecking the oil terminal]])).

---

[1]   Note: *following* is treated here as a preposition: cf. *after.*

As can be seen, the postmodifier following the head of the NP (*report*) is quite complex, consisting of a subordinate prepositional phrase which includes within it another prepositional phrase, a noun phrase, and an adverbial clause, which itself contains another adverbial clause. We can compare this with the following, the most complex NP from sample (2): *the publication of the report of the British judicial enquiry into the Bantry Bay oil tanker disaster last year, in which fifty people were killed*. This would be labelled as follows:

$$\text{NP}(\text{the publication } ^M_{\text{PP}}(\text{of the report } ^M_{\text{PP}}(\text{of the British judicial en-}$$

$$\text{quiry } ^M_{\text{PP}}(\text{into the Bantry Bay oil tanker disaster } ^M_{\text{NP}} \text{ (last year)}$$

$$^M_{\text{RCl}} [\text{in which fifty people were killed}])))).$$

Here the postmodifier following the head (*publication*) is even more complex than the NP from (1) discussed above, as there are more levels of subordination. The most subordinate items are the relative clause *in which fifty people were killed*, and the adverb phrase *last year*. These are both contained within a prepositional phrase which is contained within another prepositional phrase, which is itself contained in the prepositional phrase which constitutes the postmodifier of *publication*. There are two other NPs in (2) with subordinate relative clauses, *one of the employees at the Bantry Bay terminal owned by Gulf*, and *the lives of those who died*. The NPs in (1) have no relative clauses.

We have only made a brief and incomplete comparison of the NP structure in (1) and (2), but it is evident that the NP structure in (2) is rather more complex, particularly vertically. More striking, however, is the difference in complexity of the clause structure of the sentences, discussed above. The greater complexity in (2) reflects the greater formality of the passage.

As far as the vocabulary of the two samples in concerned, we may note that both use the kind of abstract vocabulary that you would expect in a news broadcast. But in (2) there are examples of Latinate words that have more accessible alternatives, e.g. *absent* (rather than *away*), *summon* (rather than *call*), *controversy* (rather than *row*) and (*reports* (cf. *told* in (1)). Vocabulary as well as grammar thus reflect the greater formality of (2).

The scale of politeness is not really relevant here, as the addressees are the general public, and the function of the discourse is to convey information. Politeness is of more relevance when the addressees are physically present, or when the function of the language is to have an effect on the addressee, as in advertising, for example. (For further consideration of function in language, see 9.4 below.)

Because neither the role of the speaker nor that of addressee is prominent in news broadcasts, we would expect the language to reflect impersonality. However, there is an attempt in (1) to reduce the impersonality (and formality) of the situation by the use of the personal pronoun *us*, as in *Philip Whitfield told us* (cf. *Philip Whitfield reports* in (2)). This illustrates that not only does language reflect the situation, but it can also be used to define it. The same point can be made about domain of discourse, to which we now turn.

9.4 Domain

As we said in 1.3.3, domain 'has to do with how language varies according to the activity in which it plays a part'. Or in other words, language varies according to the FUNCTION it is fulfilling.

It is a commonplace to say that the function of language is communication. But what kind of communication? Language can be used to convey information, express feelings, persuade someone to do something, make contact with someone else, write poetry, or talk about language itself. These functions can be called respectively: referential, expressive, conative, phatic, poetic and metalinguistic. Language is often used to fulfil more than one function simultaneously. For example, *I feel like a cup of coffee* could be simultaneously referential, expressive and conative. It conveys information, expresses a feeling, and tries to persuade someone to provide a cup of coffee. In general, however, language used in a given situation has a dominant function, with others subordinate to it, and we may characterise the domains of language according to their dominant functions. Table 9.2 is a partial list of some domains with the dominant and subordinate functions typically associated with them.

In fact, like the categories of tenor and mode, the category of domain does not lend itself to clear-cut distinctions. There are, for example,

Table 9.2

DOMAIN	FUNCTION	
	DOMINANT	SUBORDINATE
Journalism	Referential	Expressive, Conative
Advertising	Conative	Referential, Poetic
Religion	Expressive	Conative, Poetic
Law	Referential	Metalinguistic, Conative
Literature	Poetic	Expressive, Referential
Conversation	Phatic	Referential, Expressive

possible sub-categories of domain with no clear separation between them: the language of news reporting and the language of news commentary are both kinds of journalism, but it is not always easy to separate them. Also, domains vary in the extent to which they influence language. It is not even clear, for example, whether conversation and literature should be called domains. This is because of the wide variety of language that is possible in each case. People have more choice of language in conversation and literature than in other domains. So once again, language and situation are to some extent mutually determining. The language chosen can itself define the domain: for example, an argument (as in conversation) or a poem (as in literature). This point will be taken up again with reference to literature in 10.1.4.

9.5 Domain and discourse

The concept of domain is best further illustrated by the analysis of actual discourse from a particular domain, that of advertising. The following is a press advertisement for a car:

THE 1980 VAUXHALL CHEVETTE
    The Vauxhall Chevette has always offered a great combination of comfort, economy and enthusiastic performance.
    But this year, by realigning the rear-seat, we've conjured up extra legroom in the back.
    The result is even more space and greater comfort for passengers.
    Drivers, on the other hand, will notice that, in most respects, it remains unchanged.
    The Chevette is every bit as sure footed and sporty a performer as ever it was.
    One surprise, though, is that it's now even more economical to run.
    Because our engineers have managed to wring further fuel savings of around 4% from the already frugal 1256cc. engine.
    Think of that as around 5p off every gallon of petrol you use and you'll appreciate its value.
    In fact, recent Government figures show the Chevette saloon returning 44 mpg at 56 mph and 31.3 mpg at a constant 75 mph.
    Other thoughtful touches for 1980 include side window demisters and optional automatic transmission.
    Restyled flushline headlights accent the car's already aerodynamic lines.

If advertisements are to achieve their purpose, which is to sell a product, they have to be easy to read. The sentence structure must therefore be fairly simple. In this advertisement each sentence starts a new paragraph, and there is an average of fifteen words per sentence, which is relatively short. The clause structure of the sentences is quite simple, with more use of co-ordination than subordination. The second sentence *But this year. . .* is probably the most complex, as it has a subordinate adverbial clause and a parenthetical structure. We can summarise it thus:

$$\text{cj } A\,A \qquad S\,P\,O\,A$$
$$\overline{\text{cj } P\,O}$$

This structure in fact creates a special effect. The adverbial *this year*, coming early in the sentence, stresses the newness of the model, and the rest of the main clause (*we've conjured up extra legroom at the back*), coming at the end, gives new information (see 12.2.3) about precisely what the new feature is. A special effect is also created by the seventh sentence, *Because our engineers. . .* This sentence is really a clause subordinate to the previous main clause, *it's now even more economical to run*. However, placing *because* at the beginning of a new sentence has the effect of giving separate emphasis to the explanation for the economy.

Below the level of the clause we can look at the structure of noun phrases. In advertising language they are often fairly complex, with particularly heavy use of premodifiers. This structure has the advantage of giving precise information, yet remaining concise. Premodifiers are often nouns in advertising, as in for example, *recent Government figures, restyled flushline headlights, side window demisters. Other thoughtful touches for 1980* has both pre- and postmodifiers. The final noun phrase of the advertisement, *the car's already aerodynamic lines* has the use of the genitive *car's*, which is uncommon for inanimate nouns in many other language domains, but common in advertising. The premodifiers themselves in this case are subordinate phrases: ((*the car's*) (*already aerodynamic*) *lines*). This has the effect of conciseness and impact, as is clear if we compare an equivalent phrase with postmodification: *the lines (of the car) (which are already aerodynamic)*.

As far as verbs are concerned, tense is used effectively to convey the advertiser's message. The simple present emphasises the features of the new model (e.g. *the result is*); the perfect shows what improvements have been made (e.g. *we've conjured up*), and the future cannily makes the assumption that the car will be bought (*Drivers. . .will notice*).

The vocabulary of the advertisement can be divided into two categories: (a) words (especially adjectives) which emphasise the positive aspects of the product, and persuade the consumer to buy (conative function), and (b) those which provide technical information about the car (referential function). The modifiers *great, extra, more, greater, sure, sporty*, and *thoughtful* fall in the former category; *realigning, returning (44 mpg), side window demisters, optional automatic transmission, re-styled flushline headlights* and *aerodynamic lines* fall in the latter. *Aero-dynamic* is a technical term used almost metaphorically, and calculated to impress.

A further characteristic of advertising language is direct address, re-flected in the use of the second-person pronoun *you*, and in the impera-tive *Think*, which acts as an appeal for notice. This point draws our attention to interconnections between domain, tenor and mode. Adver-tising language is typically very informal and personal, and even when it occurs in written form (e.g. in press advertisements) it shows some of the characteristics which we associate with spoken language. Notice this in the use of interaction features (see p. 139) and of verbal contractions as in *we've, it's* and *you'll*.

There are other characteristics of advertising language that could be picked out in this sample advertisement, but our analysis should serve to illustrate the effect of domain in discourse. The exercise at the end of this chapter will give you practice in working out the effects of other domains on discourse.

9.6   Combining categories of use

So far we have looked separately at the effects of mode, tenor and domain in discourse. But in 9.5 we also noticed that a sample of discourse will be affected by all three categories simultaneously. All of the samples which we have analysed in this chapter and the last could be re-analysed, paying attention to all categories of use instead of just one.

To illustrate the point more fully, we shall analyse the effect of all three categories in the following sample of discourse:

The 1980 Vauxhall Chevette is the same car it ever was.
Same lively performance.
Same light responsive steering.
Same level handling.
But there are a few new touches you might like.
Even better fuel economy from the 1256cc. engine.
Side window demisters.
More streamlined headlights.
And as an optional extra, automatic transmission plus lots more
     rear legroom.
The 1980 Vauxhall Chevette we have changed very little but im-
     proved quite a lot.

As you may have guessed, the above is a script for a television advertisement for the same product as the press advertisement analysed in 9.5. We shall analyse it briefly from the point of view of domain, mode and tenor.

Since the domain is advertising, the television advertisement shares several characteristics with its press equivalent. For example, there is vocabulary implying the positive aspects of the product, e.g. *responsive, new, better, extra*, and some of the same technical vocabulary conveying information, e.g. *1256cc. engine, side window demisters, automatic transmission.* There is also the direct address (*you*) which is characteristic of advertising, as is the liberal use of comparative constructions: *even better fuel economy*, etc.

However, because of the impermanence of the spoken mode and the constraints on time, less information can be conveyed. Because of this, memorability of the important points has to be aimed for. This is achieved partly by repetition. For example, *The 1980 Vauxhall Chevette* appears at both the beginning and end of the script (both times in a prominent position at the beginning of the sentence), and *same* appears three times in parallel NP structures, as the first premodifier followed by one or two more.

One characteristic which the script shares with much spoken language (see 8.5) is that we cannot divide it neatly into sentence units. There are only three grammatical units with clear sentential structure, at the beginning, middle and end of the script. The other units lack verbs – most of them are just NPs and are rather like slogans, functioning as a list of the attributes of the product. This particular structure is more characteristic of advertising language than of spoken language in general, and is doubtless due to the shortness of time and the importance of conveying essential information in a concise, dramatic way.

This sample of discourse also differs from other types of spoken language (see 8.5) because it is prepared, and so is unusually fluent. It has none of the monitoring or interaction features we find in normal conversation, for these depend on an addressee being physically present (although some advertisements use such features to create the feeling that the viewer is actually there). This sample is also more explicit than spoken language in normal conversations, because the addressees are unknown and unable to give direct feedback. Another point is that it is supplemented by film and written language on the screen, which are not recorded here, but which help to determine the nature of the spoken language used. For example, the use of parallelism and incomplete sentences may be explained by the accompanying picture sequence.

Both spoken language and advertising language tend to reflect informality of tenor. The combined effect of these two categories in the script makes the language quite informal – in fact more so than in the press advertisement discussed above (9.5). The grammatical structure is extremely simple, with few subordinate or co-ordinated clauses. The vocabulary is generally concrete and accessible, and more colloquial than in the written advertisement (e.g. *new touches, plus lots more, quite a lot*). It is also quite personal (e.g. *you might like, we have changed very little*).

It is worth pointing out, however, that advertisements are not written to a formula, but to some extent have their individual styles. This advertisement adopts a casual low-key approach to the listener, as if the advertiser wants to disclaim the brash foot-in-the-door technique of the 'hard sell'. The tentativeness of *might* (*like*), *a few* (*touches*), and *quite* (*a lot*) are to some extent atypical of advertising in their moderation and even modesty.

In preparation for the next chapter, it is also worth noting that advertising language shares some features with poetry. The parallelism of

Same lively performance.
Same light responsive steering.
Same level handling.

with its reiterated first word is characteristic of both poetry and public oratory; but the alliteration of the adjectives (*lively, light, level*) is a more specifically literary device.

We have given only a brief example of an analysis using all the categories of use. By doing the exercise at the end of this chapter, you will develop a clearer understanding of how all these categories affect discourse simultaneously.

Exercise

Exercise 9
For the following samples of discourse, (i) identify the tenor, mode and domain; and (ii) show how these categories of use are reflected in the language. Remember to look at different aspects of grammar, including clause and phrase structure, as well as vocabulary.

Note that some of these samples are spoken. However, they have been written in conventional orthography so that you will have to identify the mode on linguistic grounds alone.

a.   The Black and Decker electric saw is probably the only saw you'll ever need.
It cuts out coping saws.
It cuts out tenon saws.

It cuts out hack-saws.
It cuts out bother.
It even cuts out holes.
With a set of blades the Black and Decker electric saw is probably the only saw you will ever need.

(Black & Decker television advertisement)

b.   THE WOMAN WHO HAS JUST LOST £670,000
Attractive Roberta Edgar lost a divorce settlement worth £670,000 yesterday. . . but still managed a smile.
'It won't affect my standard of living,' said the 36-year-old redhead. 'But naturally I'm very disappointed.'
The record award against her multi-millionaire ex-husband Anthony was made four months ago by Mr Justice Eastham.
But it was thrown out in the Appeal Court by Lord Justice Ormrod and Lord Justice Oliver.
They ruled that mother-of-four Roberta must be content with an agreement made in 1976, when the marriage broke up.
(*The Daily Star*, 24 July 1980)

c.   £670,000 AWARD TO EX-WIFE OVERRULED
A record £670,000 award to a multi-millionaire's ex-wife was set aside by two Appeal Court judges in London yesterday.
The £670,000 lump sum award in March this year by a High Court Family Division judge, Mr Justice Eastham, was said by lawyers at the time to be the highest cash award ever made by English courts to a divorced wife.
But Lord Justice Ormrod and Lord Justice Oliver yesterday decided the Mrs Edgar was bound by the terms of a 1976 Deed of Separation between her and Mr Edgar under which she agreed not to seek further capital or property provision from her husband.
(*The Guardian*, 24 July 1980)

d.   A GENERAL CONFESSION
to be said of the whole Congregation after the Minister, all kneeling,
Almighty and most merciful Father; we have erred, and strayed from thy ways like lost sheep. We have followed too much the devices and desires of our own hearts. We have offended against thy holy laws. We have left undone those things which we ought to have done; And we have done those things which we ought not to have done; And there is no health in us. But thou, O Lord, have mercy upon us, miserable offenders. Spare thou them, O God, which confess their faults. Restore thou them that are penitent; According to thy promises declared unto

mankind in Christ Jesu our Lord. And grant, O most merciful
Father, for his sake; That we may hereafter live a godly,
righteous, and sober life, To the glory of thy holy Name. Amen.

(*The Book of Common Prayer*)

e.   Father eternal, giver of light and grace,
      we have sinned against you and against our fellow men,
      in what we have thought,
      in what we have said and done,
      through ignorance, through weakness,
      through our own deliberate fault.
      We have wounded your love,
      and marred your image in us.
      We are sorry and ashamed,
      and repent of all our sins.
      For the sake of your Son Jesus Christ, who died for us,
      forgive us all that is past;
      and lead us out from darkness
      to walk as children of light. Amen.

(Alternative confession, *The Alternative Service Book 1980:
Services authorised for use in the Church of England in conjunction with The Book of Common Prayer*)

f.   At the Olympic Games, British sprinter Alan Wells has won the
      gold medal in the one hundred metres. It's Britain's first gold
      medal in track and field events in the Games so far, and Alan
      Wells is the first Briton to win the hundred metres for more
      than fifty years. But the result could not have been closer, with
      the first two runners recording exactly the same time, as Derek
      Thompson reports from Moscow.

(BBC Radio Four, *The World Tonight*, 25 July 1980)

10

Analysis of literary discourse

In 1.7 we spent some time looking at the language of a short poem. Now we shall examine a passage of prose, to show in more detail how grammar can contribute to the study of literature. We shall in fact refer to three extracts from novels in this chapter. The first, from D. H. Lawrence's *The Rainbow,* will be the main subject of study, and the second passage, from Dickens's *Bleak House,* will be used for further illustration. The Dickens passage and a further passage, from Virginia Woolf's *The Waves,* will provide material for the exercises at the end of the chapter. The three passages are given on pp. 166-70.

Style, viewed as the particular choice of language made by an author, in a sense embodies that author's achievement, and way of experiencing and interpreting the world. This is why the study of style has often been seen as opening a door to fuller literary appreciation. The excellence of literary artists must be evident, ultimately, in their choice of language. But we cannot study this choice of language without some knowledge of how to discuss and analyse the language itself, including its grammar.

10.1 How to analyse style

There is no foolproof technique for analysing literary style; in fact, a method will fail if it is too rigid. Each analysis of style is like an adventure of discovery, in which we combine our knowledge of language and our response to literature in order to appreciate more clearly what the writer has succeeded in conveying. But it is useful to have a flexible method of study, in which we

(a)   First of all **read** the passage carefully twice or more.
(b)   Then **identify** and **list** features of style under various headings.
(c)   And then, finally, **synthesise** these features of style in an interpretation of the meaning and effect of the passage.

Stage (b) is where the real analysis of language takes place, and this is where we can help by providing a classification of features of style. We shall note these features under one or other of the following major headings: LEXIS, GRAMMAR, FIGURES OF SPEECH, COHESION AND CONTEXT. Although grammar is represented by only one of these categories, we shall observe that it plays its part in the identification of features in the other categories as well.

10.1.1 Lexis

Under this heading we notice features of vocabulary. For example, how far is the vocabulary formal or informal, complex or simple, polysyllabic or monosyllabic? And so on. Does the passage contain unusual words, e.g. technical, archaic or dialect words?

It is useful to make lists of words belonging to the major word classes, and to note which categories (in terms of form and meaning) they belong to. We might notice, for example, that a passage has many more abstract than concrete nouns, or that it contains many verbs of movement, or adjectives of colour. Although this sounds a mechanical exercise, it can in fact provide a great deal of insight into style.

Style features, whether lexical or grammatical, tend to be a matter of frequency, or more precisely a matter of **relative** frequency. We need to compare a passage with some standard of what is usual or 'normal' if we are going to recognise what is special about its style. This is why it is particularly helpful to compare a number of different passages of approximately the same length. We have chosen three such passages, so as to make the comparison of styles easier.

As lexis is the simplest level of style, and the one which is easiest to notice and discuss, we shall say no more about it.

10.1.2 Grammar

Under this heading we look at the sentences and see how they are constructed. How complex are the sentences? What kinds of complexity are found (see 8.5)? Does complexity vary notably from one sentence to another? Are there marked uses of coordination or subordination, of linked or unlinked coordination? Is there anything to say about the kinds of clause structure or phrase structure favoured? For instance, the writer may favour [S P] rather than [S P O] patterns, premodifiers rather than postmodifiers, and so forth.

To see what role grammar can play in the effect of a passage, let us look at the first and last sentences of the *Bleak House* passage (pp. 168-9) (the sentence numbers in square brackets are those marked in the texts):

[1]   Fog everywhere.

[10]   And hard by Temple Bar, in Lincoln's Inn Hall, at the very heart
        of the fog, sits the Lord High Chancellor in his High Court of
        Chancery.

The first sentence is very short and to the point. In fact, it is not a
complete sentence at all in the grammatical sense: it has no verb, and is
simply a noun followed by an adverb of place. It expresses, in a nut-
shell, what the rest of the passage elaborates in detail – the ubiquity of
the fog. It also sets a grammatical pattern that is persisted in through
the first two paragraphs (*Fog up the river* ...) – where noun phrases,
not clauses, become the main units of the text. Why does Dickens omit
the finite verbs? Two plausible answers are these: first, the repetition of
Fog becomes in this way more forceful and dramatic; second, the
connections between the noun phrases become associative, rather than
logical – the reader's eye seems to move from one disconnected scene
to another, catching only glimpses of what lies within the fog. This is
grammar communicating at an impressionistic, 'sub-logical' level – where
explicit declarative sentences, with their implications of truth value,
are not relevant.

The last sentence [10], on the other hand, is quite long, and leads
us to an appropriate climactic conclusion of the train of thought begun
with *Fog everywhere*. The High Court of Chancery is for Dickens the
very heart of the fog, a satirical symbol for the obfuscation of the law.
Notice how he works us up to it in stages, as if we are making a journey
to the very midst of obscurity. Sentence [9] leads us as far as *Temple
Bar*, and sentence [10] completes the journey, taking us from *Temple
Bar* to the *Court of Chancery*. This sentence is a good example of the
principles of end-focus and end-weight (12.2.3), leading the reader from
given to new information. It is important for the effect that the
weighty phrases *the Lord High Chancellor in his High Court of Chancery*
come at the end as a sort of denouement, and to ensure this there is an
inversion of *S* and *P*: ... *sits the Lord High Chancellor* ... The role of
the first three adverbials (all adverbials of place) in building up the
syntactic suspense must also be noted. The order of elements in the
clause is quite unusual: [cj *A A A P S A*].

So both sentence [1] and sentence [10] illustrate, in their different
ways, a special descriptive effect that is brought about by unusual
grammatical structure: in [1] the *P*-less sentence, and in [10] the
inversion of *S* and *P*.

10.1.3   Figures of speech: irregularities and regularities

The traditional figures of speech (metaphor, etc.) are often thought of
as features of meaning and expression which are exceptional in ordinary
language, but normal in literature. There is some basis for this view, and

in the study of style we can regard figures of speech as special regularities and irregularities which are exploited in literature for their special communicative power and communicative values.

Of the traditional figures of speech, those most often discussed, such as metaphor, irony and paradox, involve communication at a non-literal level. They usually arise from some 'irregularity' of language – for example, an incongruity of meaning between elements of the same grammatical structure. This example is from the Lawrence extract (p. 166):

[14]   She saw [(the moonlight) (flash) (question) (on his face)].

In the subordinate clause, the S, P and O are strangely ill-assorted from a literal point of view. The steady gleam of 'moonlight' cannot normally 'flash' anything, and (besides) a 'question' is not something that can be literally 'flashed', nor can a 'question', literally, be on anyone's face. And perhaps the oddest feature of all, grammatically, is the use of *question* without a determiner, as a mass noun. Yet the combined effect of these incongruities is a strikingly vivid impression in which the moonlight, the sudden movement of a face out of the shadow, and the questioning expression on the face, seem parts of the same momentary experience.

But there are also figures of speech which involve exploiting extra regularities in language. These include various types of parallelism: repetitive patterns of structures and words, such as those which occur pervasively in the Dickens and Lawrence passages. A mild example is sentence [3] of Lawrence:

[3]   [^{S}(he) ^{P}(was drawing) ^{A}(near)], and [^{S}(she) ^{P}(must turn) ^{A}(again)].

Both clauses have the structure [SPA], so the sentence has a neat pattern [SPA] + [SPA]. We call this a 'mild' example of parallelism, because to some extent such patterns arise randomly in discourse, and this instance could easily occur unintentionally. But the sentence is more 'regular', more patterned, than that suggests. Note that in each clause, the phrases contain the same number of words [1, 2, 1] + [1, 2, 1], and that the subjects are both personal pronouns *he* and *she*. If such patterns were merely ornaments, or embellishments of literary style, we would not need to take much notice of them; but there is an important principle that **parallelism of form implies parallelism of meaning**, and here we can feel how the clauses, with their contrasted subjects, balance and oppose one another like the parallel movements of partners in a dance.

The image of a slow, ritual-like dance seems a particularly fitting one to associate with this passage. Look at the more striking parallelism of:

[7]   [[As he came], she drew away],
       [[as he drew away], she came].

Figure 10.1

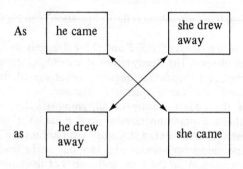

This sentence consists of a mirror-image pattern, as shown in Figure 10.1. The criss-cross pattern is called CHIASMUS after the Greek letter Chi (χ). Again, the movement of the boy and the girl is enacted in the structure of the sentence. This example is a more striking case of parallelism than that of [2], because not only the structures, but the words which occupy those structures, are repeated in the pattern.

In [7] the pattern has a MIMETIC function; it imitates the form of what it refers to: the interweaving movement of the boy and the girl. The effect of sound imitating sense, of form imitating meaning, is something we associate with poetry, but is perhaps an equally important aspect of prose writing. In prose, however, we rarely notice such effects unless we are looking for them. Who, for example, would notice the regular triple, dance-like rhythm of the following NP from Lawrence's opening sentence [1]?

      x /   x   x / x   x / x   x / x x /
[1]   a rhythm, which carried their feet and their bodies in tune.

(/ = stressed syllable; x = unstressed syllable). Or who would notice that the parallelisms we have just observed in [3] and [7] are similarly reinforced by a pattern of regular duple rhythm?

[3]   [/ × / × /] × [/ × / × /]
[7]   [/ × / × / × /], [/ × / × / × /]

Written out like this, the mimetic quality of these patterns, suggesting the regular movements of the two harvesters, is apparent. But even if readers fail to notice such an effect, they may well respond to it at a less conscious level.

If you have met the concept of mimesis in language before, it will probably have been in the more familiar form of ONOMATOPOEIA, the use of imitative sounds (particularly vowel and consonant sounds), as in *buzz* and *cuckoo*. In Lawrence [3], for instance, the use of words like *swish* and *hiss* is clearly meant to conjure up the actual sound the oats would have made when picked up and carried. Elsewhere, such phonological suggestion is more subtle and indirect: there are examples in the first sentence of the Virginia Woolf extract (pp. 169–70). But to conclude, let us notice that repetition of speech sounds can have other functions, such as ironic emphasis. One of the salient effects of Dickens's sentence [10] above is the repeated *h* sounds (followed by similar vowel sounds) at the beginning of important words:

[10a]   . . . *h*ard . . . *H*all . . . *h*eart . . . Lord *H*igh Chancellor . . . *H*igh Court of Chancery.

This helps the climax effect we have already noted in the grammar, especially through the emphasis it gives to that word *High,* which in this context is obviously sarcastic. Although *figures of speech* has often had a more limited meaning, we may interpret the term broadly enough to include all such special devices as this.

10.1.4 Cohesion and context

We look finally at features which have to do with how sentences, and indeed whole discourses, are placed within a context. This term *context,* however, like *figures of speech* in 10.1.3, will be understood in a particularly wide sense. On the one hand, it may include the way a sentence fits into the wider context of the discourse, including its relation to preceding and following sentences. This is often called COHESION. On the other hand, it may refer to the way in which parts of a discourse, and a discourse as a whole, presuppose a particular SITUATION. But it is often pointed out that whereas in other kinds of discourse (as in Chapters 8 and 9, especially 9.5) we fit our language to the situation, in literature, in general, we have to fit a situation to the language. That is, in literature, and particularly in works of fiction, we as readers 'create' a discourse situation, by inference from the text itself.

This means that for each novel, there is an implied AUTHOR - READER SITUATION, which may be formal, informal, familiar, casual, etc., and through which the novel expresses a 'point of view' towards the characters, and events in the fiction. A simple example of this is the use of the narrative present tense in the Dickens passage. This has the conventional name of 'historic present': it means that the reader apprehends the goings-on in the novel as if they were happening at the very time of reading – a device for dramatic heightening. But in the *Bleak House* description of the fog, it has a further implication of timelessness. This is, indeed, very appropriate to the pettifoggery of the Court of Chancery, where lawsuits drag on interminably.

Another peculiarity of the discourse situation in fiction is that it is complicated by situations within situations. When fiction includes dialogue, it creates a CHARACTER - CHARACTER SITUATION which takes place within the author-reader situation. There are also CHARACTER-READER SITUATIONS (e.g. the dramatic monologue of the auto-biographical novel), and possibilities of further complication by further subordination of one discourse in another, or by switching from one situation to another, or (a common technique in modern fiction) representing the 'inner monologue' of a character's mind. So a novel may have quite an intricate discourse structure.

To illustrate the point that a novel implies its own discourse situation(s), we may look at the use of questions in the Lawrence passage:

[8]   Were they never to meet?

Questions imply an answer, and therefore evoke a situation in which someone is seeking some information, or the solution to a problem, etc. When we meet this sentence, we are no longer interpreting the passage as part of the author-reader situation, but as part of a self-questioning situation which is going on in the mind of a character. The negative question (*never*), since it expects a negative answer, implies that character's frustration.

This brings us to a set of grammatical choices which are intimately connected with narrative point of view:

[8a]   'Are we never to meet?' he said.
[8b]   He asked her if they were never to meet.
[8c]   Were they never to meet?

The version which gives speech in quotation marks, [8a], supplies the actual words supposedly spoken by the character. This is called DIRECT SPEECH, in contrast to the construction with the subordinate clause [8b], which is called INDIRECT SPEECH. A third possibility for reporting the speech of a character is that of [8c], known as FREE INDIRECT SPEECH. Here the main reporting clause is omitted, but the pronouns and tenses are those which are appropriate for indirect speech [8b]. The narrative functions of these three constructions are different. Roughly speaking, [8a] allows the character to speak for himself, giving prominence to the speaker's point of view; [8b], on the contrary, submerges the speaker's point of view in the narrator's (author's) point of view; and [8c] achieves a merger of these two effects. In modern fiction, however, much attention has been given to the rendering of the 'interior monologue' of the mind, in addition to overt speech. To [8a] - [8c], therefore, we should add three corresponding variants for thought reporting:

[8d] 'Are we never to meet?' he asked himself.   (DIRECT THOUGHT)
[8e] He wondered whether they were never to meet.   (INDIRECT THOUGHT)
[8f] Were they never to meet?   (FREE INDIRECT THOUGHT)

The last of these, free indirect thought, is indistinguishable in form from free indirect speech: here again, we have to 'create' a situation to fit the words. Free indirect thought is a very common means of portraying the inner consciousness of a character. It is in this function that [8] is used by Lawrence.

With this preparation, we can return to the noting of features of style. Under the heading of **cohesion**, we note what use is made of various kinds of connection (e.g. by conjunctions and sentence adverbials); and of various kinds of cross-reference (e.g. by pronouns like *she, it, they,* by substitute forms, by ellipsis, by 'expressive repetition' and by 'elegant variation' - see 12.6). Sometimes, as in Dickens's description of the fog, it is the lack of orthodox devices of cohesion that is in evidence.

Turning to discourse **situation**, we should be aware of the role here, as in cohesion, of certain words and grammatical features by which language refers to aspects of its own situation. They include demonstrative words (*this, that, now, then, there*), first and second-person pronouns (*I, you,* etc.), tense and aspect, and verbs like *come* and *go*. One of the fascinating things about the Lawrence extract is the way these items, as well as other indicators of situation, convey a shifting or ambivalent narrative point of view. First, the characters are denoted by the pronouns *he* and *she* throughout, without any variation at all. It seems as if Lawrence wants to maintain a strict objectivity and impersonality. But in [3] (. . . *he was drawing near, and she must turn again*) we clearly see things from the girl's point of view. This is implied in the phrase *drawing near,* and also in the verb phrases: both the progressive construction *was drawing* and the modal construction *must turn* suggest the subjectivity of her viewpoint. Later, in [7] (*As he came, she drew away, as he drew away, she came*) there is a strange ambivalence of viewpoint: *came* evokes the subjective position of one person watching the other approaching, but this position switches in the middle of the sentence. Perhaps we are seeing things from the centrepoint, the stook, to and from which both he and she move. Later still, we are evidently experiencing things through the thoughts of the boy. The questions in the final paragraph can be interpreted only as free indirect thought:

[17]   Why, as she came up from under the moon, would she halt and stand off from him?

To summarise, then: under the heading of COHESION we consider (a) connections and (b) cross-references between sentences; and under the heading of SITUATION we consider features which reflect (a) the author–reader situation and point of view; and (b) the presentation of speech and thought situations within the fiction.

10.2   Illustrative extract

From: D. H. Lawrence, *The Rainbow*, ch. 4

They worked together, coming and going, in a rhythm, which carried their feet and their bodies in tune.[1] She stooped, she lifted the burden of sheaves, she turned her face to the dimness where he was, and went with her burden over the stubble.[2] She hesitated, set down her sheaves, there was a swish and hiss of mingling oats, he was drawing near, and she must turn again.[3] And there was the flaring moon laying bare her bosom again, making her drift and ebb like a wave.[4]

He worked steadily, engrossed, threading backwards and forwards like a shuttle across the strip of cleared stubble, weaving the long line of riding shocks, nearer and nearer to the shadowy trees, threading his sheaves with hers.[5]

And always, she was gone before he came.[6] As he came, she drew away, as he drew away, she came.[7] Were they never to meet?[8] Gradually a low, deep-sounding will in him vibrated to her, tried to set her in accord, tried to bring her gradually to him, to a meeting, till they should be together, till they should meet as the sheaves that swished together.[9] . . .

He waited for her, he fumbled at the stook.[10] She came.[11] But she stood back till he drew away.[12] He saw her in shadow, a dark column, and spoke to her, and she answered.[13] She saw the moonlight flash question on his face.[14] But there was a space between them, and he went away, the work carried them, rhythmic.[15]

Why was there always a space between them, why were they apart?[16] Why, as she came up from under the moon, would she halt and stand off from him?[17] Why was he held away from her?[18] His will drummed persistently, darkly, it drowned everything else.[19]

[294 words]

Between sentences [9] and [10] a short paragraph is omitted.

10.3   Outline analysis (with questions for further study)

Lexis
In keeping with the subject, the vocabulary is simple and homely, but with a slightly literary or archaic flavour here and there: *drawing near, laying bare her bosom,* etc. What is the effect of this type of lexical choice?

Compare the frequency of nouns, verbs, adjectives and adverbs in this passage with those in the Dickens passage. You will discover some marked differences. What implications do these have?

Grammar
The sentences vary from extreme simplicity ([11]) to considerable complexity ([9]), but the complexity tends to be of a progressive kind through the repetition of coordinate, particularly unlinked, constructions:

[5]   He worked steadily, engrossed, threading ..., weaving ..., threading his sheaves with hers.

Now try a skeleton parsing of sentence [9]. What is the most important feature of its structure? At word level, we notice, coordination tends to join elements in pairs: *coming and going* [1], *backwards and forwards* [5]. What other examples are there of pairing, whether by coordination or by other means? What is the relevance of all this pairing and co-ordination?

Clauses of [S P] or [S P A] structure predominate. There are few [S P O] structures. In this way, the passage tends to emphasise movements in themselves, rather than movements directed to a particular goal or purpose. It is significant that some of the clauses with objects which do occur have an inanimate subject and a human object – which is not usual: *the flaring moon laying bare her bosom* [4]; *the work carried them* [15]; and a similar case is the passive *Why was he held away from her?* [18]. What effect do these clauses have in depiction of the harvest-making?

Figures of speech
What are the predominant metaphors of the passage, and how do they fit into the description of the 'ritual' mentioned above? Metaphors are implied comparisons, whereas similes are overt comparisons. What similes occur in the passage (tell-tale words are *like, as, as if*), and how do they fit in with the metaphors?

We have already noticed, with reference to [3] and [7], that the passage contains grammatical and lexical parallelism. Look at the long sentence [9] from this point of view. What is the effect of repeating words and structures without using coordinating conjunctions?

One syntactic oddity of the passage is the use of an adjective form where normally an adverb in *-ly* would be called for: *the work carried them, rhythmic* [15]. Have you any ideas on why Lawrence should prefer this to the adverb form *rhythmically?*

Context and cohesion
We have already considered the repeated use of pronouns (*he, she*). Elsewhere it is part of Lawrence's technique to make repeated use of the same words, as if to make the most of their evocative or symbolic value. For example, the word *burden* is repeated in [2]; *sheaves* is repeated a number of times; *threading* occurs twice in [5]. The clause *But there was a space between them* in [15] is largely repeated in the next sentence: *Why was there always a space between them?* In this way the passage insists on the symbolism of the 'space' – a physical distance signalling emotional distance. At the same time, the use of free indirect thought (p. 165) in the repeated insistent *Why* questions makes the boy's longing the most dominant emotion of the passage.

Although Lawrence's language is relatively simple and accessible, he achieves intensity through the symbolism of natural or homely rhythms (the waves, the moon, the vibrating, the weaving), and the rhythmic repetitions and parallelism of the language itself, imitating the to and fro movements of the harvesters.

10.4 Further illustrative extracts for discussion

10.4.1 Charles Dickens, *Bleak House*, ch. 1

Fog everywhere.[1] Fog up the river, where it flows among green aits and meadows; fog down the river, where it rolls defiled among the tiers of shipping and the waterside pollutions of a great (and dirty) city.[2] Fog on the Essex marshes, fog on the Kentish heights.[3] Fog creeping into the cabooses of collier-brigs; fog lying out on the yards and hovering in the rigging of great ships; fog drooping on the gunwales of barges and small boats.[4] Fog in the eyes and throats of ancient Greenwich pensioners, wheezing by the firesides of their wards; fog in the stem and bowl of the afternoon pipe of the wrathful skipper, down in his close cabin; fog cruelly pinching the toes and fingers of his shivering little 'prentice boy on deck.[5] Chance people on the bridges peeping over the parapets into a nether sky of fog, with fog all round them, as if they were up in a balloon and hanging in the misty clouds.[6]

Gas looming through the fog in divers places in the streets, much as the sun may, from the spongey fields, be seen to loom by husbandman and ploughboy.[7] Most of the shops lighted two hours before their time – as the gas seems to know, for it has a haggard and unwilling look.[8]

The raw afternoon is rawest, and the dense fog is densest, and the muddy streets are muddiest near that leaden-headed old obstruction, appropriate ornament for the threshold of a leaden-headed old corporation, Temple Bar.[9] And hard by Temple Bar, in Lincoln's Inn Hall, at the very heart of the fog, sits the Lord High Chancellor in his High Court of Chancery.[10]

[276 words]

10.4.2 Virginia Woolf, *The Waves*, Penguin edn 1964, pp. 62-3

In the garden the birds that had sung erratically and spasmodically in the dawn on that tree, on that bush, now sang together in chorus, shrill and sharp; now together, as if conscious of companionship, now alone as if to the pale blue sky.[1] They swerved, all in one flight, when the black cat moved among the bushes, when the cook threw cinders on the ash heap and startled them.[2] Fear was in their song, and apprehension of pain, and joy to be snatched quickly now at this instant.[3] Also they sang emulously in the clear morning air, swerving high over the elm tree, singing together as they chased each other, escaping, pursuing, pecking each other as they turned high in the air.[4] And then tiring of pursuit and flight, lovelily they came descending, delicately declining, dropped down and sat silent on the tree, on the wall, with their bright eyes glancing, and their heads turned this way, that way; aware, awake; intensely conscious of one thing, one object in particular.[5]

Perhaps it was a snail shell, rising in the grass like a grey cathedral, a swelling building burnt with dark rings and shadowed green by the grass.[6] Or perhaps they saw the splendour of the flowers making a light of flowing purple over the beds, through which dark tunnels of purple shade were driven between the stalks.[7] Or they fixed their gaze on the small bright apple leaves dancing yet withheld, stiffly sparkling among the pink-tipped blossoms.[8] Or they saw the rain drop on the hedge, pendent but not falling, with a whole house bent in it, and towering elms; or gazing straight at the sun, their eyes became gold beads.[9]

[284 words]

Exercises

Exercise 10a
Comment in detail on the style of the passage from *Bleak House* (10.4.1), applying the general approach suggested in this chapter. Use grammatical analysis selectively, to make your commentary clearer and more explicit. The following aspects of style are among those worth examining:

1. LEXIS. Compare the types of vocabulary used with that of Lawrence. Note any unusual or technical words. Compare the frequency of nouns, verbs, adjectives and adverbs with those of Lawrence.
2. GRAMMAR. Pairing of constructions by coordination. Contrast between the last two sentences and the other sentences. Use of ellipsis and grammatical omissions.
3. FIGURES OF SPEECH. Use of similes and fanciful comparisons. Types and functions of parallelism and word repetition. Alliteration.
4. COHESION AND CONTEXT. Absence of connectives. Use of present tense.

Exercise 10b
Now try a similar stylistic analysis of the passage from *The Waves* (10.4.2).

11

Grammar and problems of usage

In Chapters 8, 9 and 10 we examined how knowledge of grammar can be used to analyse language as used by others, whether in speech or writing, in non-literary discourse or literature. In this chapter and the next we shall investigate how we can apply what we know about grammar to the choices we make in our own use of language. So the focus changes from our role as consumers to our role as producers of language, or from analysis to synthesis (see p. 114).

11.1 Opinions about grammar

Our native language is such an important part of our social existence that, like other social institutions, it easily becomes a subject for argument. Language, moreover, is intimately connected with judgements about status, and about what is good or bad, right or wrong, beautiful or ugly; this is why it is so difficult for people to be unbiased and rational when they express opinions about their mother tongue. In this chapter, all the same, we shall try to say something impartial on problems of usage about which many speakers of English feel quite strongly. For example, many people (especially older people who have gone through a traditional education in English grammar) feel quite strongly that we should not split our infinitives: for them, to separate *to* from the infinitive verb with which it belongs, as in *to flatly refuse,* is little short of a crime.

What can we say about such opinions? It is evident that, in actual practice, split infinitives are quite common. So one reaction is to shrug one's shoulders and to say there is no point in arguing about matters of taste: people who dislike split infinitives are like people who object to loud ties or who cannot stomach kippers. Another view is the one we took in 1.2: in discussing prescriptive grammar we treated received opinions as to 'good' and 'bad' usage as sociological norms, like rules of etiquette. In some situations (particularly more formal situations such as that of writing a letter of application) we shall want to be on our best linguistic behaviour, and this means steering clear of pitfalls such as the 'split infinitive', if only to avoid usages which will stigmatise us in the eyes of other people. Some precepts of 'good grammar' come to be regarded, in fact, almost as shibboleths, distinguishing the educated from the uneducated. Other precepts do have a basis of common sense, and merit serious discussion. But one thing is certain: people will not give up arguing about language usage, and it is as well to be aware of their attitudes. Knowledge of grammar can help us to describe and understand the basis of these attitudes.

11.2   Prescriptive 'rules'

First, here is a test. If you had to choose, which of the following alternatives would you use in a letter applying for a job?

(1a)   . . . the post I am applying *for.*
(1b)   . . . the post *for which* I am applying.
(2a)   *But* more recently I have been attending classes in German. . .
(2b)   More recently, *however,* I have been attending classes in German . . .
(3a)   I had to choose the *least* harmful of the two courses.
(3b)   I had to choose the *less* harmful of the two courses.
(4a)   I *will* be able to take up the appointment after 1st June.
(4b)   I *shall* be able to take up the appointment after 1st June.

If you want to improve your chances of creating a good impression, you will prefer the (b) sentence in each case, thereby obeying the following prescriptive 'rules':

1.   'Do not end a sentence or clause with a preposition.'
2.   'Do not begin a sentence with a coordinator such as *and* or *but.*'
3.   'When comparing two things, use a comparative construction; when comparing more than two things, use a superlative construction.'
4.   'After I or we as subject, use *shall* rather than *will* to express futurity.'

All these are typical prescriptive 'rules' in that they are assumed to work without exception. In practice, however, they are frequently broken by native speakers; this is why we enclose the word 'rule' in quotation marks. Moreover, if we try to apply them in every case, the result can be awkward and totally unEnglish. For example:

(a)   *For what is it?* is not an acceptable variant of *What is it for?*
(b)   *May the better man win* is abnormal and unidiomatic in comparison with *May the best man win.*

Such 'rules' may therefore have a problematic outcome, when, in an attempt to strenuously avoid a supposed offence, we fail to produce clear, idiomatic English. (As a case in point, notice that the split infinitive in the last sentence could not be happily replaced by *strenuously to avoid a supposed offence* or *to avoid a supposed offence strenuously*.) The safest course, in such out-of-the-frying-pan-into-the-fire cases, is to reword the sentence so that the possibility of breaking a prescriptive 'rule' does not arise: for example, *in a strenuous attempt to avoid. . .* would solve the problem above.

We shall not in general give solutions to problems of usage in this chapter, but we do offer one important piece of advice, which is a generalisation of the evasive tactic just illustrated:

> When you are faced with the dilemma of either disobeying a prescriptive 'rule' or awkwardly and conspicuously obeying it, reformulate the sentence so that the dilemma does not arise.

This may be called the PRINCIPLE OF GRAMMATICAL DISCRETION, because it avoids giving offence to one's addressees, whether their attitudes to usage are authoritarian or permissive. This principle applies chiefly to formal written English – the type of English in which prescriptive grammar tends to matter.

Prescriptive 'rules' like that of the split infinitive can reasonably be called superstitions: people have learned to obey them out of blind faith in authority, and find it difficult to explain *why* they obey them. When attempts are made, however, to justify such rules, these are among the reasons often given:

(a) The 'rule' helps one to communicate clearly, etc. **(a practical reason)**
(b) The 'rule' is in accordance with logic. **(an intellectual reason)**
(c) The 'rule' is in accordance with good taste. **(an aesthetic reason)**
(d) The 'rule' is in accordance with tradition. **(a historical reason)**

But such reasons rarely carry conviction on their own. If we search for the origin of such 'rules', we find that many of them began in attempts made, especially in the eighteenth century, to describe English grammar in terms of the categories of Latin grammar. The prestige of Latin was such that English constructions which differed from the Latin model were disparaged. In other cases, we find that the early grammarians, in their attempt to codify English and reduce it to rule, rationalised a situation which, in the language of their time, was variable and uncertain. So it was with the choice between *will* and *shall*. Nowadays, with the decline of traditional grammar teaching, these 'rules', if they exist in people's minds at all, are often no more than vaguely remembered folklore.

11.3   The priests of usage

One can always justify prescriptive rules, in the last resort, by appeal to authority. We are inclined to obey the *Highway Code,* for instance, because it is backed by the authority of law. But the strange thing about prescriptive 'rules' of English grammar is that they are not upheld by any official authority. (In this respect English differs from French; the *Académie Française*, even now, is regarded as the official arbiter of usage in France.) The tradition of the English-speaking world is to rely on the judgement of unofficial lawgivers, whose authority is derived simply from their reputations as scholars and writers. Among this 'priesthood' we should place many grammarians of the past; but its most famous members have been lexicographers, notably Samuel Johnson, the eighteenth-century author of the *Dictionary of the English Language*. In the present century, a somewhat similar position to that of Dr Johnson has been occupied by H. W. Fowler, author of *A Dictionary of Modern English Usage* (first published in 1926, and revised by Sir Ernest Gowers for a second edition in 1965). '*Fowler*' has become a household word, and the book is consulted for guidance not only on matters of word usage, but on matters of grammar as well. we might call Fowler the 'high priest of usage', but there are many other writers in the same fraternity: we might mention Eric Partridge, author of the popular *Usage and Abusage*.

Like his great predecessor, Johnson, Fowler is more noted for his wit and wisdom than for consistency and rationality. His attacks on some prescriptive 'rules' can be as spirited as his defence of others; in still other cases he gives up his priest's mantle and tells his readers to make up their own minds. Whether we agree with him or not, we cannot fail to find his criticisms of usage entertaining and instructive.

The great demand for books like '*Fowler*' testifies to the existence of problems of usage, and the need that users feel for guidance on these matters. How do such problems arise? In part, they seem to result from a misconception about standard English. People tend to expect that a standard language – as is generally true of spelling, but not of grammar – allows only one correct form, and that the standard can never change. So when faced with a choice between two ways of saying the same thing, they assume that one of them must be the correct one – or at least must be the preferable one. Prescriptive 'rules' help to satisfy this need for a decision procedure; but grammar is so subtle and complicated that the 'rules' do not always lead to acceptable solutions.

Hence usage problems arise: problems of when we should or should not follow the rule, or problems of which rule to follow. In the remainder of the chapter we shall discuss some examples of these problems.

11.4 The problem of personal pronouns

The main prescriptive 'rule' for subject and object pronouns runs as follows:

'RULE' A

(i) 'Use the subject pronouns *I, he, she, we, they, who* in the function of subject or complement': *I am tired; It was she who spoke first.*

(ii) 'Use the object pronouns *me, him, her, us, them, whom* in the function of object or prepositional complement': *Sarah saw them; His sister spoke to us.*

But (i) is frequently broken when the pronoun is a complement:

(5)   Who's there? It's only *me.*   (**not**: It's only *I*.)

And (ii) is frequently broken in the case of *who/whom:*

(6)   *Who* do you like best? *Who* were you speaking to?   (**rather than:** *Whom . . .*)

11.4.1   Pronouns with ellipsis

This is another difficulty. In constructions with ellipsis, prescriptive grammar argues that the correct form to use is the one which would be appropriate if omitted words were restored: that is (7a) and (8a) are correct, rather than (7b) and (8b):

(7a) Who sent this letter? *I.*	(8a) She is as tall as *he.*
(7b) Who sent this letter? *Me.*	(8b) She is as tall as *him.*
(7c) Who sent this letter? *I* did.	(8c) She is as tall as *he* is.

But (7a) and (8a) are obviously stilted and unidiomatic beside the 'incorrect' forms (7b) and (8b). According to our 'principle of discretion' (11.2), the best thing to do is to evade the problem by using a construction without ellipsis, as in (7c) and (8c).

11.4.2   Pronouns with coordination

The prescriptive 'rules' are quite often broken in coordinate phrases like *you and me, him and her:*

(9)　*You and me* must get together.
(10)　The decision will have to be made by *Christine and I.*
(11)　Susan has invited *John and I* to a party.

People who know the 'rules' find these quite blatant and excruciating violations. Such examples do, however, show the tangles and uncertainties in which native speakers find themselves over the case of pronouns. It seems that examples like (9) occur naturally and spontaneously in informal English, while examples like (10) and (11), where the subject pronoun replaces the object pronoun, arise from the user's mistaken assumption that *I* is more correct than *me*. This assumption is presumably made because of frequent correction of cases like (9). Such mistaken attempts to generalise a 'rule' are called HYPERCORRECTIONS.

11.4.3　Genitive and object pronouns
Not all pronoun problems arise over choice between subject and object pronouns. There is also the problem of choosing between the object and genitive ('possessive') forms in the subject position of NCling clauses:

(12a)　He objected to [*our* winning both prizes].
(12b)　He objected to [*us* winning both prizes].

Here prescriptive grammar favours the genitive of (12a). Fowler himself, voicing the usage priest's common conviction that grammatical standards are declining, is quite biting on the question: 'It is perhaps beyond hope for a generation that regards *upon you giving* as normal English to recover its hold upon the truth that grammar matters.' But once again there is an out-of-the-frying-pan effect when we attempt to generalise the genitive construction to nouns, and especially to complex noun phrases:

(13)　He objected to *members of the same school's* winning both prizes.
(14)　The crisis arose as a result of *recent uncontrolled inflation's* having outweighed the benefits of devaluation.

Both these sentences would improve if the *'s* were omitted.

11.4.4　Pronoun usage in formal and informal English
To conclude, there is a considerable gulf between formal and informal English in the choice of pronoun forms. While formal written English follows the traditional Latin-based rules, informal spoken English follows its own rules, which are simple enough in their own terms. According to these rules, the subject pronoun is used in the normal subject position, preceding all or part of the verb phrase, whereas the

object pronoun is used in other positions in the clause. This means that the object pronoun is the UNMARKED, neutral form in the pairs *I/me, she/her*, etc., even being used, for example, in unattached 'absolute' positions such as:

(15) How do you feel? *Me?* I feel fine.

But with *who/whom*, it is the subject form which is normal since the *wh*- pronoun normally precedes the predicator, behaving in this sense like a subject:

(16) *Who* were you talking to?
(17) I want to see you. *Who?* Me?

Difficulties of pronoun usage occur because of the conflict between these two sets of rules – the formal and the informal.

11.5 The problem of number concord

The prescriptive 'rule' of number concord is simply this:

'RULE' B

(i)   A singular predicator goes with a singular subject.
(ii)   A plural predicator goes with a plural subject.

This is nice and logical. But in a range of cases the 'rule' is commonly disobeyed:

(18) The Government *has/have* taken firm measures to protect the currency.

With nouns like *government, committee, family*, we find not only a singular verb following a singular subject, but a plural one following a singular subject. Such nouns are COLLECTIVE NOUNS: they refer to collections of people or things, and this is reflected in the choice of a plural predicator. In some cases the singular predicator cannot be sensibly used at all:

(19) In no time the audience *were* tapping *their* feet and clapping *their* hands.
(20) His family *are* always quarrelling among *themselves*.

(*The audience was tapping its feet and clapping its hands* and *His family is always quarrelling among itself* would be absurd.) Examples (19) and (20) show that there is also a problem of concord for pronouns; for example, in (20) *themselves* is exceptional in being a plural pronoun in agreement with a singular antecedent (*his family*).

It is useful, in fact, to distinguish GRAMMATICAL CONCORD – the strict rule 'singular goes with singular, and plural with plural' – from NOTIONAL CONCORD – the agreement of a pronoun or predicator with the idea of number present in the MEANING of the preceding noun phrase. Notional concord can explain not only examples like (18)–(20), but also some converse cases such as the biblical *The wages of sin is death*. Here, although *wages* is grammatically plural, the meaning it expresses ('reward') is arguably singular.

Pronouns such as *none, any, either, neither, everyone* form another set of cases in which notional concord often wins the battle against grammatical concord in ordinary speech:

(21) None of the parcels *has/have* yet arrived.
(22) His plays are popular in the West, but I doubt whether any *has/have* been performed in Japan.
(23) Everyone can vote as *they* wish.

As with the problems of grammatical case discussed in 11.4, such violations of prescriptive 'rule' are common enough in speech, but tend to be frowned on in writing.

11.6   The problem of the generic masculine

If we wished to alter (23) above in order to obey grammatical concord, we might choose between the following sentences:

(23a) Everyone can vote as *he* wishes.
(23b) Everyone can vote as *he* or *she* wishes.

Of these, (23b) is often felt to be awkward, whereas (23a) is an instance of the GENERIC MASCULINE, i.e. the use of the pronoun *he* to refer to either male or female persons. The generic masculine *he,* although traditional, is disliked by those who feel it perpetuates a masculine bias in the language. So by rejecting (23) in favour of (23a), we jump out of the frying pan of grammatical concord into the fire of feminism. The generic masculine is often used as a matter of convenience, but the principle of grammatical discretion (11.2) would lead us to avoid the possibility of giving offence in either case, by evading the problem of pronoun choice. The problem can be evaded, for example, by re-formulating the sentence in the plural:

(24) All citizens can vote as they wish.

As a matter of interest, we have tried to avoid the generic masculine throughout this book, so you may judge our success.

11.7   Problems of ellipsis

Many of the grammatical uncertainties which beset people in writing English have to do with ellipsis. Describing the rules of English in this area is not easy, and it is difficult to draw the line between prescriptive and descriptive grammar. Nevertheless, we may roughly enunciate a 'rule' as follows:

'RULE' C

A sentence with ellipsis is acceptable only if the same sentence is acceptable after the 'deleted' words are restored.

To this an explanatory rider should be added:

The words which are 'deleted' in ellipsis must duplicate words occurring elsewhere in the context.

Here is a simple illustration of this 'rule':

Version with ellipsis: (The place where ellipsis occurs is marked by ∧.)
The city can ∧, and always will, *be proud of its achievements.*

Version with 'deleted' elements restored:
The city can *be proud of its achievements,* and always will *be proud of its achievements.*

And here are two examples which violate the 'rule':

(25)   The city has ∧, and always will *be proud of its achievements.*
(26)   They are *revising* the book more thoroughly than it has ever been ∧.

The fault is clear when we try to insert the words in italics in the spaces marked ∧ in these examples. To make the resulting sentences grammatical, we should have to insert *been* instead of *be,* and *revised* instead of *revising.* Here is a parallel case involving ellipsis of a noun:

(27)   This car is one of the safest ∧, if not the safest *vehicle on the road.*

The rule requires the insertion of a singular noun *vehicle,* whereas the grammar of the sentence requires a plural one *vehicles.* This mismatch is enough to make the sentence strictly ungrammatical, though (oddly) the requirement is less strict if the elliptical phrase follows its sister construction:

(28)   This car is one of the safest *vehicles on the road,* if not the safest ∧.

The more complex a sentence is, the more liable it is to mismatches of ellipsis. It takes some time to work out what is wrong with this example:

(29) If only the litter laws were enforced, *the disgrace of our present rubbish-strewn high streets* would be eliminated overnight, and could even bring economies in the city's overstretched waste-disposal services.

The ellipsis of the subject of the second clause, after *and,* is only allowable if the second subject is meant to be identical to the first one (the phrase in italics). But it makes no sense to say *the disgrace of our present rubbish-strewn high streets could ... bring economies ...;* the intended meaning must surely be that *the enforcement of the litter laws could ... bring economies ...* This is the kind of lapse which Fowler describes as 'swapping horses' – where the writer loses track of how the sentence began, and completes it as if it had had a different beginning.

11.8   Dangling non-finite clauses

The mismatch of ellipsis most often condemned by traditional grammars and handbooks is the DANGLING PARTICIPLE (sometimes called the 'misrelated' or 'unattached participle'). In fact, what is said about the dangling participle can be extended to apply to adverbial non-finite clauses in general, whether they are Cling, Clen, or Cli clauses:

(30) [Leaning over the parapet,] a water rat caught my eye.
(31) [Lying under the table,] the secretary found a large pile of secret documents.
(32) The award went to the mountaineers who had rushed Mrs Weekes to hospital [after breaking her ribs].
(33) [Avoided by his friends and neglected by his public], Mill's faithful canary was alone the companion of his last hours.
(34) [To reach London in time,] she sent the parcel by air mail.

The 'rule' flouted in these sentences may be expressed in a loose but serviceable form as follows:

'RULE' D

An adverbial non-finite clause which has no overt subject is *understood* to have a subject identical to that of the main clause to which it belongs.

On this basis, (30) implies that the water rat was leaning over the parapet, (31) that the secretary was lying under the table, and (32) that the mountaineers broke Mrs Weekes's ribs – implications which would clearly not be intended by the writers of these sentences.

The *-ing* clauses of (30)-(32) may be described as MISATTACHED, in the sense that they are interpretable according to the rule, but the interpretation is the wrong one. The *-ing* clause of (35) illustrates, rather, the UNATTACHED non-finite clause:

(35) Walking up the hill, the view was beautilful.

There is no sensible way of interpreting this according to the 'rule'. In practice, we do interpret it, by 'stretching' the rule so that the understood subject of the infinitive is the implied AGENT or 'doer' of the action (seeing) described in the main clause. In scientific writing passive sentences which are interpreted in this way do not seem particularly objectionable:

(36) Using this new technique, more accurate results have been obtained.

There are also cases like (37) and (38), where the dangling clause is idiomatically accepted as a sentence adverbial, and where its subject is identified not with the subject of the main clause, but with the speaker of the whole sentence:

(37) *To cut a long story short,* they got married.
(38) *Considering how much it costs,* this machine is a failure.

Few people would object to this kind of unattached clause. Once more we find that problems of usage are not so simple as they appear. In the case of the 'dangling' non-finite clause, there seem to be different degrees of unacceptability, and some apparent infringements of the 'rule' seem quite normal.

11.9   Conclusion

We have continually enclosed the word 'rule' in quotation marks, as a reminder that these precepts of prescriptive grammar are not binding on either the speaker or the writer of English. None the less, there are three good reasons why it is best to keep these 'rules' in formal writing, unless there is good reason to the contrary. In breaking a 'rule', you may:

(a)   Offend against principles of good style, as discussed in Chapter 12. (For example, dangling participles can cause ambiguity.)
(b)   Produce an inappropriate usage. (For example, *Who did they see?* is inappropriate in formal written English, but not in colloquial English.)
(c)   Offend in the sense of breaking a rule of etiquette which some readers regard as important. (For example, splitting an infinitive

may be objectionable to some rather as putting one's elbows on the table or eating peas with the underside of one's fork may be objectionable.)

It is best, then, to keep to these 'rules' unless there are bad consequences of obeying them which outweigh the good consequences. In such a case, the principle of grammatical discretion (11.2) comes to the rescue once more.

Exercises

Exercise 11a   (answers on p. 212)
The following is a list of sentences which some speakers of English would condemn as being contrary to some 'rule' of prescriptive grammar. In each case, say whether the 'rule' concerns (A) pronouns forms, (B) number concord, (C) ellipsis, (D) 'dangling' non-finite clauses, or (E) some other topic. If criticised for using such a sentence in formal writing, how would you either (i) justify the sentence as it stands, or (ii) change the sentence so as to avoid the criticism?

1. It was argued that the President, in common with many other Western politicians, were dancing to the tune of OPEC.
2. Mervyn John's record is now as good, if not better than his countryman Michael Steed.
3. The risk of infection can be avoided by bathing the cut in antiseptic.
4. What worried her parents most was him being a racing driver.
5. Twenty per cent could be knocked off the fuel consumption and yet be able to keep the price at its present level.
6. Have each of you opened your parcels?
7. I believe it would be wrong to even think of it.
8. Are you sure it was them? It might have been us.
9. Margaret and he will be playing against you and I.
10. Neither the publisher nor the author know about the printer's blunder.
11. While they were talking, us girls were listening at the keyhole.
12. This error has given rise to the nation's distrust of multinational corporations and of its determination to stand on its own feet.
13. The press published a story about some Congressman from the Midwest taking bribes from farmers.
14. When removed from their normal habitat, it is advisable to treat these animals with great care.
15. The lights have to be extinguished on vacating these premises.
16. These sort of radios are very reliable.

17. Flying through the air at the speed of sound, a sudden thought struck me.
18. Which team has the best record, yours or theirs?
19. We will not object to your postponing the meeting.
20. She absolutely denies that any of her supporters have been disloyal.

Exercise 11b

This is a more difficult exercise, the purpose of which is to stimulate discussion rather than to produce solutions. There are more types of problem involving ellipsis than were illustrated in 11.7. The following sentences are felt to be unsatisfactory in one way or another. They do not, however, violate 'Rule' C as it stands.

(i) Divide the sentences below into three or more different types, according to the types of elliptical construction they illustrate.
(ii) Try to describe what might be thought unsatisfactory about each type.
(iii) Try to revise the conditions of 'Rule' C so that the 'rule' does not allow sentences of these kinds.
(iv) Revise each sentence so as to avoid the difficulty.

[A CLUE: note that all the sentences contain coordination. TIPS: (a) Insert the caret (∧) where ellipsis occurs; (b) place in angle brackets the elements which are yoked together by coordination.]

1. They captured and put him in prison.
2. She was young, attractive, and enjoyed life to the full.
3. Either the children did not know what had happened, or were trying to protect their parents.
4. The spy was in his forties, of average build, and obviously wore a wig.
5. By giving the police a pay rise, the Minister hopes to increase and make the force more efficient.
6. Had the queen lived five years longer or had given birth to an heir, the subsequent history of Ruritania would have been very different.
7. You have to weigh, count and pack the parcels in large containers.
8. Not only did she arrive late, but woke up the entire household.
9. They receive and distribute food and clothing to the homeless.
10. I am fond both of dogs and cats.

12

Grammar and composition

12.1 Grammar and Writing

How can knowledge of grammar be used to improve our style of written English? If we know something about grammar, we can criticise and discuss our own writing, and learn to improve it. Here are four maxims of good writing which we shall illustrate and enlarge upon in this last chapter:[1]

1. Make your language easy to follow.
2. Be clear.
3. Be economical.
4. Be effective.

Practical principles such as these cannot always be fulfilled at the same time. Sometimes they compete with one another. One example of this occurs whenever we open our mouths to speak: we have to speak loud enough and slowly enough to be understood ('Be clear'), but we also have to try not to waste effort by speaking too slowly for the purpose ('Be economical'). So to hit the right level of delivery, we have to weigh up the competing demands of principles 2 and 3.

Such principles are, in a way, precepts of good behaviour in the use of language. They apply to both spoken and written language; but there is less excuse for ignoring them in writing, where we have the leisure to revise and redraft, and where the addressee does not have the chance to reply and seek clarification. People understandably tend to be more critical of style in writing than in speech – which is one reason why we concentrate in this chapter on style in written composition.

12.2 'Make your language easy to follow'

Time tyrannises over the way we compose and understand messages. We

---

[1] The significance of these principles in language generally is discussed in Dan I. Slobin, *Language Change in Childhood and in History* (1975).

cannot say all that we have to say at one moment, in one fell swoop: we have to choose in which order to express things. Often grammatical choices are choices which affect order. This is notably true of choices discussed in 7.7: 'transformational' choices such as that between an active and a passive construction – for example, between *Columbus discovered America* and *America was discovered by Columbus*.

Our first principle, 'Make your language easy to follow', is designed to help the reader make sense of a text in linear form. It has three aspects, SENTENCE LENGTH, SUBORDINATION, and ORDERING.

12.2.1   Sentence length

For the reader's sake, a text should be suitably segmented into units, so that it can be understood bit by bit. In grammar, the largest unit is the sentence, and it is important to avoid sentences which are too long or too short. It would of course be wrong to prescribe an 'ideal sentence length' for all purposes, but recent studies indicate that the average sentence in written English is about eighteen words long.

In general, the longer a sentence is, the more complex it is (see pp. 137–8 for a more general discussion of complexity). Also, the more complex it is, the greater the burden it places on our attention and memory. On the other hand, if we go to the other extreme, repeatedly making use of simple sentences, the result can be monotonous, lacking in light and shade. As is the case with so many things, a happy medium is often the best course. Consider:

(1)   John Keats was fascinated by the art and literature of the ancient world. Just before his twenty-first birthday, he read George Chapman's translation of Homer. He wrote a famous sonnet on the subject. The next year, he visited the Elgin Marbles. The painter Benjamin Haydon accompanied him. This developed his enthusiasm still further. He wrote another notable sonnet after the visit. But his Greece was essentially a Greece of the imagination. It was the Greece of John Lemprière's *Classical Dictionary*. This he had read when young. He never visited Greece.

Although its meaning is clear and easy to follow, this passage suffers from the flatness of a 'short-breathed' style, with brief, one-clause sentences. On the other hand, we have:

(2)   Although John Keats had been fascinated by the art and literature of the ancient world ever since he read George Chapman's translation of Homer (which produced a famous sonnet on the subject) just before his twenty-first birthday in October 1816, and had that enthusiasm further developed by his visit to the Elgin Marbles with the painter Benjamin Haydon the following year (which also

produced a notable sonnet), his Greece was essentially a Greece
of the imagination, inspired by his early reading of John Lemprière's
Classical Dictionary: he never visited Greece.

This passage is a much more difficult reading experience than the preceding one: crammed into one sentence is all the content of the eleven
sentences of (1). But (2) has an advantage over (1) in that it indicates,
through subordination and other grammatical relations, the relations of
meaning between the different clauses. We see all the different ideas fitting into a single 'complex thought', with clear indications of how one
idea is linked to another, how one idea is subsidiary to another, etc. Now
here is a compromise between the two styles:

(3)   Although John Keats was fascinated by the art and literature of
        the ancient world, he never visited Greece. His Greece was essen-
        tially a Greece of the imagination, inspired by his early reading of
        John Lemprière's *Classical Dictionary*. Just before his twenty-first
        birthday, he read George Chapman's translation of Homer, an
        experience which inspired one of his most famous sonnets. His
        enthusiasm was further developed, in the following year, by a visit
        to the Elgin Marbles with the painter Benjamin Haydon.

Although there are occasions when we shall want to use simple sentences,
as in (1), or complex sentences, as in (2), the most generally serviceable
style will be one which, like (3), avoids the disadvantages of both.

12.2.2   Subordination
It helps the reader if we not only segment our message into units of
suitable size, but also indicate the relative importance of ideas within
those units. As (2) and (3) have already shown, subordinate clauses are
one way of making one idea less salient than another. Putting an idea in
a main clause is like shining a spotlight on it; and putting it in a subordinate clause, by the same simile, is like a placing it in the shadow:

(4)   [[Although Keats spent the last months of his life in Rome], he
        never visited his beloved Greece].
(5)   [[Although he never visited his beloved Greece], Keats spent the
        last months of his life in Rome].

The contrast between (4), which spotlights the point about Greece, and
(5), which spotlights that about Rome, is easy to notice. Often subordinate clauses state ideas which are well known, or have been mentioned
before. This 'backgrounding' effect is still felt if the subordinate clause
is placed in a final position. Compare (4) and (6):

(6)   [Keats never visited his beloved Greece, [although he spent the
        last months of his life in Rome]].

Still further backgrounding results from placing an idea in a non-finite clause or in a phrase. Compare:

(7) After he had visited the British Museum, Keats wrote his famous *Ode on a Grecian Urn.* **(finite clause)**
(8) After visiting the British Museum, Keats wrote his famous *Ode on a Grecian Urn.* **(non-finite clause)**
(9) After a visit to the British Museum, Keats wrote his *Ode on a Grecian Urn.* **(phrase)**

Coordination, on the other hand, gives equal importance to the clauses it links. We can contrast both (4) and (5) with:

(10) Keats spent the last months of his life in Rome, but never visited his beloved Greece.
(11) Keats never visited his beloved Greece, nor did he visit Rome until the last months of his life.

So there is a scale of 'backgrounding' roughly as shown in Figure 12.1. This scale is only an approximate indicator of importance; we should add that there are exceptions to it – for example, a noun clause in final position is often the most important part of a sentence to which it belongs: *Everyone thought* [*that I had made a mistake*].

Figure 12.1

Coordinate clause	Finite subordinate clause	Non-finite subordinate clause	Phrase

No backgrounding ————————————————————▶ Most backgrounding

12.2.3 Ordering: end-focus and end-weight

In fact, ordering itself is a way of indicating the relative importance of two parts of a sentence. We can see this by reversing the order of the two clauses connected by *but*:

(12) John Keats was fascinated by the art and literature of the ancient world, but he never visited Greece.
(13) John Keats never visited Greece, but he was fascinated by the art and literature of the ancient world.

Although grammatically the two clauses are of the same status, in any construction *X but Y*, the main focus of attention seems to fall on *Y*.

The final position is the most important in terms of information. Similarly, the main focus is often carried by a final subordinate clause. Compare in this respect (8) with (14):

(8)   After visiting the British Museum, Keats wrote his famous *Ode on a Grecian Urn*.

(14)   Keats wrote his famous *Ode on a Grecian Urn* after visiting the British Museum.

The emphasis typically carried by final position is best explained in terms of INFORMATION: as we read through a sequence of sentences in a text, we progressively add ideas to the store of information with which we started. This means that sentences we encounter in a text usually contain a mixture of GIVEN information (information we have met before) and NEW information (information we have not met before). In this sense, a written text is like a journey, on which the reader is continually moving from familiar to less familiar territory. In general, the reader is helped if given information is placed before, rather than after, new information. This maxim, which may be called the maxim of END-FOCUS, applies not only to the ordering of clauses, but also to the ordering of clause elements. Which of the following is the easier to make sense of?

(15)   Instead of quinine, penicillin was given to the patient, who began to get better almost immediately. Within a week, she had completely recovered.

(16)   Instead of quinine, the patient was given penicillin, and began to get better almost immediately. Within a week, she had recovered completely.

The answer should be: (16) is easier to understand than (15). There are two reasons for this: (1) *penicillin* (by its contrast with *quinine*) conveys the most important new information in the first clause, and should therefore follow the word *patient*, which is given information within this context; (ii) *recovered completely* is a better ordering than *completely recovered*, because 'recovery' has already been mentioned, and it is the adverb *completely* which brings new information at this point.

As writers, then, we have to keep an eye on two kinds of emphasis: there is the 'spotlight' effect of main clauses, and the 'focusing' effect of final position. These two visual metaphors are compatible with one another, and enable us to treat the two kinds of emphasis, the structural and the sequential kinds, independently. For example:

(17)   The patient was given penicillin, and began to recover immediately.

(18)   The patient, who was given penicillin, began to recover immediately.

These two sentences differ not in terms of the order of the two main ideas, but in treating one as coordinate (in (17)) or as subordinate (in (18)) to the other. Although they are similar in one respect, they are different in another.

There is a third kind of emphasis. It is sometimes said that the first position in a clause or sentence is more important than the final position. While this is certainly not true with regard to information focus, an initial element does have its own kind of emphasis, because it is an element which attracts the reader's attention, and which sets the scene for what follows. This is particularly clear when the initial element is a fronted object, complement, or adverbial (see 7.2):

(19) *Many of these questions* a computer can answer easily.   [*O S P A*]
(20) *Even more interesting* was their reaction to the Cuban crisis of 1962.   [*C P S*]

An initial adverbial typically has a scene-setting role for what follows:

(21) *On his 25th birthday* Keats landed at Naples on his way to Rome.

Notice that in these cases the first part of the sentence does not contain much in the way of new information – in fact, it tends to rely on what is already known. But its importance is rather that of providing a 'handle' by which to grasp what follows.

To the maxim of end-focus we may add a related maxim of END-WEIGHT:

> Place a 'heavy' constituent after a 'light' one, rather than a 'light' one after a 'heavy' one.

This maxim has to do with the weight, or complexity, of an element, rather than the amount of information conveyed; but the two measures of importance are interconnected. Naturally enough, a complex constituent (in practice, one that contains a large number of words) tends to contain more information than a simple one. Compare:

(22) The art and literature of the ancient world fascinated Keats.
(23) Keats was fascinated by the art and literature of the ancient world.

Sentence (23) is a 'happier' sentence than (22), because the complex noun phrase *the art and literature of the ancient world* is placed at the end. Often it is a good idea to use a passive construction, as in (23), in order to put the 'weight' of the sentence in final position. A marked preference for the end-weight principle can be seen in sentences like:

(24) [(I) (admire) (greatly) (the courage of the men who dared to carry out that raid)].   [*S P A O*]

(25) [(He) (has proved) (wrong) (the predictions of the country's lead-
      ing economic experts)]. [*S P C O*]

Here end-weight is so overriding that it causes the writer to rearrange
the elements out of their normal order [*S P O A*], [*S P O C*]. It is in the
light of the principles of end-focus and end-weight that we appreciate
the usefulness of having, in English, a number of transformations (see
7.7) which allow elements to be moved out of their normal position in
the clause.

12.3   'Be clear'

The principle of clarity is one of the obvious imperatives of written style.
From the negative point of view, it means avoiding ambiguities (such as
those grammatical ambiguities we noted on pp. 13, 19, and 111-12)
and also avoiding obscurity of expression which results not so much in
outright ambiguity, as in muddles and delays of interpretation. The
following illustrate temporary, 'garden-path' ambiguities – they lead the
reader up the garden path, encouraging an analysis which as the sentence
proceeds turns out to be wrong:

(26) The recruits *marched down the road* failed to return.
(27) Though Bert kept on watching *the film* frightened him.
(28) The woman shrieked at John *and his brother* started to cry.

In these examples, the constituent which is likely to mislead is in italics.
In (26) the 'garden path' is the analysis of *marched down the road* as
part of the main clause, instead of as a relative clause (= 'who were
marched. . .'); in (27) it is the analysis of *the film* as object of *watching*
rather than as subject of *frightened*; and in (28) it is the analysis of *and
his brother* as part of a prepositional phrase *at John and his brother*,
rather than as the beginning of a new clause. In each case, there is an
obvious remedy for the muddle: before the offending words, we can
insert in (26) the words *who were*, and in (27) and (28) commas.
    Another kind of delay of interpretation can occur in sentences with
SPLIT phrases (see 7.7.6):

(29) *The goods* have still not been delivered *which were ordered last
      month*.

The parts of (29) in italics constitute a single noun phrase. But what is
the point of separating them? There are occasions when the demands of
end-focus or end-weight strongly argue for discontinuity:

(30) *The time* has come *for all good men to come to the aid of the party*.

But there is no such pressing argument in (29), and in such cases the discontinuity simply adds to difficulties of comprehension, by splitting elements which belong together in meaning.

Notice that the reason for preferring (30) to (29) is a negative one: in (30) we need to sacrifice the principle of clarity for the principle of end-weight, whereas there is no such cogent reason in the case of (29). In other words, (30a) is markedly awkward in comparison with (29a), and so needs to be reformulated:

(29a)   *The goods which were ordered last month* have still not been delivered.
(30a)   *The time for all good men to come to the aid of the party* has come.

In a similar way, the principle of clarity is often at odds with the principle of economy, as we shall see in a moment.

12.4   'Be economical'

In grammar, the principle of economy can be paraphrased 'Do not waste energy.' Avoiding unnecessary words is good because it means less work for the writer and for the reader. This underlies the common objection to REDUNDANT words and structures which could be omitted without loss of meaning from the sentence:

(31)   As a rule, the negotiators *generally* manage to reach a *satisfactory* compromise which satisfies both parties.

Furthermore, a saving occurs whenever we avoid repetition, or avoid using words whose meaning could easily be inferred. The general phenomenon of grammar whereby we save words and hence simplify structures may be called REDUCTION. We have already met two kinds of reduction:

(a)   The use of PRO-FORMS: personal pronouns (*he, she, it, they*, etc.) and other substitute words, such as (sometimes) *do, so, such, that*.
(b)   The use of ELLIPSIS, i.e. the omission of words which are predictable in that they merely repeat what is said in the nearby context.

Both pro-forms and ellipsis are means of avoiding repetition:

(32)   *My brother enjoys* squash more than *my brother enjoys* tennis. (REPETITION)
(33)   My brother enjoys squash more than *he does* tennis. (PRO-FORMS)
(34)   My brother enjoys squash more than ∧ tennis.   (ELLIPSIS)

As well as reducing length and complexity, pro-forms and ellipsis help to connect one part of a sentence or text to another. Thus *he* in (33) refers back to *my brother*, which is called the ANTECEDENT of the pronoun. The maxim we should follow, in accordance with economy, is 'Reduce as much as possible.' This means, all other things being equal, 'Prefer ellipsis to pro-forms' (as in (34)), and 'Prefer pro-forms to repetition' (as in (33)). However, not all these alternatives need be available. For example, we can say:

(35) *The intruders must have* smashed the glass and *the intruders must have* broken in.   (**repetition**)
(36) The intruders must have smashed the glass and *they must have* broken in.   (**pro-form + repetition**)
(37) The intruders must have smashed the glass and broken in.   (**ellipsis**)

But the use of the pronoun in (36), for example, requires repetition of *must have* also; there is no English sentence combining a pronoun with ellipsis, such as **The intruders must have smashed the glass and they broken in.*

12.5 'Be clear but concise': clarity versus economy

Saving words can often lead to an unsuspected loss of meaning. So we should not reduce where economy conflicts with clarity. In (38), omitting the conjunction *that* after *proved* results in a 'garden-path' sentence. In (39), ellipsis leads to unclarity of constituent structure:

(38) Molesworth proved the theorem Blenkinsop had assumed to be true was false.
(39) They have been achieving their export targets and ∧ increasing home sales every year.

Does *every year* apply to the increase of home sales alone, or does it also apply to the achievement of export targets? The latter meaning is here more likely, so if we intended to convey the first meaning we should have to restore the omitted elements of the second clause, adding a comma for extra clarity:

(40) They have been achieving their export targets, and *they have been* increasing home sales every year.

Similarly, unclarity results when an ellipsis is too distant from its antecedent structure:

(41) A number of problems *will soon have been* solved, and the methods for ensuring more efficient legislative procedures in the coming session ∧ clarified.

But the most obvious types of ambiguity and obscurity are those arising from the use of pronouns:

(42)   The forwards shot hard and often but never straight till at last Hill decided to try his head. *It* came off first time.

Humorous examples like this point out the danger (increased here by the ambiguity of *came off*) of placing a pronoun too near to a 'false antecedent'. Normally the antecedent of a pronoun will be a preceding noun phrase which is either the nearest candidate, or the nearest candidate in a parallel function:

(43)   *Joan* told *her sister* that *she* would have to leave home.

The nearest potential antecedent in (43) is *her sister*, but *Joan* is also a candidate, because the function of *Joan* (subject) is parallel to that of *she*.
    Apart from this type of ambiguity, there is the opposite danger of using a pronoun where there is no antecedent at all, or where the antecedent is too distant to be recognised:

(44)   In the Elizabethan age, Roman Catholics were often under suspicion of treason, and *her* cousin Mary Queen of Scots was the chief *one*.

(Here, unless clarified by a previous sentence, the antecedents of *her* and *one* are not clear.) Yet another type of unclarity results from the repeated use of the same pronoun with a different antecedent:

(45)   When the *headmistress* visited *Pam's* home to talk to *her mother*, *she* was afraid that *she* would tell *her* about *her* misconduct.

Having stressed these pitfalls, however, we should add that common sense frequently resolves a theoretical ambiguity. There would be little chance of interpreting (45), for example, as meaning that Pam would tell her mother about the headmistress's misconduct. The unclarity in such cases lies more in the possibility of a temporary tangle which will be resolved only by re-reading. So to the maxim 'Reduce as far as possible', we must always add the rider 'unless unclarity results'.

12.6   'Be effective'

The three principles so far illustrated have to do with efficient rather than with effective communication. But to communicate effectively is to make good use not merely of the referential function of languages, but of all the functions of language (see p. 150). This brings us back to the subject of literary style, and reminds us that the artistic sense of style can be found in quite ordinary texts: there is no gulf fixed between creative writing and practical writing. So, for example, the maxim

'Reduce as far as possible' can be overruled for the sake of EXPRESSIVE REPETITION:

(46) *John Brown* was guilty of the crime, so *John Brown* would have to pay for it.

The repetition of *John Brown* here is not required for clarity, but suggests an emphasis ('that man and that man alone') which would be lost by reduction. More negatively, 'ELEGANT VARIATION' (avoiding monotony) can be a reason for avoiding both repetition and reduction:

(47) That *fight* between Ali and Liston was the most sensational heavy-weight *contest* since the Dempsey–Tunney *match* of 1926.

Variation for the sake of variation is generally treated as a vice of style; Fowler went so far as to say: 'There are few literary faults so widely prevalent, and this book will not have been written in vain if the present article should heal any sufferer of his infirmity' (Fowler, *Modern English Usage*, 1965). This view has strength if it reminds us that proper names and technical terms cannot usually be varied without artificiality, and are likely to recur in descriptive or explanatory writing. But elsewhere, variation can be a virtue which avoids both the tedium of over-repetition and the contrivance of pointless switching from one synonym to another, as in (47). Consider the italicised words in the following paragraph:

(48) The ancient civilization of India grew up in a sharply demarcated sub-continent bounded on the north by the world's largest *mountain range* – the *chain* of the Himalayas, which, with its extension to east and west, divides India from the rest of Asia and the world. The *barrier*, however, was at no time an insuperable one, and at all periods both settlers and traders have found their way over the high and desolate passes into India, while Indians have carried their commerce and culture beyond her *frontiers* by the same route. India's isolation has never been complete, and the effect of the *mountain wall* in developing her unique civilization has often been overrated.

(A. L. Basham, *The Wonder that was India*, p. 1)

Variation here is not so much a negative practice of avoiding repetition, as a positive search for different words which may appropriately high-light different aspects of the same thing. More generally, we may argue that linguistic variation of all kinds is to be welcomed in writing, so long as it is consistent with other goals. This includes variation of grammatical structure, such as:

(a)   Variation in length or complexity of sentences.
(b)   Variation in position and type of subordination.

(c) Variation between subordination and coordination.
(d) Variation in type and position of adverbials.
(e) Variation in type and position of modifiers.

If we keep an eye open for the opportunities of variation, we shall
make the most of the expressive range of the language and avoid the
temptation to fall back on stereotyped formulas and clichés. To be aware
of the manifold possibilities of English grammar, as outlined in Part B
of this book, is to become aware of how the use of those possibilities
can be varied, for varied effect, in our own writing.

Exercises

Exercise 12a   (answers on p. 213)
In view of the principles of style discussed in this chapter, all the following sentences may be regarded as less than successful. What is the
stylistic weakness of each example, and how would you avoid it? (It will
be useful to refer to the three principles examined in 12.2-12.5: a. 'Make
your language easy to follow'; b. 'Be clear'; c. 'Be economical'.)

1. Mr and Mrs Smith bought a collar for their dog with studs all over
    it.
2. Once the war started, the powers that were needed human cannon
    fodder.
3. The pipe was leaking so badly that it ran all over the kitchen.
4. She argues in her latest book Iris Murdoch has produced a master-
    piece.
5. In the long run, we shall one day eventually win the battle against
    poverty.
6. They have given their plans for improving the sports facilities up.
7. No one will ever know how Dickens meant *Edwin Drood*, the novel
    on which he was working when he died, to end.
8. The detective swore that he had seen the accused when he was
    checking in, which was evidence of his presence in the hotel.
9. The Inland Revenue no longer allows you to give tax-free presents
    to your children of any size you like.
10. The desultory conversation in the drawing room among guests who
    had regarded Miss Manning's superb performance of *Ave Verum*
    as a mere interruption revived.

Exercise 12b   (answers on p. 214)
Ambiguities, including those of the temporary, 'garden-path' variety,
can often be eliminated by the insertion of commas or other stops. In
other cases, they can be eliminated by changes in the grammar of the

sentence: e.g. deletions, transformations, re-orderings. How would you insert punctuation or otherwise clarify the structure and meaning of the sentences in the following cases? Provide (i) an improved version of each sentence, (ii) an informal description of each ambiguity, and (iii) a description of the change you have made.

1. Before we started eating the table was absolutely loaded with delicacies.
2. It is best to reduce your overheads and work, as far as possible, alone.
3. As we soon discovered the ambassador was not interested in discussing armaments.
4. I fed the dog and Harry the budgerigar.
5. Inside the house looks almost as it did when Darwin died.
6. Her parents Lord and Lady Boothroyd refused to meet.
7. The party was attended by the Melchetts, some cousins of ours, and William, of course, arrived late.
8. Middlesex having already won the Schweppes Championship, looks like winning the Gillette Cup as well.

To conclude the exercises in this book, the following two supplementary exercises are designed to provide more wide-ranging material, for practice and discussion of written composition.

Supplementary exercise 12c

The following passage consists of short, repetitive sentences, which as they stand do not hold together as a reasonable piece of English prose. Make what grammatical and lexical changes you wish – including re-ordering by changing active into passive, etc., combining sentences by subordination or coordination, deletion, substitution of pronouns, etc. – to make these sentences into three coherent paragraphs of an article or essay on Brook Farm. You may also add sentence adverbials. Be prepared to justify your changes, in terms of the principles outlined in this chapter.

Utopian communal experiments flourished in nineteenth-century America. The idealism and freedom of a young country inspired utopian communal experiments. Religious sects founded some utopian communal experiments. Other utopian communal experiments promoted radical sexual and marital arrangements. Few utopian communal experiments endured for more than a year or two. Brook Farm was in Massachusetts. Brook Farm was one of the more notable utopian communal experiments.

Brook Farm was one of the nobler failures of American social history. Brook Farm was begun by George Ripley and a small band of eminent followers. The followers were teachers and preachers, musicologists and writers. The writers included the celebrated

novelist, Nathaniel Hawthorne. The founders included high-minded
ladies and two experienced farmers.

Hawthorne signed his early letters from Brook Farm as
'Nathaniel Hawthorne, Ploughman'. Hawthorne was soon disabused
about the glamour of farm work. Milking the cows seemed a
comic occupation for a literary man. Hawthorne could joke about
it in his letters to his family and to his fiancée. Mowing hay in the
sweltering heat or shovelling in the manure pile proved to be ex-
hausting work. At the end of the day, Hawthorne felt little incli-
nation for writing stories. The always precarious financial situation
of the community discouraged Hawthorne. Hawthorne left after
seven months. Hawthorne chose not to remain through a long
winter.

(excerpts freely adapted from James R. Mellow, 'Brook Farm: an
American Utopia', *Dialogue*, 13.1, 1980 pp. 44–52)

Supplementary exercise 12d

The following are two passages for comment. The first is an extract
from a story by a 12-year-old girl. The second is a letter written to
a newspaper. Discuss each passage critically from the point of view of
usage (Chapter 11) and from the point of view of good style (Chapter
12). If you were the author, and were asked to make revisions, what
grammatical changes would you make to each passage?

1. As I was coming home one evening on the bus from school there
    in front were two children. One was shabby and thin looking
    and the other tubby and medium looking.

    These children were talking about a circus which had come
    to town which they had been to. The shabby girl's name was
    Sheila and she thought it was very funny. She liked the little
    short clowns and the giraffe-necked ladies and thought it was
    wonderful how all the animals were trained, especially the sea-
    lions, and thought how lovely they looked balancing the balls
    and for the first time in a circus she had seen giraffes taking part.

    But Anna, the posh, fancy, high-school looking girl had dif-
    ferent ideas. She thought it was cruel to keep lions and eleph-
    ants, polar-bears, grizzly-bears, sea-lions, seals, giraffes and all
    the other kinds of animals that used to roam on their own round
    ice-bergs in the sea and the jungle in a cage.

    (quoted in James Britton, *Language and Learning*, Penguin,
    1970, p. 252)

2. The major problem of socialism (and I am beginning to think
    it is insoluble) is to advocate liberal socialism in a capitalist
    society which has produced in the working class a form of ac-
    quisitiveness which uses capitalist blackmail in a way that could

destroy capitalism without replacing it by a society where mankind could collectively control those of its members who have
inordinate acquisitive instinct (and most people are not grossly
greedy) without wholly suppressing man's normal self-interest,
as has already been done in many large institutions.

(from a letter to a newspaper)

Answers to exercises

Exercise 1a

1. False. We can learn about grammar by studying Latin, but also by studying any other language.
2. True. (See 1.1.)
3. True. (See 1.1.)
4. False. Spelling has to do with the written representation of the sounds of a language, rather than with how whole words are put together to form sentences.
5. False. (See 1.1.)
6. False. Children learn how to speak without formal tuition, by listening to the speech they hear around them. (See 1.1.)
7. False. This would be a prescriptive approach. Studying grammar in fact involves describing how people DO speak.
8. False. Notions of incorrectness are irrelevant to descriptive grammar. (See 1.2.)
9. False. American English is simply DIFFERENT from British English, and identifies its user as American. For example, the verb form *gotten* is used in American English, but not in British (where *got* is used instead). (See 1.3.1.)
10. True. Language varies according to the characteristics of the user. (See 1.3.2.)
11. False. (See 1.3.3.)
12. False. (See 1.3.2.)
13. True. (See 1.3.2., under 'Social-class membership'.)
14. False, at least in the context of grammar. (See 1.3.3.)
15. False. Speech and writing are equivalent in some ways, but not in others. (See 1.3.3 and Chapter 8.)
16. True. Doctors have specialised terms, barely comprehensible to patients, which they use when talking to one another.
17. False. (See 1.4.2.)
18. False. (See 1.5.)
19. False. (See 1.6.)
20. False. (See 1.7.)

Exercise 1b

1. **C.** Ambiguous as to who has the confidence.

2. **B.** Prescriptive grammar dictates that multiple negatives should be avoided. However, many non-standard dialects allow them, and it is estimated that they are used by 80-90 per cent of speakers in Britain.

3. **C.** Ambiguous as to whether there should be more schools, or whether they should be more comprehensive.

4. **A.** Parts of the verbs are used ungrammatically.

5. **A.** This is actually a line from Hopkins's poem *God's Grandeur*, and so illustrates 'poetic licence'.

6. **A.** This is actually a sentence produced by a foreign learner of English.

7. **C.** The sentence is too long and complex to process easily.

8. **B.** Prescriptive grammar would insist on subject pronouns *He* and *I*.

9. **C.** Ambiguous as to who has laid the eggs.

10. **C.** Difficult to understand. This sentence demonstrates that following a rule of prescriptive grammar (i.e. not to end a sentence with a preposition) can actually lead to ineffective communication. (A wry marginal comment which Winston Churchill wrote on an official document.)

Exercise 1c
1. Formal; written; journalism.
2. Formal; written; religion.
3. Informal; written; advertising.
4. Informal; spoken; advertising.
5. Informal; spoken; journalism.

(SOURCES: 1. *The Guardian*, 25 July 1980; 2. *The Book of Common Prayer;* 3. a British Rail advertisement in *Radio Times;* 4. a television advertisement; 5. BBC Radio One *Newsbeat*, 25 July 1980.)

Exercise 2b
1. See Figure A.1.

2. See Figure A.2.

(a) The abbreviated tree diagrams would leave out the labels Wo and Se (or Cl).

(b) The unlabelled tree diagrams would leave out all the labels.

3. [(Tawny owls) (were hooting) (loudly) (in the wood)].

4. [(The critics) (have slated) (his plays) (without mercy)].

Exercise 2d
1. Cl[AvP($_{Av}$Typically), NP($_N$Aunt $_N$Belinda) VP($_V$had $_V$been $_V$uttering) NP($_N$platitudes) NP($_d$all $_N$evening)].

2. See Figure A.3.

Figure A.1

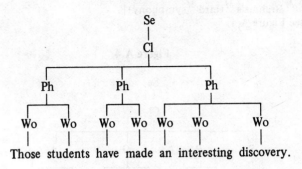

Figure A.2

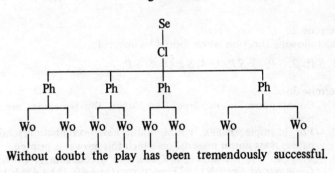

Figure A.3

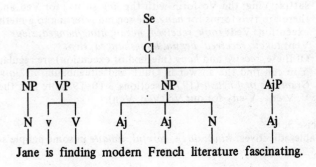

3. Cl[^{A}(^{H}Next) ^{S}(^{M}the ^{H}orchestra) ^{P}(^{Aux}will ^{Mv}perform)
    ^{O}(^{M}Brahms's ^{M}third ^{H}symphony)].
4. See Figure A.4.

Figure A.4

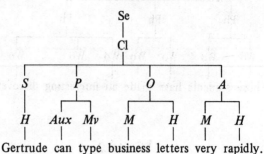

Gertrude can type business letters very rapidly.

Exercise 2e

The following function labels should be inserted:

1. *S P;* 2. *S P;* 3. *S P O;* 4. *S P O;* 5. *S P.*

Exercise 3a

1. Count nouns: *weed, laugh, employer;* the remainder are mass
    nouns.
2. For example, *paper:* count noun: news/examination/scholarly
    paper; mass noun: material on which this answer is printed.
3. You can find the answer in Quirk and Greenbaum, *A University
    Grammar of English* (1973) sections: (a) 4.40, (b) 4.48; (c) 4.50,
    (d) 4.42-45.

Exercise 3b

1. Vo: the form given in the question; Vs: the Vo form with the *-s*
    suffix; Ving: the Vo form with the *-ing* suffix; for Ved and Ven
    there are two forms for *hang,* the second referring to a method of
    execution: Ved: *took, received, began, hung/hanged, slept*
    Ven: *taken, received, begun, hung/hanged, slept*
    Of these, *receive* and *hang* (method of execution) are regular.
2. You can find the answer in Quirk and Greenbaum, *A University
    Grammar of English* (1973) sections 3.10-19 (note that they use
    V, V-ed$_1$, V-ed$_2$ for our Vo, Ved, Ven).

Exercise 3c

Gradable adjectives: *kind, dirty, careful, unique* in some people's usage
(see 3.2.3).

Exercise 3e

1. *1* Aj, *2* Av; 2. *1* Av, *2* Aj; 3. *1* Aj *2* Av; 4. *1* Aj, *2* Av; 5. *1* Aj, *2* Av; 6. *1* Aj, *2* Av; 7. *1* Aj, *2* Av; 8. *1* Av, *2* Aj.

Exercise 3f

1. *1* N, *2* V; 2. *1* Aj, *2* N; 3. *1* V, *2* Aj; 4. *1* V, *2* Aj; 5. *1* V, *2* Aj; 6. *1* Aj, *2* V, *3* N; 7. *1* V, *2* N, *3* Aj; 8. *referee: 1* N, *2* V; *match: 1* N, *2* V.

Exercise 3g

N   *cruppets, spod, vomity, Podshaw, glup, whampet, mimsiness, manity, gooves*

V   *whozing, priddling, vipped, brandling, gumbled*

Aj   *gleerful, groon, flupless, blunk*

Av   *then, huffily, podulously, bindily, magistly* (it is perhaps possible to conceive of *magistly* as a noun, but this is an unlikely interpretation).

Exercise 3h

1. [$_{cj}$But $_{jj}$alas, ($_d$the $_e$two $_{Aj}$ugly $_N$sisters) ($_v$had $_v$gone) ($_{Av}$home) ($_p$without $_{pn}$her)].

2. For example, [$_{ij}$OK, $_{cj}$although ($_{pn}$I) ($_v$am $_v$feeling) ($_{Av}$rather $_{Aj}$bored) ($_p$with $_d$these $_e$eleven $_N$classes)].

Exercise 4a

Main phrases: 1. (Mary), (had), (a little lamb); 2. (the fleece of the little lamb), (was), (as white as snow); 3. (everyone in town), (admires), (the whiteness of the fleece of Mary's little lamb).

Subordinate phrases: 1. none; 2. (of the little lamb), (as snow); 3. (in town), (of the fleece of Mary's little lamb), (of Mary's little lamb), (Mary's).

Exercise 4b

1. b; 2. c; 3. b; 4. a; 5. a; 6. a; 7. c.

Exercise 4c

A. We give only the most unmarked (or normal) orders: other, more marked orders are possible. In order to help in determining the premodifier ordering rules (B), we have have indicated the class of each word.

1. $_{Gp}$Cinderella's $_e$two $_{Aj}$ugly $_N^H$sisters.

2. $_d$A $_{Aj}$small $_{Aj}$green $_{Aj}$carved $_{Nj}$ade $_N^H$idol./$_d$A $_{Aj}$small $_{Aj}$carved $_N$green-jade $_N^H$idol. (If 'green jade' is a substance.)

3. $_d$All $_d$those $_{Aj}$intricate $_{Aj}$interlocking $_{Aj}$Chinese ^H_Ndesigns.

4. $_{Av}$Quite $_d$a $_d$few $_{Aj}$disgusting $_{Aj}$old $_{Aj}$Victorian ^H_Ndrawings./

     $_d$A $_d$few $_{Av}$quite $_{Aj}$disgusting $_{Aj}$old $_{Aj}$Victorian ^H_Ndrawings.

5. $_{GP}$Moldwarp's $_{Aj}$brilliant $_{Aj}$new $_{Aj}$geological ^H_Nhypothesis.

6. $_{GP}$Morgan's $_e$second $_{Aj}$revolutionary $_{Aj}$cylindrical $_N$steam ^H_Ncondenser.

7. $_d$An $_{Aj}$ancient $_{Aj}$grey $_{Aj}$Gothic $_N$church ^H_Ntower.

8. $_{Av}$Almost $_d$all $_d$the $_e$first $_e$hundred $_{Aj}$foreign ^H_Ntourists.

9. $_{GP}$His $_{Aj}$heavy $_{Aj}$new $_{Aj}$moral ^H_Nresponsibilities.

10. $_{GP}$My $_{Aj}$hectic $_N$London $_{Aj}$social ^H_Nlife.

B.   Here is a rule which covers the normal order of the premodifiers in examples 1–9 above, and in many other English NPs. (Superscript 'n' in the rule indicates that there may be more than one of the category: e.g. 'Aj^n,' means 'one or more adjectives'.)

$$NP = \{Av\}\ \{d\}\ \{^d_{GP}\}\ \{e^n\}\ \{((\{Av\}Aj)^n\}\ \{N^n\}\ ^H_N$$

The only example not covered by the rule is example 10, *My hectic London social life,* where the Aj *social* occurs after the N *London* rather than before it. Adjectives like *social* and *geological* which are derived from nouns and mean 'relating to' in some sense often come immediately before the head N, after any modifying noun. (See Quirk and Greenbaum, *A University Grammar of English* (1973), section 13.40, for more details.) Within the category of adjectives that do occur in the place our rule predicts, the order of a string of adjectives is based on meaning, as follows:

general	age	colour	verb participle	provenance	denominal

e.g.   *intricate   new   green   carved   Gothic   geological*

(This is based on Quirk and Greenbaum, 1973, section 13.41.)

Exercise 4d

1. ($^H_{pn}$she); 2. ($^M_d$the ^H_Nskeleton $^M_{PP}$(in . . .)); 3. (^M_dthat $^M_{Aj}$strange ^H_Nfeeling); 4. (^M_dhalf $^M_d$the ^H_Npeople $^M_{Aj}$present); 5. ($^M_{GP}$(Stanley's) $^M_{Aj}$historic ^H_Nmeeting $^M_{PP}$(with . . .) $^M_{PP}$(at . . .); 6. (^M_dall ^M_dthose $^M_{AjP}$(utterly fruitless) ^M_Nafternoon ^H_Nmeetings $^M_{PP}$(of . . .) $^M_{NP}$(last year)).

Exercise 4e

1. *I;* 2. *we;* 3. *you;* 4. *you;* 5. *he;* 6. *she;* 7. *it;* 8. *they;* 9. *me,* 10. *us,* 11. *you;* 12. *you;* 13. *him;* 14. *her;* 15. *it;* 16. *them;* 17. *myself;* 18. *ourselves;* 19. *yourself;* 20. *yourselves;* 21. *himself;* 22. *herself;* 23. *itself;* 24. *themselves;* 25. *my;* 26; *our;* 27. *your;* 28. *your;* 29. *his;* 30. *her;* 31. *its;* 32. *their;* 33. *mine;* 34. *ours;* 35. *yours;* 36. *yours;* 37. *his;* 38. *hers;* 39.—; 40. *theirs.*

[The OBJECT form of the pronoun is in fact the form that occurs in the greatest variety of places in grammatical structure, for example (a) as *O,* (b) as head of a PP (i.e. after a p), (c) in one-word answers (*Who is coming? Me.*), and (d) in most people's casual speech after cj (*John and him*), (e) as *C* (*That's him.*); other functions of the object pronoun will be seen later.]

Exercise 5a

1. [*S A P O A*]; 2. [*S P*]; 3. [*S P A*]; 4. [*S P O C*]; 5. [*S P O A*]; 6. [*A S P C*]; 7. [*A S P O O A*] (for the possibility of a second *O*, see 5.6).

Exercise 5b

1. [NP AvP VP NP PP]; 2. [NP VP]; 3. [NP VP PP]; 4. [NP VP NP AjP]; 5. [NP VP NP AvP]; 6. [PP NP VP AjP]; 7. [NP NP VP NP NP AvP].

Exercise 5c

1. [*S P Oi Od*] and [*S P O C*]; 2. [*S P O*] and [*S P O A*] (*A* = (*with brazen audacity*)); 3. [*S P C*] and [*S P O*]; 4. [*S P Oi Od*] and [*S P O C*] (it is also possible to understand this sentence as [*S P Oi Od*]); 5. [*S P A*] and [*S P O*].

Exercise 5d

1. [*S P O*]; 2. this is a passive clause (see 5.5) – the passive clause pattern is [*S P*], the corresponding active clause pattern is [*S P O*]; 3. [*S P*]; 4. [*S P O*]; 5. [*S P O*]; 6. [*S P C*], 7. [*S P Oi Od*].

Exercise 5e

1. ^{A}(for a man ^{M}(with one eye)), or ^{A}(for a man) ^{A}(with one eye), where second *A* is a *manner adverbial*; if you took *looking for* to be the verb, the analyses would be ^{O}(. . .^{M}(. . .)), ^{O}(. . .) ^{A}(. . .).

2. ^{A}($_{Av}$down), or ^{O}($_N$down).

3. *What* in the question was intended to elicit an *O*, but a *C* was given in answer.

4. (*the day* [*he was born*]) is an *O* (what he cursed), or an *A* of time.

Exercise 5f
(In the tree diagrams we have used the more general labels v, V, and *Aux*, rather than more specialised labels such as m, Ving, *Prog*, etc.)

1. See Figure A.5.

2. See Figure A.6.

3. See Figure A.7.

Figure A.5

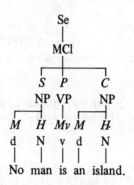

No man is an island.

Figure A.6

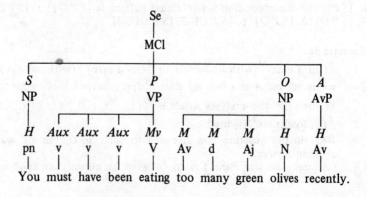

You must have been eating too many green olives recently.

Figure A.7

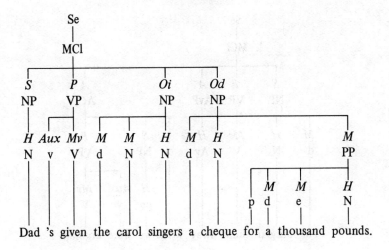

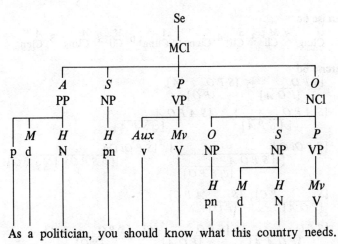

Exercise 6a

See Figures A.8 and A.9.

Figure A.8

Figure A.9

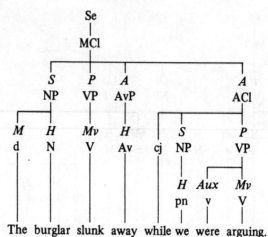

The burglar slunk away while we were arguing.

(*While* is a cj rather than an *A*, for it does not really answer the question *When?* for *we were arguing:* the ACl answers that question for *the burglar slunk away*.)

Exercise 6b

1. ACl[cj *S P O*], time; 2. ACl[cj *S P A*], purpose; 3. NCl[*S P Oi Od*];
4. RCl[*S P Oi Od*]; 5. RCl[*A S P O A*]; 6. NCl[*A S P O*]
7. ACl[cj *S P A C*], contrast; 8. NCl[*S P A*]; 9. RCl[*S P A*].

Exercise 6c

1. $\overset{O}{\text{Cling}}$; 2. $\overset{M}{\text{Cli}}$; 3. $\overset{S}{\text{Cli}}$; 4. $\overset{O}{\text{Clen}}$; 5. $\overset{A}{\text{Cling}}$; 6. $\overset{M}{\text{Cli}}$; 7. $\overset{A}{\text{Cling}}$; 8. $\overset{A}{\text{Clen}}$.

Exercise 6d

1. [*S P O* ___], [*S P O* ___ *A*]
    [$\overline{P\,O\,A}$]   [$\overline{P\,O}$]

2. [*S A P O*___], [*S A P O A*___].
    [$\overline{A\,S\,P\,A}$]   [cj *S P A*]

3. [*S P Oi Od* ___], [*S P Oi Od* ___ *A* ___].
    [$\overline{\text{cj } S\,P\,O\,A}$]   [cj *S P O*] [cj *S P O*]
        [cj *S P O*]

4. [*S* ___ *P C*], [*S* ___ *A P C*].
    [$\overline{P\,O\,A}$]   [$\overline{P\,O}$]

5. [*S P O* ___], [*S P O* ___ *A*], [*S P O* ___ *A A*].
    [$\overline{P\,O\,A\,A}$]   [$\overline{P\,O\,A}$]   [$\overline{P\,O}$]

6. $[S\ P\ Oi\ \underline{\hspace{2cm}}\ ]$, $[S\ P\ Oi\ Od\ \underline{\hspace{2cm}}\ ]$,
   $\underline{\underline{[S\ P\ O\ \underline{\hspace{1cm}}\ ]}}$ $\qquad$ $\underline{\underline{[S\ P\ O\ \underline{\hspace{1cm}}\ ]}}$
   $\quad\quad [A\ S\ P]$ $\qquad\qquad\quad [A\ S\ P]$

   $[S\ P\ Oi\ \underline{\hspace{1cm}}\ \ Od\ \ ]$.
   $\underline{[S\ P\ O]}\ \ \underline{[A\ S\ P]}$

7. $[S\ P\ \underline{\underline{O}}\ \ ]$, $[S\ P\ O\ \underline{\underline{A}}\ \ ]$, and finally one in which [*the dog*
   $\quad\ \underline{[P\ O]}$ $\qquad\quad \underline{[P\ O]}$

   smoking a cigar] was the event which I found:

   $\qquad [S\ P\ \underline{\underline{O}}\ \ \ ]$;
   $\qquad\quad \underline{[S\ P\ O]}$

   This is a 'catenative' construction (see 7.5.2).

Exercise 6e

1. $[S\ P\ O\ \underline{\hspace{2cm}}\ ]$, $[S\ P\ O\ \underline{\hspace{2.5cm}}\ ]$
   $\quad\quad (M\langle\ H + H\ \rangle)$ $\qquad\quad \langle\ (M\ H) + (H)\ \rangle$

2. $[S\ A\ P\ O\ \underline{\hspace{2cm}}\ ]$, $[S\ A\ P\ O\ \underline{\hspace{2cm}}\ ]$
   $\quad\quad\ \ \langle\ (M\ H) + (H)\ \rangle$ $\qquad\quad\ (M\ \langle\ H + H\ \rangle)$

3. $[S\ P\ O\ \underline{\hspace{2cm}}\ ]$, $\quad [S\ P\ O\ \underline{\hspace{2.5cm}}\ ]$
   $\quad\quad (\text{p}\ \langle\ H,\ H\ + M\ H\ \rangle)$ $\quad\quad (\text{p}\ \langle\ M,\ M + M\ \rangle\ H)$

   (It is also possible to interpret the PP (*in French* ...) as a C, characterising (*her exams*), or an A, though it is unclear what kind of A. This would change the **clause** structure to $[S\ P\ O\ C]$ or $[S\ P\ O\ A]$; the structure of the PP remains as above.)

4. $[S\ P\ C\ \underline{\hspace{2cm}}\ ]$, $[S\ P\ C\ \underline{\hspace{2cm}}\ ]$.
   $\quad\quad\ \langle\ (M\ H) + (H\ \underline{M}\ )\rangle$ $\quad\quad (M\ \langle\ H + H\ \underline{M}\ \rangle)$
   $\qquad\qquad\qquad [P]$ $\qquad\qquad\qquad\ [P]$

5. $[A\ S\ P\ A\ A\ \underline{\hspace{2cm}}\ ]$, $[A\ S\ P\ A\ A\ \underline{\hspace{2cm}}\ ]$.
   $\quad\quad\ \ \langle\ [P] + [P\ O]\ \rangle$ $\qquad\quad\ [\langle\ P + P\ \rangle\ O]$

6. $[S\ P\ A\ \underline{\hspace{3cm}}\ ]$,
   $\quad\quad \underline{[S\ P\ \langle\ O + \underline{O}\ \ \ \ \rangle]}$
   $\qquad\qquad \underline{[S\ P\ \langle\ O + O\ \rangle]}$

   $[S\ P\ A\ \underline{\hspace{4cm}}\ ]$,
   $\quad (\text{p}\ \langle\ M\ H\ M\ \underline{\hspace{1.5cm}} + H\ \rangle)$
   $\qquad\quad \underline{[S\ P\ \langle\ O + \underline{O}\ \ \ \ \rangle]}$
   $\qquad\qquad\qquad \underline{[S\ P\ O]}$

   $[S\ P\ A\ \underline{\hspace{5cm}}\ ]$,
   $\quad (\text{p}\ \langle\ M\ H\ \underline{M}\ \ \ \ \ + M\ H\ \underline{M}\ \ \ \ \ \rangle)$
   $\qquad\quad \underline{[S\ P\ O]}\ \ \ \ \ \ \underline{[S\ P\ \langle\ O + O\ \rangle]}$

$$[S\ P\ A\underline{\hspace{4cm}}].$$
$$(\text{p}\ \langle\ M\ H\ \underline{\underline{M\hspace{1cm}}}\ +\ M\ H\ \underline{\underline{M\hspace{1cm}}}\ +\ H\ \rangle\ )$$
$$\underbrace{\qquad}_{[S\ P\ O]}\qquad\underbrace{\qquad}_{[S\ P\ O]}$$

7. $[S\ P\ \underline{A\hspace{2cm}}]$, $[S\ P\ \underline{A\hspace{2cm}}]$,
    $\quad(\text{p}\ M\ \langle\ H+H\ M\ \rangle)\qquad(\text{p}\ \langle\ M\ H+H\ \rangle\ M)$

    $[S\ P\ \underline{A\hspace{2cm}}]$, $[S\ P\ \underline{A\hspace{2cm}}]$.
    $\quad(\text{p}\ M\ \langle\ H+H\ \rangle\ M)\qquad(\text{p}\ \langle\ M\ H+H\ M\ \rangle)$

(Note that we have not further analysed the postmodifier PP (*of questionable parentage*).)

8. $[S\ P\ \underline{C\hspace{4cm}}]$,
    $\quad[M\ \langle\ M\ H+M\ H\ \rangle\ \underline{M\hspace{2cm}})$
    $\qquad\qquad\qquad(\text{p}\ M\ \langle\ H+H\ \rangle)$

    $[S\ P\ \underline{C\hspace{4cm}}]$,
    $\quad(M\ \langle\ M\ H+M\ H\ \underline{M\hspace{2cm}}\ \rangle)$
    $\qquad\qquad\qquad(\text{p}\ M\ \langle\ H+H\ \rangle)$

    $[S\ P\ \underline{C\hspace{4cm}}]$,
    $\quad(M\ \langle\ M\ H+M\ H\ \underline{M\hspace{2cm}}\ \rangle)$
    $\qquad\qquad\qquad(\text{p}\ \langle\ M\ H+H\ \rangle)$

    $[S\ P\ \underline{C\hspace{4cm}}]$.
    $\quad(M\ \langle\ M\ H+M\ H\ \rangle\ \underline{M\hspace{2cm}})$
    $\qquad\qquad\qquad(\text{p}\ \langle\ M\ H+H\ \rangle)$

Exercise 7a

1. (a) $^{M}_{\text{Cling}}$ [*standing at the door*] should **post**modify ^{H}*girl*; (b) $^{Mv}_{V}$ *making* requires an *O*, but there is none.

2. (a) $^{S}_{\text{NP}}(^{H}_{\text{pn}}my)$ should be **subject** pn *I*, and $_{Vs}$ *has* should show subject **concord** and be $_{Vo}$*have*; (b) $^{M}_{\text{Aj}}$*interesting* should **pre**modify $^{H}_{job}$.

3. (a) $^{O}_{\text{NP}}(very\ good\ reputation)$ requires $^{M}_{d}\ a$, the INDEFINITE ARTICLE; (b) $_{\text{p}}for$ requires a NP or NCl after it.

4. A Cli is not usually a MCl in a sentence. But it could occur as a SCl, or as an **elliptical** sentence (e.g. in reply to a question or as the heading of an article).

5. A Cl without a *S* is not usually a MCl in a sentence. But it might occur as an **elliptical** sentence, e.g. in very casual conversation, or perhaps in an advertisement, for instance *Have gun, will travel.*

Exercise 7b

1. 'DO SUPPORT'. All the following transformations require a finite operator verb, v = m, be, hv (see 4.5.2 and 5.4.1). If there is none,

use the **dummy operator** *do*. It will be the finite element, carrying tense and agreeing with *S*.

2.   CLAUSE NEGATION. Place negative *not* immediately after the first (finite) v of *P*. If it is *n't*, attach it to this v.
3.   YES-NO INTERROGATION. Place the first (finite) v of *P* before *S*.
4.   CLAUSE EMPHASIS. Place the main stress on the first v.
5.   TAGS. Add an unlinked second Cl (see 6.7.1), consisting of the first v of the *P* of the original Cl, with *n't* attached, followed by the subject pn that would stand for the *S* of the first Cl. (If the *P* of the first Cl is negated, the tag will not be negative, i.e. the tag is opposite in **polarity**, positive or negative, to the original Cl. There are also emphatic tags, which have the **same** polarity as the original Cl (*You like cheese, do you? He hasn't finished his homework, hasn't he?*).
6.   ELLIPTICAL COMPARATIVES: There are a number of different kinds of elliptical CCl, but the kind represented by the data on p.74 consists of $_{cj}$*than* followed by a *S* (normally not identical to the MCl *S*), followed by the first v of the MCl *P*.

Note: (a) ^{Mv}do is not an operator v, hence it needs dummy *do* (*I didn't do it*); (b) $^{Mv}have$ is an operator v in some varieties of English, a full V in others: hence, for example, *Have you a match?* or *Do you have a match?*

Exercise 7c
1. $[A \ S \ \langle \ P\,A + P\,A \ \rangle]$;   2. $[Aux \ S \ Aux \ \langle Mv \ A + Mv \ O \rangle]$;
3. $[S \ P \ \langle O\,A + O\,A \rangle]$;   4. $[A \ \langle \ S\,P\,A\,A + S\,P\,O \rangle]$;
5. $[A \ \langle \ S \ P \ O + S \ Aux \ \text{not} \ \rangle]$ (note that dummy operator $^{Aux}_{vs}does$ 'stands for' $^{Mv}_{Vs}likes$).   6. $[A \ \langle S \ P \ C + S \ C \rangle]$.

Exercise 7d
We give a fairly general description of the transformation, using symbols (you may have used a less abstract description), but we do not attempt to give the rather complex restrictions on their application.

1.   *Fronting of subordinate clause object*

it be $C \ ^{S}_{Cli}[\ldots Pi \ \underset{NP_1}{O} \ldots] \longrightarrow \underset{NP_1}{S}$ be $C (\ldots \underset{Cli}{M} [\ldots Pi \ldots])$

For example,

It is ^{C}(interesting) $^S_{Cli}[^{Pi}$(to study) $^O_{NP}$(grammar) in depth] $\longrightarrow$

$^S_{NP}$(Grammar) is ^{C}(interesting $^M_{Cli}[^{Pi}$(to study) in depth]).

2.   *Postponement of indirect object*

$S \ P \ Oi \quad Od \longrightarrow S \ P \ Od \ A_{(p \ NP_1)}$, where p = *to* or *for*.
$\quad\;\; NP_1$

For example,

$[^S(\text{We})\,^P(\text{are teaching})\,^{Oi}(\text{you})\,^{Od}(\text{grammar})]. \longrightarrow [^S(\text{We})\,^P(\text{are teaching})\,^O(\text{grammar})\,^A(_p\text{ to you})].$

3. *Postponement of postmodifier*

NP(...H M) $\longrightarrow$ NP(...$\underbrace{H......M}$), where M must be a Ph or Cl.

(This transformation is hedged about with restrictions which are only poorly understood.)

For example,

$^S_{NP}(\text{The }^H\text{road }^M_{PP}(\text{to a mastery of grammar}) \,^P(\text{is}) \,^C(\text{very thorny}).$

$\longrightarrow ^S_{NP}(\text{The }^H\text{road }^P(\text{is}) \,^C(\text{very thorny}) \underbrace{^M_{PP}(\text{to a mastery of grammar})).}$

Exercise 7e

1. [it be C S _____],
    [cj A _____ S A P A A A]
    [cj S A P A]

2. [there be S A A _____].
    [cj it be A that S P A]

Exercise 11a
(The error-type is followed by a suggested revision.)

1. B. It was argued that the President...*was* dancing to the tune of OPEC.
2. C. Mervyn John's record is now as good *as,* if not better than, *that of* his countryman Michael Steed.
3. D. (It is difficult to avoid the 'dangling' non-finite clause, which is in any case not seriously objectionable.)
4. A. What worried her parents most was *his* being a racing driver.
5. C. We could knock twenty per cent off the fuel consumption and yet keep the price...
6. B. Have *both/all* of you opened your parcels?
7. E. (Split infinitive.)... it would be wrong *even to* think of it.
8. A. (No obvious way of evading the object pronouns: subject pronouns would look extremely odd here.)
9. A. Margaret and he will be playing against you and *me.*
10. B. Neither the publisher nor the author *knows* about the printer's blunder.
11. A. ... *we* girls were listening at the keyhole.
12. C. ... and *to* its determination to stand on its own feet.

13. A. (The genitive . . . *some Congressman from the Midwest's* . . . would be very awkward here. Either leave the sentence as it is, or substitute a relative clause construction: . . . *about some Congressman . . . who had taken* . . .)
14. D. When *they are* removed from their normal habitat, it is advisable to treat these animals with great care.
15. D. Put the lights out when you leave. (A simpler and more direct style is preferable, and avoids the usage problem.)
16. B. Radios of this sort are very reliable.
    This sort of radio is very reliable.
17. D. *As I was* flying . . . a sudden thought struck me.
18. E. (Superlative in place of comparative.) (To change *best* to *better* here would seem rather pedantic.)
19. E. We *shall* not object to your postponing the meeting.
20. B. . . . any of her supporters *has* been disloyal.

Exercise 12a

1. b. The object *a collar with studs all over it* is discontinuous.
2. b. 'Garden-path' ambiguity: *that were needed* reads like a passive relative clause.
3. b. *It* lacks an antecedent such as *water*.
4. b. Ambiguity: the adverbial *in her latest book* can belong to the main clause or to the noun clause.
5. c. Redundancy: *in the long run, eventually* and *one day* are all similar in meaning.
6. a. End-weight: *up* follows a long object.
7. a. End-weight: *to end* follows a long object.
8. b. Unclear antecedents for *he, which* and *his*.
9. b. The object *tax-free presents of any size you like* is discontinuous.
10. a. End-weight: the predicator *revived* follows a very long subject.

Suggested revisions

1. Mr and Mrs Smith bought their dog a collar with studs all over it.
2. Once the war started, the 'powers that were' needed human cannon fodder.
3. The pipe was leaking so badly that the liquid ran all over the kitchen.
4. She argues that in her latest book Iris Murdoch has produced a masterpiece.
5. In the long run, we shall win the battle against poverty.
6. They have given up their plans for improving the sports facilities.
7. No one will ever know how Dickens intended to finish *Edwin Drood*, the novel on which he was working when he died.
8. The detective swore that he had seen the accused checking in. This sighting was evidence of the presence of the accused in the hotel.

9.   The Inland Revenue no longer allows you to give your children tax-free presents of any size you like.
10. The desultory conversation in the drawing room revived among guests who had regarded Miss Manning's performance of *Ave Verum* as a mere interruption.

Exercise 12b
(i)   **Suggested revisions**
1.   Before we started eating, the table was absolutely loaded with delicacies.
2.   It is best to reduce your overheads, and to work as far as possible alone.
3.   As we soon discovered, the ambassador was not interested in discussing armaments.
4.   I fed the dog, and Harry the budgerigar.
5.   Inside, the house looks almost as it did when Darwin died.
6.   Lord and Lady Boothroyd refused to meet her parents. OR Her parents, Lord and Lady Boothroyd, refused to meet each other.
7.   The party was attended by the Melchetts, some cousins of ours; William, of course, arrived late.
8.   Middlesex, having already won the Schweppes Championship, looks like winning the Gillette Cup as well.

(ii)   **Description of ambiguities**

(All are 'garden paths' except 4 and 6.)

1.   *The table* is initially read as object of the adverbial clause, not as subject of the main clause.
2.   *Work* is initially read as a noun coordinated with *overheads*, rather than as a verb.
3.   *The ambassador* is initially read as object of *discovered*, rather than as subject of *was*.
4.   EITHER *Harry the budgerigar* is a noun phrase coordinated with *the dog*, OR *Harry* is the subject, and *the budgerigar* the object, of an 'ellipted' verb *fed*.
5.   *Inside* is read initially as a preposition, and *inside the house* as a prepositional phrase. In fact, *inside* is an adverb, and *the house* is subject of *looks*.
6.   EITHER *Lord and Lady Boothroyd* is in apposition to *Her parents*, OR *Her parents* is the 'fronted' object of *meet*.
7.   *William* is read initially as coordinated with *the Melchetts and some cousins of ours*, rather than as subject of *arrived*.
8.   *Middlesex* can be read initially as the subject of the adverbial *-ing* clause *Middlesex . . . Championship*, rather than as subject of the main clause.

Further reading

The list of references which follows includes a selection of books which might be consulted by students wishing to pursue some of the topics we have touched upon in this book.

The items are listed by author, in alphabetical order, and are also numbered consecutively for easy identification according to topic:

Topic	Reference numbers
Language and linguistics	3, 7, 8, 15, 16, 26, 30, 36, 40, 41
Language variation	18, 19, 29, 37, 38
English grammar	1, 6, 16, 17, 25, 32, 33, 44
Speech versus writing	9, 11, 35
Discourse analysis	5, 10, 17, 22
Analysis of literary discourse	12, 14, 20, 23, 24, 36, 39, 43
Opinions on usage and correctness	2, 13, 21, 27, 31
Written composition	4, 28, 42

References

1. Adrian Akmajian and Frank Heny, *An Introduction to the Principles of Transformational Syntax* (Cambridge, Mass.: MIT Press, 1975).
2. Albert C. Baugh and Thomas Cable, *A History of the English Language* (London: Routledge & Kegan Paul, 1978) ch. 9, 'The Appeal to Authority, 1650–1800'.
3. Dwight Bolinger, *Aspects of Language*, 2nd edn (New York: Harcourt Brace Jovanovich, 1975).
4. G. V. Carey, *Mind the Stop: A Brief Guide to Punctuation* (Harmondsworth: Penguin, 1976).
5. Malcolm Coulthard, *An Introduction to Discourse Analysis* (London: Longman, 1977).
6. A. P. Cowie and R. Mackin, *Oxford Dictionary of Current Idiomatic English. Volume 1: Verbs with Prepositions and Particles* (Oxford: Oxford University Press, 1975).
7. David Crystal, *Linguistics* (Harmondsworth: Penguin, 1971).

215

8. David Crystal, *A First Dictionary of Linguistics and Phonetics* (London: Deutsch, 1980).
9. David Crystal, 'Neglected Grammatical Factors in Conversational English', in Sidney Greenbaum, Geoffrey Leech and Jan Svartvik (eds), *Studies in English Linguistics: for Randolph Quirk* (London: Longman, 1980).
10. David Crystal and Derek Davy, *Investigating English Style* (London: Longman, 1969).
11. David Crystal and Derek Davy, *Advanced Conversational English* (London: Longman, 1975). (Accompanying tape available.)
12. Edmund L. Epstein, *Language and Style* (London: Methuen, 1978).
13. H. W. Fowler, *Modern English Usage*, 2nd edn, revised by Sir Ernest Gowers (Oxford: Oxford University Press, 1965).
14. Roger Fowler, *The Languages of Literature* (London: Routledge & Kegan Paul, 1971).
15. Victoria Fromkin and Robert Rodman, *An Introduction to Language*, 2nd edn (New York: Holt, Rinehart & Winston, 1978).
16. H. A. Gleason, *Linguistics and English Grammar* (New York: Holt, Rinehart & Winston, 1965).
17. M. A. K. Halliday and Ruqaiya Hasan, *Cohesion in English* (London: Longman, 1976).
18. M. A. K. Halliday, Angus McIntosh and Peter Strevens, *The Linguistic Sciences and Language Teaching* (London: Longman, 1964) ch. 4, 'The Users and Uses of language'.
19. Arthur Hughes and Peter Trudgill, *English Accents and Dialects* (London: Arnold, 1979).
20. Roman Jakobson, 'Closing Statement: Linguistics and Poetics', in Thomas A. Sebeok (ed.), *Style in Language* (Cambridge, Mass.: MIT Press, 1960).
21. Samuel Johnson, *A Dictionary of the English Language* (London, 1755).
22. Geoffrey N. Leech, *English in Advertising* (London: Longman, 1966).
23. Geoffrey N. Leech, *A Linguistic Guide to English Poetry* (London: Longman, 1969).
24. Geoffrey Leech and Michael Short, *Style in Fiction: A Linguistic Introduction to English Fictional Prose* (London: Longman, 1981).
25. Geoffrey Leech and Jan Svartvik, *A Communicative Grammar of English* (London: Longman, 1975).
26. J. E. Miller and E. K. Brown, *Syntax: A Linguistic Introduction to Sentence Structure* (London: Hutchinson, 1980).
27. W. H. Mittins *et al.*, *Attitudes to English Usage* (Oxford: Oxford University Press, 1970).
28. Walter Nash, *Designs in Prose* (London: Longman, 1980).
29. W. R. O'Donnell and Loreto Todd, *Variety in Contemporary English* (London: Allen & Unwin, 1980).
30. Frank Palmer, *Grammar* (Harmondsworth: Penguin, 1971).

31. Eric Partridge, *Usage and Abusage*, 5th edn (London: Hamish Hamilton, 1957).

32. Randolph Quirk and Sidney Greenbaum, *A University Grammar of English* (London: Longman, 1973).

33. Randolph Quirk, Sidney Greenbaum, Geoffrey Leech and Jan Svartvik, *A Grammar of Contemporary English* (New York: Seminar Press and London: Longman, 1972).

34. Dan I. Slobin, *Language Change in Childhood and in History* (University of California, Berkeley: Working Paper No. 41, Language Behaviour Research Laboratory, 1975).

35. Michael Stubbs, *Language and Literacy* (London: Routledge & Kegan Paul, 1980).

36. Elizabeth Closs Traugott and Mary Louise Pratt, *Linguistics for Students of Literature* (New York: Harcourt Brace Jovanovich, 1980).

37. Peter Trudgill, *Accent, Dialect and the School* (London: Arnold, 1975).

38. Peter Trudgill, *Sociolinguistics* (Harmondsworth: Penguin, 1974).

39. G. W. Turner, *Stylistics* (Harmondsworth: Penguin, 1973).

40. J. F. Wallwork, *Language and Linguistics* (London: Heinemann, 1969).

41. J. F. Wallwork, *Language and Linguistics, a Workbook* (London: Heinemann, 1972).

42. John E. Warriner and Francis Griffith, *English Grammar and Composition* (New York: Harcourt Brace Jovanovich, 1973).

43. Henry G. Widdowson, *Stylistics and the Teaching of Literature* (London: Longman, 1976).

44. David J. Young, *The Structure of English Clauses* (London: Hutchinson, 1980).

Index

Notes

1. Major or defining page references are printed in bold type.
2. See pages xiv–xvi for symbols and conventions.
3. The abbreviations s. and S.a. mean 'see' and 'See also' respectively.

218